DIAL BOOKS
An imprint of Penguin Random House LLC
1745 Broadway, New York, NY 10019
penguinrandomhouse.com

Title page and jacket art copyright © 2026 by Dana Ledl
Text copyright © 2026 by Tsultrim Dolma and Rebecca Wei Hsieh

Penguin Random House values and supports copyright. Copyright fuels creativity, encourages diverse voices, promotes free speech, and creates a vibrant culture. Thank you for buying an authorized edition of this book and for complying with copyright laws by not reproducing, scanning, or distributing any part of it in any form without permission. You are supporting writers and allowing Penguin Random House to continue to publish books for every reader. Please note that no part of this book may be used or reproduced in any manner for the purpose of training artificial intelligence technologies or systems.

Dial & colophon are registered trademarks of Penguin Random House LLC.

This book was edited by Rosie Ahmed and Michelle Lee, copyedited by Regina Castillo and Aaron Burkholder, proofread by Kenny Young, and designed by Maya Tatsukawa. The production was supervised by Jayne Ziemba, Nicole Kiser, and Vanessa Robles. Text set in FS Brabo.

Library of Congress Cataloging-in-Publication Data is available.

First published in the United States of America by Dial Books, 2026

Manufactured in the United States of America
BVG

ISBN 9780593615959
1st Printing

The authorized representative in the EU for product safety and compliance is Penguin Random House Ireland, Morrison Chambers, 32 Nassau Street, Dublin D02 YH68, Ireland, https://eu-contact.penguin.ie.

*To my friends and family,
whose real identities I can't share in order
to ensure their safety. I hope to sing your names
from the mountaintops of Tibet one day.*

Defying China is the true story of Tsultrim's journey as a Tibetan activist. However, Tibet remains a sensitive topic, so we have changed all names and tweaked some minor details to protect everyone involved in Tsultrim's story.

This memoir also includes mentions of physical, emotional, and sexual violence. We hope you prioritize taking care of yourself, even if it means putting down the book. Please be patient and kind to yourself, and know that you are not alone.

CHAPTER
ONE

The place I call home has tall mountains and long rivers. Even the small stream in my hometown flows past the village boundaries, disappearing into the grassy plains of the Kham region of Tibet. Some days, I imagined it pouring into a lake as a waterfall. Others, I dreamed that it unfurled into a river and carved the steep valleys of the Tibetan Plateau, finally snaking its way back to the ocean. Or maybe it simply went on forever. All I knew was that it flowed beyond the borders of a little village called Pelbar Dzong, and that, more than anything, I wanted to follow that stream and see its end for myself.

Very rarely, airplanes would soar across the sky like birds, and I wondered if they could see me going about my day. Every morning, for as long as I could remember, I stepped down the squeaky stairs of our squat house, wooden bucket in hand. My breath appeared in puffs of cool air against the pink sliver crawling over the horizon as I let out our livestock.

We had a variety of animals under our care: a single

horse, cattle, sheep, yaks, and female yaks, called dri. Yaks and cattle belong to the same family of animals, but to my eyes, they couldn't be more different. Yaks have long horns that reach high toward the sky and a pronounced hump on their back, covered by long, warm wool. On the other hand, cattle tend to have shorter horns and hair. Sometimes they're crossbred to create a hybrid called a dzo for males and dzomo for females.

We had one such dzomo, and she was my favorite among them all. She had a sleek black coat and a pair of curved horns. Maybe I adored her because she reminded me of myself: just a shy little thing that nonetheless stood out like a sore thumb. She snickered anxiously as I smoothed a hand over her head. I was still a child at around eleven years old, but I'd grown up caring for two younger siblings, so the sweet murmurs came naturally to me.

"Hey, it's okay," I cooed. "You're such a cute little baby, such a good girl."

One by one, I milked the livestock, the rhythm of milk hitting the bucket a soothing *thump thump thump* as they grazed lazily outside our home. Normally, I'd move on to other tasks afterward: churning dri butter, making tsampa bread out of barley flour, gathering firewood and dried yak dung for fuel.

Today, however, I was to forgo those chores, leaving them to my siblings Bhuti and Yeshe instead. It was the day my father and I would depart for a pilgrimage to Lhasa, the capital city of Tibet, west of our humble little village. In the Tibetan language, *Lhasa* literally translates to "land of the gods"—the city was more than a governmental hub. It was also the spiritual center of our faith, Tibetan Buddhism.

I'd tossed and turned all night. And yet, I'd never felt so awake in my life as I sat by the front door. From our house, I could see villagers slowly emerging from their own homes. They were like tiny ants, milling about in preparation and streaming steadily to the main path, where we'd agreed to meet for the journey. Father was well respected in the community, so it came as no surprise that at least a dozen people had leapt at the chance to travel with him.

"Punjun," he called from the house, "give Bhuti the bucket and get your pack. It's time to leave."

My brother Bhuti was around four years younger than me, and our sister Yeshe was a little younger than that. We didn't keep track of the years with a calendar, so I was never quite sure of our exact ages. He trudged down the stairs and took my spot by the dri.

"I got it," he mumbled, before giving her a fond little pat and continuing to milk her.

It seemed like only yesterday when he and Yeshe were still infants, babbling nonsense and blowing raspberries.

After invading Tibet in the fifties, the Chinese government had seized control of land from Tibetans, including my own family. For as long as I could recall, like many other Tibetans, my parents left each morning to work on other people's fields until nightfall. These fields were farther from home, so I'd spent the first few years of my very young life taking care of my two baby siblings. On days when my parents worked especially late, I'd strap the babies to my chest with a blanket, banging on pots and pans to lull them to sleep.

But now, around four or five years later, things were different. Better. We had our land back, our parents were home more often, and we were about to embark on a major spiritual journey.

My friend Pema was already waiting by the time Father and I arrived, wearing a determined look on her round face. Her hair was tied up neatly for the arduous trip, and a large pack, filled with barley flour, dried meats, and water, towered over her. It was covered in a large cloth that would be her sleeping roll as we made our way to Lhasa. Her parents had allowed her to join us, entrusting her to Father's care. At around fourteen, Pema was already of marrying age, and this would be her only chance to see Lhasa. It would most likely be my only chance to travel as well. Though Father never said so, I had an inkling that he'd meant the trip as a final gift before I married. I shook off the thoughts before they could spiral out of control. Parting gift or not, I didn't want to waste time focusing on the negative.

I adjusted my own pack and took a deep breath until my lungs felt close to bursting. I stuck by my father's side as the adults chatted amicably: the weather, the route we would take, the towns we could stop at for supplies. The excitement in the air was almost palpable, shot through with apprehension.

There were four mountains we had to cross, each tipped in a thick layer of snow. Even with the mild spring weather, it would take us at least a month to reach Lhasa on foot. Some pilgrims even died on the way there. The journey was not for the faint of heart. I was the youngest, but I knew from past experience that I had what it took to complete the journey.

My friends and I were collecting firewood one day, chatting and squealing as we always had. It had been a day like any other: We sang as we picked splinters out of our gloves. We played silly games, making up the rules as we went. We spotted the occasional berry bush and plucked off the ripe berries as a treat. We were in our own merry bubble, cracking jokes as we hacked at tree stumps with our little axes.

Nyima huffed as she tossed away another piece of wood. "Too damp," she declared bitterly. I picked it up, examining it before adding it to my own bundle of kindling. I tied the kindling together with a leather rope and placed it into the large basket on my back.

The bubble burst when I made eye contact with my older brother, Gelek. I closed my mouth mid-song, teeth clacking together, suddenly hyperaware of what I was doing. I'd forgotten that he'd tagged along that day.

Gelek was almost a stranger to me. My brother was a bit older, although I never learned by exactly how many years. He'd lived with our grandparents on the other side of the village for as long as I could remember. Every spring, the villagers would take their livestock to higher ground to prevent them from grazing in the newly planted barley fields. It was a massive undertaking that spanned months until the harvest was over in the early autumn. Our grandparents owned a particularly large herd of animals, and as they grew older, they needed the extra help to maintain their flock. As a result, Gelek had grown up with them, and he felt more like a distant cousin, one who was kind and cordial, but always at an arm's length.

We meandered up the mountain in awkward silence, me taking care to stay closer to my friends. But I couldn't avoid him forever. For some reason, we'd decided to venture farther than usual, following a beaten path that eventually led to a terrifying drop. I can't quite remember how large the gap was, only that alarms sounded in my brain the moment I laid eyes on it. We had to jump across, onto the opposite ledge that was higher than the one we were standing on. Loose rocks and dirt slid under my feet as I shuffled behind my friends in single file.

Gelek crossed without hesitation. Just one clean jump, and he was on the other side, helping the other kids onto the ledge. I tried not to think too much about the stones that scattered off the edge and into the river below.

Wiping my clammy hands, I approached the ledge and looked down.

These were not the placid waters of the village stream. The river below us, frothing mad and white, crashed down the mountain at a dizzying speed. Even if I were to survive the fall, I was sure to be swept away by the river.

I stared. This close and with a basket weighing me down, the gap felt twice as big. I swayed, from the gusts of wind or from dizziness, I wasn't entirely sure. My shirt was beginning to soak through with sweat, and suddenly three layers of clothing felt stifling even on a chilly day.

One by one, my friends jumped across the gap, sending small rocks flying as they landed on the other side. Nyima had been quick to follow Gelek across the gap; Dawa had made the leap with an excited squeal. Sangye had let out a whoop and was chatting animatedly as I stood frozen in fear.

"Punjun!" Gelek called my name and opened his arms. He gestured to our surroundings, so casually as if I was missing something obvious. "You can do it."

"No, I can't," I said.

"You'll be fine."

My jaw ached from how hard I clenched my mouth shut, and I stared at him with eyes round as saucers because clearly, he was the one who missed the obvious.

Gelek reached out a hand, ready to grab me once I got close enough. *If* I got close enough. I still had to take the leap, hang in the air for a split second with nothing under my feet.

Heart hammering, I stepped back a few paces for a running start. Twigs crunched beneath my feet, the roar in my ears growing louder as I tensed my muscles, and then—

No no no no absolutely not.

I skidded to a halt, my leather shoes slipping on the ground, which only spiked my pulse with a fresh wave of fear. It hadn't rained today, but the air was humid enough to make everything just a little more slippery than I'd have liked. Shoulders raised to my ears in embarrassment, I looked up to see Gelek gesticulating at me.

"Come on," he said, firm but not unkind. "It's not that bad."

My eyes must've been bulging by then. But I didn't want to wait here as everyone else went ahead without me, and I had no intention of heading back home, not when the sun was still glaring down overhead.

I stepped back, took a deep breath, and threw myself at the ledge. My eyes squeezed shut the moment my feet left the ground, and I held my breath, biting back a scream in my throat.

For a single, breathless moment, I was flying. And in the next, I was falling. Then I felt the sharp bite of gravel on my knees and a strong grip crushing my fingers, pulling me away from the ledge. I stumbled, lurching forward on shaky legs as Gelek led me away. Mind buzzing, I looked back at where the last few kids were crossing the gap. My brother was right; it wasn't that bad, now that I'd made it to the other side. A bundle of wood slid out of someone's basket, disappearing in the river with a dull splash, and I shuddered. No, it was definitely that bad.

"Told you you could do it," my brother said, a proud smile on his face. And as much as I hated to admit it, he was right.

The wind tugged at my clothes as we climbed higher. The sun dipped toward the horizon, the towering mountains casting long dark shadows onto a slope of gold.

The view was yet another reminder that there was life outside of Pelbar Dzong. There were taller mountains in the distance, so tall that they reached the clouds. There were sights hiding beyond the horizon, lush forests and billowing waters and towns full of people I'd never get to meet.

But at the same time, everything looked so small from up here: the houses, the people, the squabbles and inconveniences of daily life. From this vantage point, anything seemed possible. As we made our way home, I carried a piece of that scenery with me, nestled in my chest like a little seed of hope.

Now that seed had begun to sprout.

Each step I took brought me farther from my hometown than I'd ever dreamed of. By midday, Pelbar Dzong had already vanished beyond the horizon. Turning back to see my tiny village—my whole world—out of sight should've been terrifying. But all I could do was marvel at the scenery around us.

Trees I never learned the names of dotted the landscape, sometimes growing into the kind of thick, lush forest my great-aunt Jampa had once described to me. Thin leaves dangled from squiggly branches. I jumped up, trying to grab hold of one. I could hear the gurgle of a stream nearby and wondered if it merged with the one in the village or a different river entirely. Excitement quickly overruled any initial nervousness I'd felt; I didn't have time to be scared when there were so many new things to take in. It didn't matter to me then that I didn't know the names of a plant. It didn't matter that I didn't know how the terrain looked, or the exact flow of a river close by. What mattered was putting one foot in front of the other, and a voice in my head saying, *Punjun, you can do it.*

CHAPTER
TWO

It wasn't so long ago that religious displays had been banned entirely.

In my village, people mostly kept their doors wide open; we were free to come and go as we pleased. I would spend my free time wandering in and out of people's homes, shyly saying hi and chatting when prompted. And every now and then I stumbled upon elders mid-prayer.

Restrictions had been lifted by then, allowing for some religious festivals and public prayer, but they still scrambled to hide the evidence of their faith: the prayer books, the prayer beads, the mantras that slipped from their lips with a heart-aching familiarity. Their eyes would widen in fear, seeing phantom soldiers in their doorways, until they calmed enough to recognize me. Though they never shooed me away or said anything, the message was always loud and clear: I'd seen something I wasn't supposed to. I'd merely lower my gaze and turn around, pretending I hadn't seen a thing.

Then, when I was around eight, an announcement came that seemed to signal progress.

"They're allowing us to go to Lhasa on pilgrimage," Mother said, her eyes bright.

Even though I had no idea what *Lhasa* or *pilgrimage* meant back then, I'd gotten caught up in the flurry and excitement of preparations. We bartered for meat with the traveling butcher and laid out the strips to make jerky for the road. We churned yak butter, making sure the whole group had enough to last the trip.

Mother and Uncle Tenzin were going with almost twenty other people, the first to go to Lhasa in years. The group was mostly men; it was typical for men to enjoy privileges like that. Father, however, insisted that Mother go first.

"She's worked so hard, giving birth and taking care of you. She deserves the peace and quiet," he said when I asked him about it later. He was working on a pair of new leather boots for my mother. I watched, entranced, as he stacked pieces of leather together to form the thick soles. He punctured the leather, inserting rigid string through the holes to bind all the pieces together. More materials lay scattered around him: cotton, wool, and different kinds of animal hide. The boots wouldn't be fancy, but they would keep Mother safe and warm.

Though we rarely spoke of relationships, I knew that my parents did not have an arranged marriage, unlike many other couples. They'd married out of love. We hardly expressed our love through words, but I saw the way Father poured his care and affection into each minute detail. I wanted to do that too.

"Can you teach me how to make shoes like that?"

"No," he said firmly. "It's a boy's job. You already know how to spin yarn and the like."

But it's not the same, I wanted to argue, but I knew from his tone that he'd already made up his mind. My father had always been a reserved man, cautious with his words. He rolled his thoughts around in his mouth as if savoring a particularly delicate tea, before letting them out in a measured trickle. If he said no, then that was the end of it.

It was baffling. Going on a pilgrimage was a once-in-a-lifetime event, and yet Father allowed Mother to go first, not knowing when or if his own opportunity would come. At the same time, he refused to teach me a "boy's job." As far as I could tell, there was nothing about cobbling that was inherently hard for girls to do.

Still, I observed in silence day after day as he transformed raw materials into a pair of functional shoes. His hands were calloused, his knuckles swollen, and he had to take breaks to stretch his fingers and roll his neck. He wouldn't have to work so hard if he'd just let me help. He continued working himself to the bone, even after Mother's departure, as if channeling his anxiety into something useful. He grew restless, as did the rest of the village. Pilgrimage was a joyous occasion, but Pelbar Dzong was small enough that we felt the group's absence. We had no means of communication with the travelers, no way to check in on them. They could be snowed in or starving, and we wouldn't know until it was too late. All we could do was pray for their safety, day and night.

And after three months of agonizing waiting, the pilgrims finally returned, safe and sound.

Mother fished out a small cloth bundle, unfolding it reverently with a look of awe on her face. Sitting in the middle of her palm was a handful of pure white beads.

"A monk from our village was recently released, so I visited him while I was in Lhasa," she explained. "He blessed a long string of prayer beads, and we decided to divide them among the group."

Her face dropped when she realized what she'd let slip. Curiosity burned in the pit of my stomach. What did she mean by "released"? And why had the monk been captured in the first place?

That's not for me to know, I reminded myself, and pretended I didn't catch her slip of the tongue. I'd heard that phrase so often that it felt engraved in me like a mantra. Instead, I focused on the white gleam of the beads, the little swirls and patterns that danced across the rounded surfaces.

Mother continued, "I can't make full strings of these for all of us, so I'll find some other beads to fill it out."

She bartered for some wooden beads and spent the next few days carefully stringing them into necklaces. She added the white beads at regular intervals, keeping count to make sure each necklace had 108 beads. They looked like little orbs of light that stood out among the brown wooden beads.

She tied the ends of the string together and placed it gently into my hands. "These are for you."

Finally, prayer beads to call my own. I could slip them through my fingers, one by one, to help keep count as I recited mantras. They'd help me focus, and the repetitive movement would ground me in the moment, clearing my mind of distractions.

The beads hung around my neck now, years later, as I put one foot in front of the other toward Lhasa.

CHAPTER
THREE

Just like in other religions, a pilgrimage in Tibetan Buddhism is a trip to a holy or sacred site. It's a ritual that allows one to gain "merit," a positive force that can also be accumulated by doing good deeds. It's a grand occasion, and in most cases, a once-in-a-lifetime chance. Something so monumental that it was worth the risk, especially for those from remote areas like us.

Among our group was an elderly couple, Gyatso and Lhakyi. They had embarked on the journey with a sense of joy that made them seem younger than their sixty-odd years. But that joy was short-lived. We were barely a couple days into the journey when Lhakyi began to falter.

The dirt path we'd been following was flat, but each step she took seemed to siphon all the energy out of her, even with all of us taking turns carrying her pack. Gyatso helped her along, saying nothing about the way her face had begun to swell. She panted with each shaky step, as if she'd just run a marathon.

The evening before our departure, the sun was sinking into the horizon, leaving the sky bruised with purple-orange light. As my friends and I splashed around in the river, I looked up to see two shadowy figures at the foot of a hill. It was Gyatso and Lhakyi, their travel packs two dark lumps lying by their feet.

Gyatso was a tall man with a long face, old enough to be my grandfather. He reminded me of Father—Gyatso, too, was highly respected in our village. My neighbors would make a beeline for him whenever they needed help deciphering a phrase in a prayer book or for advice for their daily troubles. Unlike Father though, he was more expressive, more outwardly cheerful. To Gyatso, reading didn't seem like a meditative experience; it was joyous, an exciting adventure to unearth new information.

Lhakyi, on the other hand, was alarmingly frail, her silhouette almost ethereal in the twilight. She bent down as her husband helped her shoulder her pack, and I could see her limbs shaking, even from a distance. Gyatso picked up his own pack, and the two began to slowly ascend the hill, as though checking if they could bear the weight. Even Gyatso, who was healthier, struggled to climb.

I bit my lip. This was a soft slope compared to the terrain that we'd have to traverse. But nobody could fault them for taking the risk. We all understood the enormity of a pilgrimage.

Father called me inside. With one last glance at Gyatso and Lhakyi, I turned to say goodbye to my friends. Dawa and Wangmo chirped and squealed, making me promise to regale them with tales of my adventure. Nyima wished me luck with a carefully neutral expression, but she couldn't quite hide her envy.

Pema, who wasn't particularly religious, could barely contain her anticipation. She and I would be the only minors in our group, and it was reassuring to have someone closer in age to keep me company, even if she, like me, wasn't very talkative.

The only person who didn't seem to share the excitement was Thubten. She was sitting on the riverbank, looking at me with a wistful smile on her face. She could hardly join us in the river with her chronic fatigue and general poor health; a months-long trip to Lhasa was out of the question for her. But merit could be shared. Although I was fuzzy on the details, so long as I was sincere, I could share any merit I gained with not just Thubten, but all other beings.

"I hope you have fun," she said earnestly. I thanked her with a small smile, and as I trudged back to the house, I offered up a quick prayer, hoping that she would get to see Lhasa someday too.

I never did see if Gyatso and Lhakyi made it to the top of the hill.

Lhakyi could walk no farther. We found shelter in a small town, a dozen of us cramped in a small barn house. Gyatso quickly laid out some blankets, carefully laying Lhakyi down. By now, her limbs had begun to swell too. Her breaths came out harsh and jagged as she nestled into a pile of blankets for days. The warm glow of a lamp only cut deeper shadows into her face.

The last time I'd seen someone this sick, my mother had just had a miscarriage. I still remember the way my aunt had frantically helped her through the door, shouldering her weight as they rushed back from the fields as quickly as possible. Mother had looked feverish, sweat pouring down her ashen face as she floated in and out of consciousness.

I might not have fully understood life and death then. But I did now, and I watched in horror as a human being wasted away before my eyes.

There was no hospital to take Lhakyi to, no doctor to explain why her face was now swollen beyond recognition. We could only feed her bits of food and water, and burn incense as we prayed for her recovery.

Gyatso just sat by her side, praying silently. And I sat beside him, still not sure if I was praying properly. I hung my head and mumbled the mantras I'd learned as days blended into nights, hoping it really was the thought that counted. This wasn't like the peaceful prayer sessions I shared with Father. I mixed up the words as my anxiety grew, but if Gyatso hadn't lost hope, I wouldn't either.

When Father wasn't discussing the logistics of the journey, he sat with his eyebrows furrowed, deep in thought. Mulling over the most tactful way to phrase something we all knew but didn't have the heart to say out loud: We needed to move on. Every day, we nibbled on smaller and smaller pieces of tsampa as we began to ration our flour.

Finally, one week into our stay, he called a meeting. "We understand if you wish to continue your journey," he said. A few muttered in agreement, but there was no further discussion. What else was there to say, really, when someone lay dying just a few feet away, and you were helpless to do anything?

Over the next few days, the travelers formed little groups of their own, each promising to pray for Lhakyi before departing. There were no apologies, no arguments, no resentment. Simply a resigned acceptance that there was no chance of Lhakyi traveling onward. Soon, only a handful of people, including me, Father, and Pema were left in that barn, keeping Lhakyi company during her last days.

The locals did all they could to supplement our food. One of them even gave me yogurt as a treat to cheer me up, but the town had limited resources. No matter how many times someone tried to distract me, no matter how mindfully they spoke about Lhakyi's condition in front of me, I knew from the lightness of our packs that, this time, my thoughts and prayers alone wouldn't be enough.

One week later, we had barely enough food to see us through to Lhasa if we were mindful about pacing ourselves. There was nothing to do here. Nothing we *could* do. So, we left, Gyatso still holding a silent vigil by Lhakyi's side.

I stuck close to Father, still reeling from how quickly things had gone wrong. As I put one foot in front of the other, I wished so desperately that I'd been capable of more.

Pelbar Dzong used to have a modest little school staffed by teachers that came and went. At around five years old, I was too young to take classes, but I loved to stand by the door of the room and listen as best as I could. The sight took my breath away every single time.

Older kids sat on long wooden benches in a wide room, small blackboards in hand. They fixed their eyes on the tablets, writing symbols with stubs of chalk made from soot and ashes. They chanted in stilted voices, repeating after the teacher, who stood at the front.

I squinted, trying to get a better look at the chalk markings. A symbol like three little icicles inching toward the ground; another, two cherries joined to a single stem; and yet another, the same cherries with a leaf added on top. The children wiped away the markings and carefully drew new ones.

I crept into the back of the room to get a better look. If it had been any other teacher, I wouldn't have dared to do so, shy as I was. But my uncle Tenzin had just replaced the previous teacher. Whenever I tried to sneak in, the teacher before him would shoot me a stern look; Uncle Tenzin simply let me be. He was my mother's brother—a loud, lively man who took to teaching like fish to water. He'd try to teach me to read every now and then, but he lived on the other side of town and couldn't visit very often. Without consistent lessons, I wasn't able to learn. I couldn't discover something new with each letter, let alone create stories of my own.

I was peering over the shoulder of a boy in the back row when suddenly he turned to look at me. It was Sangye, one of the boys I would play with by the village river. He narrowed his eyes at me and moved his blackboard, hiding it from view. My cheeks flushed with indignation, and I glared at the back of his head. He was so petty!

I didn't know when exactly I would be allowed to start school, but for now, all I could do was wait until I was old enough to attend. We didn't celebrate individual birthdays at home, so I counted the seasons instead. But by the time I finally turned six, the classes stopped. Uncle Tenzin went back to working in the fields full-time. I didn't know why, and nobody explained. Maybe they'd run out of resources. Maybe there was some complex political situation. All I knew was that I'd lost my one chance at receiving an education.

CHAPTER
FOUR

We walked for another day or two, and grass and unruly shrubs soon gave way to gravel as we began climbing the first of four mountains. There was still plenty of wildlife: small animals that burrowed in the dirt or hid in hollow trunks, unfamiliar plants that stuck out between jagged rocks. Someone had strung prayer flags along the cliff face, the faded fabric fluttering as the wind blew their blessings across the land.

I didn't know exactly what sort of prayers had been written on these particular flags, but I imagined them enveloping Lhakyi as she moved on to the next life, wherever that might be. I let these blessings wash over me, felt them fluttering through strands of loose hair. The colors were faded, the edges threadbare and unraveling, but I still watched in awe. Despite being worn, the prayer flags seemed to come alive in the wind, so full of life, so different from the ones I'd seen four years ago.

Pema was around ten years old then, and I was around seven. The air was heavy with the scent of rain. Above us, a blanket of clouds shrouded the land in gray. I could still see my parents working in the barley field with my younger siblings strapped to their backs. The adults were too busy to notice a pair of children wandering away.

We could hear our friends shrieking by the river somewhere. Normally, I'd join them, flinging handfuls of dirt, pretending to be soldiers in a game of make-believe. But that day, Pema decided to take me on an adventure. She guided us a little farther, toward the outskirts of the village, where an old Buddhist monastery lay in ruins.

The monastery had sat abandoned for as long as I could remember. It comprised multiple buildings, almost like a small village in itself. The roofs had collapsed, leaving behind a skeleton of walls made of stone and mud. I'd avoided it for the most part, but I had ventured in a few times when our livestock wandered inside. I'd follow the pitiful bleating of a lost yak, goose bumps crawling across my skin as I stepped over splinters and stones.

To my relief, Pema stopped right outside of the ruins. The ruins were surrounded by low mounds of dirt. I'd never paid them any mind; who cared about piles of dirt? But Pema got on her hands and knees and began to dig. I watched in utter confusion as she used a rock as a makeshift shovel, the pointy end digging into the ground. Then, I picked up a rock as well and followed suit.

We dug for a few moments in silence, save for the whisper of wind through a nearby tree. Finally, my fingertips met something hard and smooth.

"I found something!" I called. I was apprehensive, but I couldn't contain the excitement of discovering something new. Something unknown. I tugged it free and brushed off the dirt. It was a stack of paper covered in dark script. I passed it to Pema, who was one of the few girls who'd learned how to read.

Pema frowned, flipping the sheets back and forth, squinting at the squiggles and symbols. Then she tossed them aside. "It's nothing, really."

We continued to dig. More paper. I picked one up and squinted. Not for the first time, I wished I could read. But then Pema tossed another one aside. *Well, it had to be boring,* I tried to convince myself, burying my curiosity as we continued to dig up page after page.

A light rain began to fall and the wind picked up. A loose page drifted on the breeze, swirling across the plain and toward the mountains. Then, I spotted a flash of color through the damp soil. It was a rectangular piece of cloth in a dull red. I tugged on it, and another flag followed, this time green. I gaped as I continued to pull, unearthing a seemingly endless string of flags in every color imaginable. They hung on by a thread, and if I looked closely, there seemed to be some sort of writing on the frayed fabric, faded from age.

Pema wasn't particularly interested in the flags either, seemingly content to just dig, but I was entranced. I'd never seen anything like it. I coiled the string up as best as I could and stuffed it into my pocket. I ran home as the sun set behind thick clouds, little feet carrying me as fast as they could. I bounded up the wooden steps of the house, the old wood creaking under my weight.

In the middle of the family room was a giant wooden pillar. Though we'd decorate the house for special occasions, the central pillar stood bare and boring at the time. Carefully, I wound the flags around it. They took on a golden glow from the firewood stove, and the muted colors seemed to come alive. It was exciting to make art like this, to bring something beautiful into our home.

Moments later, I heard the footsteps at the door, and my siblings' wails pierced the thin walls as my parents fussed over them. Then, they entered the family room.

"Mother, look what I found!" I presented my masterpiece with a flourish. I was practically vibrating with excitement, waiting for my parents to tell me that I'd done a good job.

Mother's eyes followed the string of flags.

"Oh." The color drained from her face. "Oh, no. Punjun, what were you thinking?" She looked down at where the tail end of the string had fallen on the floor and made a pained noise. "And you dragged it on the ground?"

I stood there, stunned and confused. This was the exact opposite of what I'd expected. I'd done something good, hadn't I? The flags had been buried in the ground; they would've continued to waste away if I hadn't dug them up. They were beautiful and deserved to be on display.

Mother grabbed me roughly, eyes wide with terror. "Don't do this ever again."

"Why not?"

"Just don't."

"I don't get it. It's just some pretty flags."

She tightened her grip. I flinched. Through the pain, I could feel her hand trembling on my arm. "You don't need to get it," she said in a hushed voice. "Some things are not for children to know."

The next morning, the flags were gone. It wasn't until years later that I learned that they were Buddhist prayer flags. Prayer flags hold prayers and mantras, and we believe that blessings spread across the land as they flutter in the wind. They belong strung across ravines and rivers, over mountains and between buildings, not stuffed in half-forgotten dirt mounds.

Some things aren't for children to know. I hadn't known then that the Chinese government had inflicted decades of brutality on Tibetans. I hadn't known that they were destroying the land with their economic ambitions. I hadn't known that there were prisons full of innocents, crimes being committed, lives being taken. Mother and Father did a good job of shielding me from the horrors of the world.

Yet despite their efforts to protect me—or maybe even

because of them—I knew, down to the marrow of my bones, that being Tibetan was something to hide. Something to fear. Something to be ashamed of.

Some things aren't for children to know, but I knew those things well enough.

I never found out what happened to the prayer flags. Maybe my parents buried them back in the ground, in a hole deep enough to hide all sorts of stories and secrets.

CHAPTER
FIVE

I tugged at my hat, making sure it fit snugly, and braced myself as the incline grew steeper, the air colder and thinner. My lungs felt scraped raw, somehow burning and freezing at the same time.

We'd been on the trail for two or three weeks by now, sticking to a steady rhythm each day: walk, rest, walk, rest, walk, rest. I knew the pilgrimage didn't start in Lhasa. The journey itself was part of the merit-making process, so I did my best to keep my mind occupied, taking in the scenery, listening intently as the adults chatted. But there was only so much repetition I could take as an eleven-year-old.

Though my routine at home was also repetitive, it was by no means static. I could spend my time playing with a whole group of friends around my age: Nyima, Wangmo, Dawa, Pema, and even mean, bratty Sangye.

"Sniffles is down! Sniffles is down!" he liked to yell as we pretended to be soldiers, whooping when a dirt-filled cloth ball smacked me square in the face. I'd wave my hands frantically, trying to dispel the worst of it while I coughed and sputtered. Sangye cackled in glee and made exaggerated sniffling noises.

I flung my own makeshift bomb at him. Sangye shrieked, and my friends charged ahead, making gun noises as they pointed their branches and sticks this way and that.

"You should tell him to stop calling you that," Dawa said one day. She hauled me to my feet, doing her best to brush away the layer of grime on my shirt. She picked a twig out of my hair.

I grimaced and scrubbed my sleeve across my face. Where the cold gave Dawa an endearing red flush, it gave me a perpetually runny nose. There was nothing to do about the nickname, and I truly didn't care all that much. "It's fine." Dawa seemed to disagree, her frown almost a pout, but she said nothing more, simply grabbing a handful of dirt to fling at the opposing team.

At the time, none of us had actually witnessed this kind of violence firsthand—things like explosions, gunfire, and the agonized screeches of fallen soldiers. We'd only seen the propaganda films that Chinese officers would bring to the village. We mimicked the flickering images of rugged warriors, each of us screaming dramatically as we flailed on the ground.

Not all of our sessions of make-believe were so violent. We also loved playing house. It was one of the only activities that our friend Thubten could participate in, as she had trouble running around due to her poor health.

My friends and I would stretch across a patch of grass by the water. We scoured its edge for perfect little pebbles to use as play-pretend rice, piling them onto flat stone "plates." Sometimes, if I squinted, I could see hints of greens and reds under the rocks' dull gray exteriors. Those made the best imaginary vegetables and meats.

During these games, I loved playing the father. I loved pretending to be a boy, period. There was something liberating in the way I'd pitch my voice low, trying to mimic my father's mannerisms. I'd put my hair up, wrapping it with a strip of cloth to keep stray strands out of my face like Father did. Sometimes, I even borrowed some boys' clothes from Sangye so I really looked the part.

"Your face is all dirty." Nyima scrunched up her nose. "That's no way to come to the dinner table."

Normally, I would do as told without a peep. Nyima was a year older than me and seemed so much more worldly. She could be blunt, but she was a radiant, feisty young girl. She never hesitated to voice her thoughts, and took charge with such ease. She was a North Star that we looked to for guidance even when the light burned our eyes a little. I wiped my face on my sleeve as best as I could.

As the play-pretend father, however, I could at least shoot back a retort or two. Punjun would never speak up like that, but for now, I wasn't Punjun. I made up intricate little backstories, living out dreams that seemed completely unobtainable—dreams like seeing the world beyond our rural village.

But now that I was actually outside of Pelbar Dzong, there was nobody to play house with while we trudged through the snow, nobody with whom to spin stories and crack jokes. Without Nyima or Dawa to lead the way with their effortless enthusiasm, Pema and I walked on in silence. The difficult climb had been a welcome distraction at first, but now it was just getting tedious. It was taking *forever.*

Just past the tree line, the mountain was a sea of white glitter. I squinted, the sun reflecting harshly off the snow. It crunched under my feet, the chill seeping into my shoes despite the thick padding. I flexed my fingers and toes, the joints feeling swollen and tight.

We cut zigzags across the face of the mountain, careful to test our footing before resting our weight on it. Or at least, that was what the adults did.

I spotted a smooth patch of snow that led downhill and grinned. I was already near the front of the group, and now I could extend my lead by sliding down the mountain. Was I actually competing with anyone? No. Was I still determined to win? Yes.

Pulling my clothes tight, I sat on the icy, hard-packed snow and pushed myself off the top. I barreled down the slope, my cheeks red from the wind. I shrieked in delight as the trees flew by in a flurry of white and muted green. The snow flew in my face, and I swiped it away over and over, determined to remember every second.

Finally, I ground to a halt, lying in a bed of snow so soft, I would've curled up in it had it not been freezing cold. My ears still roared from the rush, and I felt a little dizzy with the thin mountain air.

Pelbar Dzong was hilly, but it didn't have steep slopes like this. At the very most, we could slide up and down the river when it froze over.

I sat up and brushed the snow off my hat, cheeks burning pleasantly from the rush and the wide grin on my face. I turned back toward the group, ready to gloat over my successful slide.

Father came hurtling at me.

"Punjun!" He was furious. "What do you think you're doing?"

"It's a little race!"

He stared at me as if I'd grown another head. "A what?"

"A race," I said, trepidation beginning to creep in. "We were going so slow, and you said we were behind schedule..."

"You could've..."

He didn't have to finish for me to understand. Lhakyi's gaunt face came to mind. The sound of her labored wheezing cut through the roar in my ears.

So I just nodded, the tips of my ears burning from cold

and shame. I stuck close to Father the rest of the afternoon as we descended one mountain and ascended the next.

For the rest of the journey, I snuck glances at his face, watching as it subtly shifted back into his usual pleasant, neutral expression.

The only time I felt truly connected to my father was during our morning prayers. For as long as I could remember, Father would rise at dawn and pray every day without fail. He shaped yak butter into candles and placed little goblets of water onto our modest altar the same way he mended our shoes—lovingly, carefully, yet without fanfare, like it was the most natural and obvious thing to do. His faith was quiet and unsuspecting, as pedestrian as it was precious, and because of it, I lived and breathed faith like an innate instinct.

He owned a few prayer books, the edges worn and their spines cracking. He flipped through them with calloused fingers so delicately that the paper barely whispered as he turned each page. The back of his sun-spotted hands flexed as he cradled one of the books reverently.

"This one." He pointed to a line in the book. Father wasn't fully literate, but he knew enough to recognize the basics. The writing danced across the page, the lines twisting this way and that. "Om mani bêmê hum."

"What does it mean?"

He paused for a moment, before saying, "It's a mantra to help other people and ourselves."

I nodded sagely and mumbled the syllables with all the wisdom of an eight-year-old.

"No, no. Listen carefully. Om mani bêmê hum."

I repeated, tripping a little over the unfamiliar sounds.

"And you have to mean it when you say it."

I spoke the words with a little more gusto, eliciting a smile from my father.

"You'll get it in time."

I sat beside him and muttered along as he recited different mantras. Even if I couldn't get all the words right on the first try, surely the prayers would still work if I really put my heart into them.

Prayer was soothing. It helped settle the frantic thoughts ricocheting through my head. Maybe it was the repetition, the simplicity: Speak the words with all your heart, and the world would be a better place. The knowledge that somewhere out there, someone else was doing the same. A stranger you might never meet was wishing you nothing but the best.

Small plants began to sprout as we descended the last mountain. Pristine white snow melted into a sludgy brown mess, and I kept slipping with all the grace of a newborn calf. The ground leveled out and the unmarked path we were on opened into a road, the dirt packed tightly from decades of use.

In the distance rose a sprawl of white and red buildings, cradled in a vibrant green, set against a backdrop of fog-covered mountains: Lhasa.

CHAPTER
SIX

Lhasa was stunning.

It was *loud*.

As we entered the city, rows of white buildings towered over us, lining the streets. Locals and visitors chattered and yelled and sang. Throngs of people came and went: a stonemason, a merchant, a gaggle of kids squealing as they play-fought. Automobiles kicked up dust in their wake, hulking metal boxes on wheels that carried crates like they weighed nothing.

We noticed other pilgrims prostrating themselves on the street in practiced motions. Bikes and passersby swerved smoothly around them as the pilgrims pushed themselves up, held their hands to their faces, and lowered themselves to the ground again.

I huddled even closer to Father and Pema, afraid I'd get swept away in the chaos. There were just the three of us now, our companions having broken off at various points of the journey, and Father was stopping here and there to ask for directions.

The plan was to stay at a friend's place, or rather, in her garage, where there was more room. But it was growing darker. Brow furrowed, Father finally stopped us with a sigh.

"I can't find them," he said apologetically. "We'll have to sleep rough one more night."

We settled on the edge of Barkhor Square, spreading our blankets onto the dark gray flagstone. There was a large building on the other end of the square—a temple, judging by the stream of pilgrims circling it. Other passersby crossed through the plaza, eyes skidding over us as I nibbled on some tsampa.

Then, suddenly: "Under your blankets. Hurry!" Father's voice was strained. "And don't make a sound." I followed his gaze into the distance, squinting until I saw the silhouette of a soldier approaching us. The toll of the day was creeping up on my father as he blinked hard and stretched his back with a slight wince. Still, he got to his feet, carefully keeping a neutral face as the stranger approached.

Pema's eyes went wide for a split second and she hastily pulled her blanket over her head. I followed suit, ducking under my own covers and curling into a ball.

"You there!" the soldier demanded. "You aren't from here, are you?" He was definitely Tibetan—he spoke with the confidence and fluidity of a native speaker. But his accent was so different from my own that my curiosity got the better of me.

I couldn't help it. I snuck a few furtive glances from under my blanket. The officer paced slowly in front of my father, the lit end of his cigarette winking in and out. His face was obscured by a military-issue hat that sat low over a nest of dark hair. The metallic barrel of a gun peeked over his shoulder, unmistakable even in the semidarkness. The man didn't even bother looking at Father as he continued his questioning.

"And where are you coming from?"

"The Kham region, sir."

The officer paused. "That's in the east."

"Yes, sir."

"That's where the Chushi Gangdruk are from, isn't it?"

"Yes, I think so, sir."

My heart leapt up my throat. The man's demeanor changed in a heartbeat, disgust writ large on his face. The officer spat the name like a curse, as if trying to get a bitter taste off his tongue. I only had a vague understanding of the Chushi Gangdruk. They were a group of fighters who resisted Chinese occupation. He parted his lips, taking a leisurely drag from his cigarette. Smoke billowed in a long exhale. "So you're rebels like them, out to destroy the Chinese."

"No, sir."

"Insurgents."

"No, sir."

"Then what are you doing here?"

"We're here on a pilgrimage."

"Just you?"

"No, we came with a group, but we went our separate ways. That's why we're sleeping rough tonight, sir."

Beside me, Pema was tense as a bowstring, fighting to keep her breath steady under her blanket. For a moment, a wave of nausea threatened to overwhelm me.

Pema was a pretty girl, already brushing off unwanted advances back home. I'd seen the way older boys threw themselves at her or whichever girl caught their eye. I'd heard of boys forcing themselves on a girl, as if she were nothing but a piece of meat to be consumed.

The officer could rape her, and we wouldn't be able to do a thing.

I bit my lip hard and squeezed my eyes shut, fighting the sting of tears. I didn't dare move any more than that.

"You're animals, the lot of you," the soldier spat. "Dangerous, filthy animals who don't belong here."

Father said nothing. There was nothing he could do but murmur the occasional agreement as the man hurled insult after insult. Nothing he could do but keep his head down and gaze lowered as the man got right up in his space.

After more insults I didn't understand, the officer finally walked away with a scoff. Perhaps I shouldn't have been so surprised by the turn of events. After all, there were also soldiers stationed at Pelbar Dzong.

Gingerly, I pulled the covers down and watched as my father prepared for bed. His face was drawn, his gaze dark and distant as he smoothed out his blanket. I looked away, trying to ignore the lines around his mouth that deepened as he clenched his jaw.

"Go to sleep. We have an early day tomorrow," he said softly, before turning on his side.

I did as told, facing the other way.

That night, I dreamed of incense smoke and cigarette butts.

The Tibetan Plateau is one of the highest places on Earth. As you go higher and higher, the oxygen in the air becomes thinner. If you're not accustomed to the thin air, you can get altitude sickness, which can cause vomiting, headaches, and sleep issues. In severe cases, it may also be fatal.

As born-and-raised Tibetans, everyone in my village was used to the high altitude. In contrast, Chinese personnel often couldn't stay for very long because they could barely breathe. But the few days they did stay were particularly miserable for everyone in the village.

We had mandatory meetings where officials would lecture us harshly about everything under the sun. The centerpiece of each meeting was public shaming. They singled out individuals, making them stand in front of a crowd as they hurled insults and listed all their supposed transgressions. Dorje was seen murmuring a prayer in public. Doad complained about grain taxes. Tsering had a picture of someone called the Dalai Lama. I would just stand there in silent confusion. I was bursting with questions, but the somber looks on my parents' faces made it clear that they were not meant to be voiced, even in the privacy of our own home.

Why exactly were any of these bad things? The officers continued their verbal assault with vague explanations. Something about keeping the motherland whole, something about causing trouble and dividing the people. But weren't the officers the ones disturbing the peace? They could have just spoken nicely to the villagers instead of humiliating them in front of everyone. The officers didn't seem to know how to hold a civil conversation.

Sometimes, officers even brought people from neighboring villages, parading them in our streets as cautionary tales. The poor souls always had a placard hanging from their necks, their heads bowed from the weight. Some recoiled with every minor movement. Some didn't so much as flinch as officers hurled insults right in their faces.

Every now and then, Chinese officers hauled a projector to my village after sunset. A generator gurgled and groaned by the machine, filling the air with the stench of gasoline. Most of the time, they projected brief clips of propaganda onto the side of a house: montages of happy Tibetans, ever thankful to the Chinese government for swooping in and saving them from themselves. Other times they showed us miserable scenes from overseas, outside the benevolent influence of the Chinese government. A Tibetan voiceover described to us how lucky we were to be a part of China, but in truth, we barely registered the staticky sounds. Instead, we sat enraptured with the way colors danced on the plain wall, mesmerized by the way the irregular surface distorted the images. The sun had already gone down, yet we bathed in light so bright it almost made our eyes hurt.

But one night, they brought us an action-packed movie. The images danced across the wall like pale ghosts. I had no idea what was going on—the movie had been dubbed in Mandarin Chinese. Foreigners in hard hats were running around, ducking into trenches and behind barricades. They hurled makeshift explosives toward the enemy, and mud splattered everywhere.

Like dung, I thought, wrinkling my nose. Then, a plan formed in my mind. I knew just the way to fight back against the officers who made our lives miserable.

I was older now, around nine or so, no longer the helpless little girl who could only watch in silence as settlers abused us with impunity. *Only a few more years before you're old enough to marry,* a treacherous voice whispered in my head. *Soon, you'll be tied down with a family of your own, without time or energy to speak up.* I tamped down on it. Now was not the time to worry about some nebulous future. It was the time to take action like the heroes in the movie and protect my community.

First, I borrowed clothes from Sangye. It would be harder to get caught if I was in disguise, and if I covered my face a little, I could even be mistaken for a boy. Then, I made mud balls like the ones we used to play make-believe, except this time, I mixed in hefty chunks of yak manure. I stuck them into my borrowed trousers and crept into one of the buildings the officers were using.

I tiptoed into the pitch-black coatroom, heart thumping in my chest. But my excitement started to ebb away as I waited. It must've been time for the town meeting, but the officer still hadn't arrived. I was beginning to lose patience, and the ball of manure was really starting to stink.

Finally, the muted thud of boots came from the hallway. I held a hat in one hand and raised it above my head, hoping it would make me look taller in the darkness. I readied my throwing arm. I only had one shot and I had to make it count. Then, the door opened. Light came flooding in, and a man appeared, his face cast in shadow. I hurled the ball of yak dung at the officer. It landed on his face with a satisfying *splat!*

He let out a yelp, hand flying up only to feel a handful of dung. I darted out of the room as he squirmed in confusion and disgust, making my daring escape. A few seconds later, footsteps came thundering behind me.

I did it. I'd fought back against our oppressor.

Their angry shouts and disgusted noises filled me with glee as I ran home, taking detours just in case I was being followed. Soon enough, I could no longer hear my pursuers. This was *my* home, after all, and I knew it like the back of my hand. I shook the officer off my tail as easily as I breathed the thin mountain air.

For the next few days, I began plotting more missions, each more audacious than the last. I rode that high until one morning when a uniformed man came knocking on our door. He strode in as if he owned the place and settled himself on a cushion, his disdain thinly veiled.

"Fetch me some milk," he ordered in an unfamiliar accent. He could've been Chinese, or he could've been from a different region of Tibet. It wasn't unheard of for Tibetans to work for the occupiers. Mother nudged me toward the jug while she greeted the stranger.

"How can I help you, officer?"

He ignored her. Instead, he turned to leisurely examine our little house, taking in my younger siblings playing on the floor. I placed the wooden cup down, next to where he drummed his fingers against the tabletop. His sharp eyes met mine, and even that brief look seemed to stab right through my chest. "These are your children?"

"Yes, sir," Mother murmured.

He wrapped his fingers around the cup, taking a long, deliberate sip. Then he fixed me with a knowing look that dug straight into my soul. "I hope this doesn't upset my stomach," he said quietly, venom laced through every word. "I'm sure you gave me the best you have, didn't you, little girl? You'd get into quite a bit of trouble if you made me sick."

"It's the same milk we drink," Mother cut in hastily. "It's not much, but I can assure you it's harmless."

"That's good to hear. It would be a pity if anyone in your lovely family were to fall ill."

We stood in silence as the man slowly sipped his drink. My body was frozen, but my thoughts raced, smashing into one another until my head was a jumbled mess. Then, they screeched to a halt when I remembered what the meeting had been about that day.

They'd announced evictions. Houses had been confiscated and redistributed to other, more occupier-friendly families. The original inhabitants would have to live in a run-down barn, sharing their space with livestock. We were a family of five, two of whom were still toddlers. I would be okay with living in a dirty shack alone. The idea of dragging my entire family into a life of squalor, however, made me sick to my stomach.

The man didn't outright accuse me of anything. It had been dark and I'd been in disguise. Surely, he couldn't have known I'd pelted him with yak dung. I trembled like a leaf. He suspected, and suspicion was more than enough to earn some punishment.

His visit was a pointed reminder: *Your little stunt changes nothing.*

It was a warning: *Do anything stupid, and your whole family pays the price.*

I had never felt so small in my life. The officer was right. The Chinese occupiers still came, the meetings continued, and yet more families were kicked out of their homes.

And all I could do was watch in silence.

CHAPTER
SEVEN

In the morning, we wandered through labyrinthine alleyways on our way to the temple. The Barkhor was a historic hub in Lhasa, a bustling marketplace full of goods both familiar and strange. I clutched my pack close to my chest. The marketplace seemed even busier than it had yesterday evening. While some vendors had brick-and-mortar storefronts, others had ramshackle stalls or simply floated around the streets, waving their goods at locals and pilgrims alike.

Even the yak products seemed unfamiliar because of the sheer amount that was on display. I'd never seen stalls full of yak butter and pristine pelts. As self-sufficient as we were at home, we never sold our goods like this, and we certainly didn't buy food or drinks from vendors who hawked their wares at the top of their lungs, not when we could make them ourselves. When Father fished out a few coins to pay for a sweet frozen treat, my eyes practically bugged out of my skull.

"Are you sure?" I asked, although I was already eagerly holding out my hand.

Father smiled and handed me my portion. "Of course. It's not every day that we get to come to Lhasa. This is the trip of a lifetime."

I tensed up then. Father was right. This would most likely be my only trip to Lhasa, if not my only trip outside of Pelbar Dzong, period. I wouldn't have the time to go on another months-long pilgrimage once I married and had children. That was the whole point of this journey. It was a gift from my father before I left my family for another.

I shook the somber thought from my head and shoved the treat into my mouth. My eyes widened at the taste: sweet and tangy, like yak yogurt made into a frozen treat. I resisted the urge to just shovel the rest into my mouth and took another careful bite instead. If this was my last time here, I wanted to savor each moment as much as possible, sear each memory into my mind.

After months of anticipation, I'd imagined this part of the pilgrimage would be a solemn affair. I would pay my respects at temples and hermitages, learn about major figures in Tibetan Buddhism, and circle around sacred sites on foot, holding tightly to the prayer beads Mother had given me. My understanding of religious concepts was murky at best. But I knew that circumambulating a sacred site was important. When I finally took my first proper look at Jokhang Temple, a wave of giddiness washed over me, all thoughts of *serious, respectable grown-up business* gone.

I wasn't prepared for how breathtaking Jokhang was.

My first thought was that it was huge. I'd never seen any building as large as Jokhang Temple. The temple faced west, haloed in light softened by a fine shroud of early morning mist. Whitewashed walls towered over the square, bathing the passersby in shadow as they went about their business. Like the stores in the surrounding Barkhor, the walls of the temple were topped in red and gold.

There had to be five, ten, twenty different shades of red, and as many shades of white and gold. Even the black paint framing the windows seemed to come in a dozen different variations. Then there were the prayer wheels, gilded and large enough to be seen from a distance. Above it all, two golden deer held up a dharmachakra wheel, one of the most important symbols in Tibetan Buddhism, used to represent the Buddha's teachings.

"If you keep gaping like that, you'll get flies in your mouth." Pema giggled. She nudged me gently. "Come on. The line for the temple is getting really long."

Father led the way as we looked for the end of the queue. My heart soared as I eyed the hundreds, if not thousands, of visitors waiting to enter Tibet's spiritual center. Although we had the occasional sanctioned religious celebration in Pelbar Dzong, I could never have imagined a sight like this.

The air was rich with the scent of burning wood, sweet

and earthy. Smoke poured out from stone furnaces, worshippers feeding the flames with pieces of juniper and sandalwood. Vendors hovered near the long line of pilgrims, selling water and prayer wheels and pieces of fragrant wood.

A steady stream of pilgrims circled clockwise around the temple, a meditative practice known as kora. Some held prayer beads and prayer wheels; others prostrated each step of the way, heedless of the sweat on their brow as the sun crossed the sky. Although they muttered the same prayers, they spoke with different accents, their vowels twisting this way and that. On more than one occasion, I had to ask Father what they were saying.

Monks and nuns came and went, some also circling the temple, others simply going about their day. I could distinguish them based on their shaved heads and robes, another sight that had me staring in awe. My own great-aunt Jampa was a nun, and yet I'd never seen her wear a nun's robes in Pelbar Dzong.

Tibet was much bigger and more diverse than I ever could have imagined. It was a far cry from the way elders in my hometown only dared to pray under the cover of night. I was almost vibrating with excitement at the thought of joining the worshippers after our tour of the temple.

It wasn't until midday that we were finally admitted into the temple proper. A monk in maroon and saffron-yellow robes greeted us and took us around the complex. My feet ached from standing in line for hours, but I practically skipped as he guided us past the threshold.

Murals adorned the walls, meters and meters of art stretching from one end of a room to the other. They depicted historical scenes that I'd never seen before in vibrant shades that rivaled the exterior of the temple.

Jokhang Temple had been established in the seventh century, the monk said, by King Songtsen Gampo in honor of his two brides: Princess Bhrikuti of Nepal and Princess Wencheng of China.

The monk explained in great detail, and I nodded vigorously, silently urging him to move on to the next colorful mural. This was my one chance to bask in the grandeur of Jokhang Temple. I had to remember everything: every crack, every paint chip, every story behind every vivid painting.

Great-Aunt Jampa never spoke about her training or religious knowledge, so now I listened attentively, drinking in all the information that she wouldn't—or couldn't—tell me.

The monk took us through the center courtyard, to various altars, up and down dozens of stairs. Everywhere we went, statues of Buddhas and deities looked over us. Some had visible cracks that ran through their torsos and limbs like deep wounds; others were untouched or had been painstakingly restored, piece by tiny piece. I wondered if the run-down monastery in Pelbar Dzong had ever had statues like these. The rooms here were thick with the scent of butter lamps and centuries of stories. The hum of prayer followed us everywhere. But instead of feeling suffocated, I felt a wave of calm wash over me.

It was warm in here, intimate, even though we shared the space with countless strangers. Or maybe it was their very presence, the knowledge that we were all connected, that made the room feel like a familiar embrace. We went from room to room, chapel to chapel, Father pouring the melted yak butter we'd brought into large goblets as offerings to the gods.

We stopped in front of a mural that depicted Gushri Khan and Sonam Chopel, side by side. They wore splendid robes of red and yellow against a backdrop of clouds and flora. My mind began to swirl with questions as the monk explained the history behind the mural.

The Dalai Lama was the title of the most important leader in Tibetan Buddhism, an incarnation of the bodhisattva of compassion. After the passing of the Fourth Dalai Lama, a ban had been placed on searching for his reincarnation. Without a successor to its most important leader, the Gelug school of Tibetan Buddhism would have suffered immensely. Yet Sonam Chopel led the effort to find him despite the threat of punishment and succeeded. Later, the Gelug school would come under attack again. This time, with the help of Gushri Khan and his Mongol army, they were able to fend off their foes and ensure the survival of the Gelug tradition.

"That is how we've come to stand here today, through the resilient spirits of our ancestors," the monk concluded.

I frowned. He'd announced it with such finality, like everything was fine and dandy now, but that didn't quite square with what I'd experienced.

Taking a deep breath, I began to list out the things I knew in my head.

The elders in my village prayed in secret because religion had been banned. But now we were openly visiting the spiritual center of Tibetan Buddhism. So, was religion permitted now? But then where was the current Dalai Lama? Surely, we would have heard from him if he were alive. And if not, there must be a search for the next reincarnation. But then why would Father be so hesitant to tell me more about His Holiness? And what about the destroyed monastery and the missing statues? So, was religion *still* not permitted? But we'd celebrated religious festivals at home before . . .

I wondered if a similar struggle was happening right now, like the monk said had happened with the Fourth Dalai Lama. Father had mentioned the Dalai Lama before, but never in detail. He was a big deal. He was the incarnation of an important bodhisattva.

I wanted so badly to ask where he was or if he was even alive. Surely, such a question would be okay, if the monk was comfortable enough to speak openly about religious figures, if crowd after crowd prostrated around the temple in public. I looked to my father. He chanted along as we paid our respects to each idol, his face belying none of his fear from last night.

For a moment, the sweet, earthy scent of incense turned into something else, something harsh and acrid, like tobacco smoke from the end of a cigarette winking red and hot in the twilight. I bit back the questions at the tip of my tongue and swallowed them whole. They tasted like a thinly veiled threat and churned in my stomach like dri milk gone sour.

You don't need to get it. Some things are not for children to know.

No, I couldn't ask. Better to be silent and safe than vocal and vulnerable.

Finally, the monk steered us toward one last chapel. My mind screeched to a halt. Father, who'd stayed calm and collected throughout the tour, drew in an audible breath.

"The Jowo Rinpoche," the monk said softly, reverently. "The historical Buddha at twelve years old, consecrated by the Buddha himself."

Before us stood a sculpture of the Buddha, its golden sheen glowing in the candlelight. The figure sat serenely, legs crossed in the lotus position. His royal-blue hair was topped with a crown embedded with turquoise and coral. I marveled at the gentle set of his mouth, the graceful curve of his eyebrows, his soft gaze. He looked at peace.

"What does *consecrate* mean?" I whispered, eyes still glued to the statue.

"It's like waking up a statue so it's not just a statue anymore," the monk replied, voice low as if he might disturb the still, calm air of the chapel. "Like it's the Buddha himself who is with us."

The Buddha, right here with us in spite of all the troubles in the world. We would be okay.

For the rest of our stay, we visited every temple, monastery, and nunnery in the city. Some were major places of worship, like Sera Monastery, while others were little more than a stone plaque bearing a name I couldn't read. We paid our respects to each one regardless, stepping around rubble as we walked around the site clockwise, shifting our prayer beads as we went.

By far my favorite was Potala Palace. Mother had briefly explained that it used to be the home of the Dalai Lama. I'd taken the comment to mean that he had passed away, and it had been a depressing thought. But now, with the palace standing right before me, I could only think about how majestic it was.

Sets of crisscrossing stairs led up to the building, whitewashed and topped with red, just like Jokhang Temple. The sheer grandeur seemed to embolden me. I needed to know what the world looked like from up above, to take in as much as my eyes could see. I flew up the stairs, breathless with anticipation, narrowly dodging a few visitors in my rush to get to the top. A few people shot me dirty looks, while others simply looked on, bemused as my father rushed after me and apologized for his unruly daughter.

As I stood at the top of the palace, the entire city seemed so small and so big at the same time. If I stretched my arms wide enough, it was like I could touch the city boundaries and hold Lhasa to my chest. A little wider, and I could trace the gray-green outlines of the mountains beyond with a finger. Shielding my eyes from the sun, I turned east.

This had to be the top of the world, with nothing above me but a blue sky and thin, wispy clouds. My shoulders relaxed and my jaw unclenched. My confusion and anxiety melted away, and I was simply a girl basking in the sun's rays on the Roof of the World.

CHAPTER
EIGHT

Life resumed in Pelbar Dzong. Although we'd been away the whole summer, it was as if we'd never left, and we returned seamlessly to our routine. That sense of normalcy was shattered when Father brought up the prospect of marriage.

"She's not getting married until she's ready, end of discussion," Uncle Tenzin snapped. He was normally such a jovial man, cheerfulness making him seem younger than his sparse gray mane would suggest, but now his annoyance seemed to deepen the lines on his face.

I kept my eyes trained on my dinner, fighting to keep the relief off my face. I'd been expecting the topic to come up. I was almost thirteen now, but hearing everything spoken out loud filled me with a sense of dread. At least there was no way I would be married off without Uncle's blessing. I took another bite of dumplings. I had a sleepover planned with my friends. The sooner we finished dinner, the sooner I'd get to leave.

Father's voice was strained as he replied, "Brother, she's twelve. The boys in the village are already eyeing her. It's time for her to move on, get a husband to protect her."

"Punjun can stay with us for as long as she likes."

"And who will protect her when we are gone?"

My stomach twisted with unease. My faith had taught me that death was nothing to be afraid of—it was simply the end of this life and the beginning of the next. But it was hard to wrap my head around the thought of my parents dying, let alone accept it.

Father had a point. Who would protect me when they passed on? Who would ward off the boys who followed me home or pinned me to the ground? To me, the obvious solution was to teach boys not to do any of that. Realistically, the best deterrent for harassment or assault was the presence of a male chaperone. Marriage wouldn't completely protect me, but it would afford me an extra layer of security.

To my relief, Mother cut in. "It's getting late. Let's just finish up dinner and talk about this some other day. Punjun, come help me with the dishes."

I leapt to my feet, gathering the bowls and hurrying over to her. *Finally.* If I had to hear one more word about marriage, I was sure I was going to lose my mind. I rushed outside, blanket in hand, eager to start the sleepover. The crisp night air was cool on my face, helping me clear my mind as I headed over to Pema's house. Still, I couldn't get the thought of marriage out of my head completely. It had wormed its way into my brain, an unwelcome visitor determined to stay.

I tried to imagine myself caring for a family of my own and quickly pushed the thought away with discomfort. It wasn't that I looked down on married women; I loved and respected Mother for all she'd done for us. It just wasn't for me.

Father had taken me to Lhasa to see the world before I married, but his plan had backfired. The brief taste of the world outside had only whetted my appetite even more. It seemed as if the village had shrunk around me, or maybe I'd grown a little too big for it. The idea of spending the rest of my life taking care of a husband and children sent a wave of dread through me. I didn't want to stuff myself into a life that was two sizes too small.

Wangmo, Dawa, Pema, and Nyima were already waiting on the roof when I arrived. The roofs in our village were flat, so we often had sleepovers out in the open, pointing out funny shapes among the stars. I climbed up and laid down my blanket, eager to listen to some chatter to distract me. But I was out of luck.

"I haven't seen Jetsun in forever," Wangmo said. I barely knew Jetsun, but Wangmo was friends with everyone and had mentioned her before.

"I saw a wagon parked outside her door a few days ago. The same one that appeared a few weeks back." Dawa leaned in conspiratorially. "I bet that was a suitor."

Pema gasped. "Do you think that's why Sangye moved away? Did he get married too?"

I could practically hear Nyima's eye roll. "Don't be stupid. That was ages ago. Besides, who'd want to marry him? He was such a brat."

"Exactly," Dawa said. "He kept calling Punjun 'Sniffles' even though I told him not to. Isn't that right, Punjun?"

"Huh?" I rolled onto my side to face her. The stars overhead glittered like a canopy of jewels. Dawa's big brown eyes gleamed in the starlight, staring expectantly at me. "Yes? I think?"

"Aww, you're no fun, Punjun. Were you even listening?"

Before I could answer, Wangmo cut in. "Don't mind her, she's been spacing out more often lately."

I fiddled with the corner of my blanket as they continued to chatter. Nyima jumped in with another quip; even Pema came out of her shell to giggle along and fantasize about her future spouse. It was light-hearted gossip, something to fill the silence as we stared at the night sky. But the more I listened, the more certain I became that I was not interested.

No, what I wanted more than anything was an education. After the pilgrimage, I was desperate to know more. Surely, there were more stories than the ones our guide had shared, hidden between pages or etched into stone. But since the little village school shut down, it wasn't an option. Uncle Tenzin was too busy to teach me, and without consistent lessons, I couldn't learn to read or write properly.

Students often received their education at monasteries and nunneries as well, but we had none left in Pelbar Dzong. Great-Aunt Jampa even had to join a nunnery in Lhasa to continue honing her religious knowledge.

Her kind face appeared in my mind as I began to fall asleep. I missed her boisterous voice and booming laugh, the way the lines on her forehead softened in rare moments of silence. Then I remembered another wrinkly face, another elderly villager who seemed to exude scholarly grace. Perhaps there *was* someone else who could teach me.

Sherab was an elderly man who lived near the river, and that was more or less all I knew about him. He'd step out of his shack, back hunched over as he went about his business. As far as we could tell, he had no family. No wife, no children, not even a distant relative with whom to sit in awkward silence. He had an otherworldly air about him, as if he'd seen the world twice over. Even though he never uttered a word about his life, I was absolutely convinced that he'd received an education in his youth. His silence only intrigued me more.

"Where are you going?"

Nyima stopped me when I stood and dusted off my pants. We'd been chattering away by the river. Or rather, my friends gossiped as I sat in uninterested silence. What did I care about who had a crush on whom or the new shoes that someone got?

I pointed to the old shack. Like clockwork, Sherab came ambling out, hunched over like an ancient tree heavy with fruit. He plopped down on a log and proceeded to stare into the distance.

"Again?" she asked, a hint of impatience creeping into her voice. "All you do is stare at each other. Stay here and stop pestering him."

"I'm not pestering him, I'm just sitting with him," I said.

"You don't even talk! Why won't you play with us instead?"

"Stop it, Nyima," Wangmo said, resting a hand on her shoulder. "If Punjun doesn't want to join us, she doesn't have to."

"She's gotten so distant," Pema muttered with a frown, and turned to me with a forlorn look. "We just want to include you, you know."

I did know, but I didn't know how to tell them that I didn't really mind the distance growing between us.

The thought caught me off guard. I wasn't being condescending, was I?

Dawa eased my worry when she flashed a reassuring smile before turning back to her conversation. We were different, that was all. Nyima liked playing house, Wangmo liked running around the field, and I liked going to school. Or rather, I would've liked going to school.

All the more reason, then, to observe Sherab. Maybe I would gather the courage to ask him to tell me everything he knew about the world.

When I approached Sherab, he took one look at me, nodded, and settled his gaze back on the mountains. Figuring that he didn't mind my company after all, I sat on a log opposite him and studied his face.

He had a pair of deep-set eyes, his eyebrows two great white bushes atop them. Like my parents, his face was dusted with sunspots, his hands calloused from hour after hour of manual labor. He had to be old enough to be my grandfather, with deep wrinkles carved into the corners of his eyes and mouth.

I had asked Mother about this enigmatic man, but like every other time I'd asked about the village elders, she simply said, "I don't know." He kept to himself, but it was hard to imagine Pelbar Dzong without him. He'd lived here for decades, and he would surely stay here for even more.

I tried to imagine my own face with those same wrinkles, or perhaps I'd get those sunspots. Would I grow the same shock of full white hair, or would my hair grow thin like the other elders I'd met?

Suddenly, Sherab stood with a grunt, startling me out of my reverie, and hobbled back into his shack. I sat there nervously, scuffing my shoes against the dirt. Was I bothering him after all? Surely, he would tell me if I was.

Sherab emerged from the doorway just as I stood up to leave, a steaming cup in each hand. He held a cup out to me. I stared. After a beat, I sat back down gingerly and accepted the proffered cup.

Father would sometimes share his butter tea with me, but it tasted absolutely disgusting to me, the salt accentuating the bitter brew. But the cup in my hand let off a more fragrant scent, earthy and thick with yak butter. Perhaps Sherab prepared his tea differently. Not wanting to seem rude, I held the cup up to my lips, the steam settling on my face in a fine layer of moisture. I tipped it back just a smidgen, and a full-body shudder ran through me. Tea really was gross, no matter who made it.

The silence was as thick as the buttery aroma wafting in the air.

I wanted to ask why the monks in town never wore robes, why old ladies rushed to hide their prayer beads when I saw them praying in the dark. As far as I knew, life had taken a turn for the better. We owned our own land now, for the most part, and though we were poor, we never starved or lacked shelter. The Chinese officers who did come to Pelbar Dzong never stayed for long.

I wanted to ask why I wasn't allowed to ask in the first place.

I knew how to spin wool into yarn and the perfect flour-to-water ratio for tsampa. I knew the amount of firewood we needed to last the winter, and the best place to collect water. I knew everything I was supposed to know as a girl from a rural Tibetan family, but not the things that I wanted to know.

For a moment, I imagined myself as someone bolder, braver. Someone who wasn't Punjun.

I found prayer flags and books in the ground, I might say without even batting an eye. *We should dig them up.*

Sherab would nod, and I'd lead the way to the old, ruined monastery. He'd tell me all about Pelbar Dzong, the good and the bad. We'd talk about his travels.

Slowly, we'd go through the tattered books together. He'd teach me how to read and explain each of the books. I would keep a few for myself and painstakingly copy each word and symbol. I'd finally learn how to tell stories of my own.

My thoughts were still a jumbled mess as I settled into my blanket that night. I didn't *have* to get married. Not technically. There was no decree or law forbidding me from becoming an old spinster.

I thought of my great-aunt Jampa. *She* wasn't married, and she was doing just fine! I thought of my own parents. They'd married out of love. So, if I didn't love anyone, I wouldn't get married, simple as that!

But Father's concerns weren't unfounded. The teenagers in the village were growing rowdy, restless. A boy had flung himself at me, pinning me down and clawing at my clothes in a tangle of limbs and screams. I'd managed to fight him off that time, but who was to say I would be so lucky the next?

I buried my face in the blanket. *The next,* I thought, because assault seemed all but inevitable.

Beside me, Mother had already fallen asleep. I studied her face. She seemed happy. For all the hardships in her life, she loved her family, and that seemed enough for her. I tried to picture myself in five years, as content as my mother and accepting my lot in life. But my mind drew up blank.

Maybe it was through playing house and imagining and pretending to be something other than Punjun that made me realize that Punjun could be someone different. The problem was I didn't know how exactly to get there.

CHAPTER
NINE

The family room smelled of sugar and butter, and a siz-
zling sound filled the air as Father lowered another piece of dough into a pot of hot oil.

We were making khapse, a kind of deep-fried Tibetan snack that resembled cookies. Sugar was rare, but it was Losar—the Tibetan New Year celebrated over several days—and Father had bought us a pouch as a treat. The dough was made of flour, eggs, butter, and sugar, and then shaped. Some khapse were also finished off with another dusting of sugar on top.

"Are you done with the next batch?" Father called over his shoulder.

"No . . ." I looked forlornly at the gooey mess of flour and eggs in my hands. Next to him, Yeshe was happily sprinkling a generous amount of sugar on the finished cookies. My mouth watered. Maybe there would be some left over that I could eat straight out of the pouch.

For now, I focused on shaping the dough. There were

many different designs, from simple shapes to complicated twists, and this year, I was determined to master a braid.

"Fold the dough in half and cut it into strips," Mother said, demonstrating. "Then you take the left strand here and pull it across here. And then you twist it like this—no, no, like *this*, Punjun." There was laughter in her voice as she watched my sad attempts at emulating her movements.

I, on the other hand, was pouting. I could braid hair just fine! Maybe it was the texture of the dough that was throwing me off, or the part where I had to flip it over, or the other part where I needed to worm the right strand under the middle strand, and now the right strand was the new middle strand, and the left strand went over the middle strand but did that mean the right strand or—

"I'm done!" Bhuti declared triumphantly, interrupting my thoughts. I was about to scold him for making me lose track of the braid when he proudly presented his shapeless lump of dough. I burst into laughter.

"What's *that?*" I said, streaking flour on my cheek as I wiped away tears.

"Khapse. Obviously."

I pointed at Mother's immaculate khapse. "Weren't you trying to do that too?"

"Who cares? It all tastes the same. Now hurry up and finish yours."

I pinched the ends of my dough together and looked at my lopsided braid. Bhuti had a point. It was just a snack we made together to enjoy as a family, so there really was no need to fuss over the appearance. I passed my khapse to Father, who added it to the pot of oil.

My stomach growled as I started my next attempt. Khapse wasn't the only food we had for Losar, of course. We had noodle soups and momo dumplings, pastries packed with cheese and butter, yak meat and rice. We'd gather with family on the first day of Losar, making sure to eat our fill to manifest a year of abundance. Then, the village would hold festivities for the rest of the holiday, full of prayer and song and more good food. My favorite part was the dancing.

All the children in the village were dressed up in the finest garments their families had to offer: intricately embroidered jackets, robes in magenta and green and black. For me, that included a pair of large stone earrings. They were grayish turquoise, old but well-loved as they were passed down through generations.

We were dancing with all the other kids, giggling as we flailed this way and that. Nyima noticed that I'd been reaching for my ears throughout the day.

"Are you okay, Punjun?" she asked, an expression of genuine concern on her face.

"Yes, it's just that . . ." I ducked my head, sheepish. "My earrings are kind of heavy." The stones had been pulling on my earlobes all day, occasionally even smacking the side of my face.

Nyima's face softened when I reached up to fiddle with the earrings again, my discomfort clear as day. "Do you want to wear mine instead?"

"Can I really?"

She took off her jewelry without a moment's hesitation. The earrings also had dangling stones, but they were smaller and more manageable. I accepted them gratefully and offered mine in return. "Here. You can wear mine."

She put them on with a smile. "I'll give them back after the new year."

We went straight back to the celebrations. I twirled and skipped, waved my arms, and fluttered my fingers. My ears rang from the clash of cymbals and the thundering drums. I marveled at the swirl of vibrant fabrics and the glittering ornaments. I'd always felt like a fish out of water, but as I spun around and around in a crowd of flushed, smiling faces, I knew that Pelbar Dzong would always be my home.

The festivities wound down, and the village settled back into its usual rhythm. We'd prayed for abundance after all; it was time to put the work in.

The snow had melted away by early spring, and Nyima and I were out collecting firewood. We hacked at tree stumps, occasionally stopping to show off a particularly good chunk of wood.

"Oh, before I forget," I said, tossing a handful of sticks into my basket, "here are your earrings."

I pulled them out from my pockets carefully and offered them to her. Nyima's wide smile froze when she reached out. She squinted at the earrings in my palm, her face so close I could feel her light breaths against my fingertips. The squint turned into a frown, and the frown turned into a glare so heated, I swore I could feel the heat radiating from her flushed cheeks.

"You broke them." She held up the pieces, and sure enough, one of the stones had broken off from the wire. Guilt twisted my stomach. I really thought I'd been careful.

Then I lit up. "Actually, Mother can probably fix it! All she has to do is attach the stone back on, right?"

"But you broke it."

"Yes, and I'm really, really sorry. So let me take it home for my mother to fix."

Nyima huffed, her glare now growing cold. "It's broken, Punjun. I don't know what else you want me to say, but you broke it, and I don't want it back."

"Well, I'll ask Mother to fix them anyway. She can fix anything." Pride swelled in my chest. Just the other day, Mother had patched up the holes in our clothes in the blink of an eye. The earrings would be a piece of cake.

"Do what you like. I'm keeping your earrings," she said, and stomped away.

"You can't do that." I stared at her, waiting for her to burst into laughter and say she was just teasing me. She couldn't just do that. I chased after her, anxiety twisting thick in my belly. "They're not just mine, Nyima. Those belong to my family."

The earrings weren't just some silly little trinkets. Those were not mine to lose.

Nyima ground to a halt. "You think I don't know that? My earrings belong to my family too, and you broke them!"

I thrust my hands toward her again, trying to show her how Mother might fix it. "Look, it's not *broken* broken, the stone just fell off, so we can just glue it—"

"I don't want it!"

"But it belongs to your family. You should take it back once we fix it." My desperation was growing. Nyima could be prickly sometimes, but I'd never seen her mad like this before. Her face was bright red with anger now. "I'll bring it to your house—"

"I said *I don't want it!*" Nyima shoved my hand away. The next thing I knew, the air was knocked from my lungs as I hit the ground.

She sat her weight on my chest, straddling me as her fists rained down in a flurry of blows. She was screaming at me, garbled and barely intelligible. "You broke it! It's my family's treasure and you broke it!"

"I'm sorry! Mother can fix it, I promise!" But Nyima didn't seem to be listening. I raised my arms to my face to protect myself from the worst. She was relentless, her hair was falling out of her neat bun, the stray pieces framing wide, furious eyes.

Reaching up blindly, I got a solid fistful of her hair and yanked as hard as I could.

Nyima screeched in pain and scrambled off me.

I wheezed, finally getting a decent gulp of air, and dropped my head to the ground with a dull thud. We'd had our disagreements, but I'd never gotten into a physical fight with a friend before.

Still in a daze, I pushed myself up, wincing from the cuts and bruises beginning to form. In my hand was a tuft of soft brown hair. On her scalp was a bare patch of angry red skin. I watched in horror as Nyima clamped a hand over her new bald patch, her face contorted from the pain. Her eyes were swollen and red-rimmed, and she fixed them on me.

"You've done it now," she hiccupped. "I'm getting my brothers, and they're going to teach you a lesson!" She then clambered onto her feet and ran toward the village.

I hugged my knees to my chest, reality finally sinking in properly. I'd ripped Nyima's hair out. *I'd ripped Nyima's hair out.*

For a second, I thought of getting my own brother. But what good would that do? Running home would take me right past Nyima's house, and Gelek was too busy taking care of my grandparents. I didn't want to bother him. I buried my face in my hands. Not for the first time, I wished I had someone not just to protect me, but to fight for me as well.

All too soon, Nyima's voice returned, this time accompanied by two deeper voices.

"Come on out, Punjun!" they called. "And you better get ready for the beating of your life!"

I scrambled onto all fours to stay hidden, clamping my mouth shut and breathing through my nose. My heart hammered in my chest, and I held back a wince of pain as I began crawling, searching for a thick bush to hide in. It would be unpleasant, but anything would be better than being beaten to a pulp by someone bigger than me. I slipped right into the bush, wincing as twigs bit into the fresh scratches on my body. For the next few hours, I sat there, curling into myself as much as possible until their voices faded into the distance.

Night had already fallen by the time I got home.

Mother wiped my face with a washcloth, scrubbing the back of my ears, making sure to get every speck of dirt. "Punjun," she started, and my shoulders tensed. She was going to ask me what happened. And I would have to tell her that I lost our precious earrings and pulled a girl's hair out. But the question didn't come. She just fixed her gaze on me, eyes searching. Then she shook her head, lips in a tense line, and started wiping my arms.

Father sat at the table, sipping his tea as he watched Mother clean me off. He took in the sorry state I was in: covered in scrapes and bruises, clothing torn and muddied, my hair practically a bird's nest. His eyes met mine, and I flicked my gaze away, sheepish and guilty for having come home late in such a mess. I braced myself for a harsh lecture as the silence stretched on.

"Punjun," he said finally, "sometimes we have to be the bigger person." He swirled his cup, considering his next words. "People will do what they do. We can't control them, and we can't always reason with them."

So, Nyima's parents had already told mine what had happened. I opened my mouth to explain, but stopped short at the look on his face. Father often came home exhausted, but this was more than exhaustion. It was resignation. The lines on his face seemed to deepen. He looked worn down by something other than manual labor and children's squabbles.

I nodded. Whatever was troubling him, it was yet another of those things that were not to be talked about. Just one more question, never to be asked, itching under my skin like an insect bite.

Once again, we would carry on as if nothing had happened. Mother then placed a small wooden bowl of yogurt in front of me. It was rich and creamy as always, but tonight, it felt just a little too heavy on my tongue.

CHAPTER
TEN

I spent the next few days agonizing whether or not to apologize to Nyima. I really was sorry for ripping her hair out and for breaking her earrings. At the same time, the bruises on my body still felt tender. She hadn't needed to resort to violence like that.

But the next time we saw each other on a wood-gathering trip with the other girls, Nyima only shot me a dirty look before carrying on as usual. Like the adults, she had already perfected the art of pretending nothing was wrong, at least not in public. We were to live our lives like the plants in our yard: rooted firmly in the ground, ordinary and inconspicuous. We were to blend in with our surroundings, even if invasive species began to cover the land.

"We're going home," she declared, nudging her chin upward. Sure enough, the sky was blanketed in a dense gray even though it was just past noon. The smell of rain grew stronger as the girls packed up their belongings.

I adjusted the basket on my back and paused. It was

woefully light. We had some wood in the house, but I didn't want to come home practically empty-handed.

"I'll keep going," I said.

Nyima furrowed her brow. "You'll get sick."

"Leave her be. You know how hard-headed she can be," Wangmo called over her shoulder, and then turned to me. "Just make sure you get home safe, Punjun."

Nyima looked unimpressed. "If you want the rain to ruin what little firewood you collected, go ahead."

"I'm staying with Punjun!" Dawa marched over, as if the idea of getting caught in a downpour was no big deal.

"You don't have to," I mumbled. I didn't want to impose.

"I want to," she insisted, eyes bright and sincere.

I offered a small smile, and we headed deeper into the mountains without another word. With the other girls gone, the only sounds left were twigs snapping underfoot and small animals burrowing in the brush. Dawa would occasionally comment on the growing scent of rain, or how the sticks she found were all damp and useless. I simply nodded. Not for the first time, I wondered if I was being terribly boring. But Dawa seemed content to work in silence.

It began to drizzle, and we started toward a nearby cave, not wanting to ruin our firewood. The mountainside was riddled with caves and alcoves. Apparently, monks used to meditate in solitude up in the mountains, away from the distractions of the material world. I could almost picture it:

a solitary monk clad in humble clothing, legs crossed in the lotus position, breathing deep with only the soft patter of rain to keep him company.

I'd like that, I thought as we settled in just past the mouth of the cave. *To devote myself to my religion.*

But that, of course, was impossible. I had younger siblings to care for, livestock to herd, barley to harvest. A man to marry and children to carry, eventually. I picked at the dirt, growing restless with each thought. The feeling of unease crept up my spine until I jumped up to walk it off.

With my hands slightly outstretched, I ventured to the back of the cave in the semidarkness. Nothing but a pile of rocks. Well. I didn't exactly have anything else to do as we waited for the rain to stop.

Carefully, I ran my fingers over the pile as my eyes slowly adjusted to the dimness. The rocks were a little slick and slimy from having been in a damp cave for goodness knows how long. They were mostly large chunks around the size of my fist, but varied wildly in texture. I closed my eyes, trying to focus on the sensations.

This other one had little bumps on it, and another chunk had divots instead. This one was even, unnaturally so. Crevices stretched across the surface, too uniform and delicate to be cracks. The contour dipped and crested, the surface smooth until it broke off in a jagged edge. I brought my face right up to the stone and squinted.

I gasped, and Dawa came running over in alarm.

"Punjun, are you—" Her eyes widened as she looked past my shoulder. "Wow."

It wasn't just a pile of boring gray rocks. In the dim light, we could make out the outlines of broken statues, covered in a layer of grime that barely budged when I tried to wipe it off. Massive cracks ran through some of them, and others were even missing a limb or two.

Dawa and I dragged a stone figure to the mouth of the cave, cupping puddled rainwater in our hands to clean off the dirt.

The statue was a little over a foot tall, battered and damaged, but with all its limbs miraculously intact. The figure sat serenely with its hands in its lap, draped in silks hewn out of stone. Most of the colors had faded, but there were unmistakable patches of red and blue paint that had hung on stubbornly. Our fingers slowed as we revealed each detail, each intricately carved line that withstood years of damage and disrepair.

So this was where the authorities had hidden our religious icons.

"I'm going to bring it home," I said, staring at the statue in awe. It was nowhere as grand as the ones at Jokhang Temple, but we would clean it, fix it, take care of it as best as we could. I wanted to put the pieces back together again, just like Mother had fixed Nyima's earrings with ease. After all, the statue was a representation of the Buddha. Or, at least, I thought it was the Buddha. In any case, it had to be someone important, if the Chinese thought to discard it out in the middle of nowhere.

"Are you sure?" For the first time since we left the village, Dawa seemed uncertain.

"Father would love it. Unless you wanted it!" I added hastily, secretly hoping that she would let me take the statue. I didn't know how religious her family was, but if she really wanted it . . .

To my relief, she shook her head with a soft smile on her lips.

"I'll help you put it in your basket."

My back hurt so bad as we hiked home. The basket was so much heavier with the statue. My hair stuck to the back of my neck, tacky and itchy like dozens of tiny damp fingers on my skin. But I couldn't bear to rest for too long, eager to share my discovery with my family

When I got home, my aunt and uncle were at the house again. I fought the grin off my face, not wanting to spoil the surprise. They were also profoundly devout Buddhists. I'd only brought home one statue, but they'd no doubt still be pleased to see it even if they couldn't have one themselves. This would be even better than I'd planned.

After dinner, we prayed in silence as usual, but I could hardly sit still.

Now, I thought as we wrapped up our ritual. *Now is the perfect time to show them my gift.*

"Mother, Father, Uncle, Aunt," I said, giddy. My heart was about to leap out of my chest. "I have something to show you."

Uncle chuckled. "It better be something good, Punjun. I've never seen you this excited."

I hurried over to reach into my basket, but my muscles were like jelly after the hike, and I couldn't lift the statue out. Mother stood from her cushion and slid her hands next to mine. "This certainly does not feel like firewood."

Suddenly, the tips of my ears felt unbearably hot. Oh. Right. I was supposed to get kindling for the stove. I'd completely forgotten. But surely this would more than make up for the lack of firewood. So, I looked up at her, not wanting to miss the moment her eyes lit up as she lifted the statue from the basket.

Instead, Mother's face went blank. She took a deep, shuddering breath through parted lips and called out softly to my father. Father kept his expression neutral, but his hands shook as he cradled the statue in his hands. Realization dawned on me, as cold as a bucket of snowmelt. It was like the prayer flags all over again.

This was worse than coming home empty-handed. I'd marched proudly down the mountain with a confiscated religious icon. Not a modest little figure that Father had sequestered away or a simple string of prayer beads. This was not some government-sanctioned religious display. No, I'd brought home a solid stone statue that Chinese soldiers had clearly meant to destroy and leave to rot.

"There's . . ." I cleared my throat and tried again. "There's some firewood at the bottom of the basket," I offered feebly.

Mother swallowed hard. "We can't keep this." Her eyes were wide with panic and awe as they met my father's. "There's no way."

Father shook his head, running a gentle hand over the statue. "No, we can't."

But I want to. The unspoken message was so loud and clear on his face. Something in my chest twisted, as if someone had reached in and squeezed my heart. I began to shrivel in on myself as I watched the adults share pained, furtive glances.

"We'll take it," Aunt finally said after a long stretch of silence.

"It wouldn't be right to just put it back in that cave," Uncle added. "Though we'll have to borrow the basket."

After putting the statue away, the adults eased back into their small talk, finding their usual rhythm despite some initial awkwardness. They'd smoothed away the edges of the problem and tucked it on a high shelf, never to be spoken of again.

Everything was fine now.

We laid out our blankets that night, same as always. Bhuti and Yeshe were already fast asleep, blissfully unaware of the tension I had caused. I listened to the steady rhythm of their breathing, the occasional whistle as they took in one breath after another.

Everything was fine. I'd done something incredibly stupid, but they were fine. We were fine. No harm had been done.

"If you find any more of these, you leave them," Mother said firmly.

"But the monk at Jokhang Temple said that statues—"

"Punjun."

She looked me square in the face. The conflict was clear in her deep brown eyes, and I knew from the tiny reflections in them that my expression was the same.

This time, nobody had caught me as I hauled the contraband home. This time, my brother and sister still had a family to look over them as they slept. This time, everything had turned out fine.

And that was why there could never, ever be a next time.

CHAPTER
ELEVEN

The door to the house was open, letting in a cool breeze. It caressed my heated cheeks as I tried not to fidget with self-consciousness. The elaborate outfit Mother had put me in was a far cry from my usual plain garb. She layered a loose white robe over my pink top, the robe's edges embroidered in gold and red. The wide sleeves ran past my fingertips, all the way down to my knees, and I wondered how anyone was able to do anything with their hands hidden. Mother then wrapped a long brown skirt over the robe, tugging here and there to make sure the delicate wool sat correctly at my ribcage.

Last, she gave me a meaningful look as she placed necklace after necklace around me, the coral beads large as my thumbs. I looked away sheepishly.

"I'll keep them on this time. Promise."

A high lama had come to town for a religious festival. In Tibetan Buddhism, lamas are spiritual teachers. Some are monastics who have taken their vows and live in hermitages;

other lamas are laypeople who have not taken monastic vows and are allowed to get married. This high lama was also an ordained monk. I couldn't quite remember what the specific occasion was, but the entire village had been buzzing, and I was no exception. It wasn't every day that such an esteemed monk came to the Middle-of-Nowhere, Kham Region.

When Mother finally finished fussing over me, we headed toward the modest town hall where the festival was to be held. I stepped as lightly as I could, skirt in hand, trying not to soil the hem with dirt or mud.

The town hall had once been a temple, but I'd only ever known it as a broken-down meeting place for the village. According to Dawa's grandmother, the Chinese had ransacked the place when they arrived, emptying the life out of it and leaving us with wood and stone. It wasn't the only building that had been destroyed.

Pelbar Dzong had once been an administrative center before the Chinese invasion, but now it was a husk of its former self. We passed large residences that used to belong to Tibetans, now relegated to housing livestock. The administrative office had been reduced to rubble, a collection of chipped bricks and overgrown weeds. Then there was the local nunnery, farther up in the mountains, that had been destroyed so thoroughly, it was barely recognizable as a place of worship. I wouldn't have known if my great-aunt Jampa hadn't mentioned it in passing. Questions bubbled up my throat, and I shoved them back hard. After all, today was a day of celebration. There was no use dwelling on the past.

The little hall was almost unrecognizable. Butter lamps had been placed throughout, lending a warm, intimate atmosphere. Rows and rows of cushions had been placed on the ground. An altar had been set up with small religious statues and golden goblets of water, simple but regal all the same. Sunlight streamed through the open doorway, the light winking in and out as people shuffled by.

We settled onto the floor, legs crossed, and faced a low platform that had been erected at the far end of the chamber. I imagined I had a string attached to the top of my head, gently pulling my spine up straight, even though the heavy necklaces made me want to slouch all the way to the ground. I was determined to be on my very best behavior today, especially since Father and Uncle Tenzin had been in charge of preparations.

The high lama was already sitting, his expression solemn. He wore a pair of simple robes, as was customary. But the monastics at home so rarely wore those clothes that I couldn't help but stare. The red and gold fabrics cascaded off his thin frame like waterfalls. In his right hand was a dorje scepter, and in his left, a tribu handbell. I'd seen the bronze instruments in passing in Lhasa, but now I could pick out more details.

The dorje fit neatly in the lama's liver-spotted hand. It had a cylindrical handle and curved prongs that sprouted from both ends before meeting again in a spherical shape. The metal had become slightly dull, a dark patina having settled into the fine bronze ornamentation from years of use.

The bell was cast from the same bronze. At the tip of the handle, the metal split into curved prongs like the dorje. The lip of the bell flared out in a gentle slope, carved decorations lining the edge. The monk flicked the handbell in a practiced move, and the bright, brassy sound filled the air, signaling the beginning of puja.

The lama initiated the chant, and we joined in until our voices merged into one. I copied Mother's posture, holding my own prayer beads in both hands, thumbing the beads each time I recited the prayer. This was a sanctioned religious event, I reminded myself. The Chinese government permitted it. We had nothing to fear. I focused on that thought, willing myself to transmit the reminder to everyone else in the room.

We were always to pray for others, Father had taught me, to let go of our egos. The world was made of hundreds, thousands, millions of other sentient beings. Why focus on yourself when there were so many others just as complex and deserving of good fortune?

Eyes closed, I sank into that calm place that only prayer could bring me. My breath slowed. The words melted on my tongue, the vibrations building to a pleasant buzz that sank into my bones. I pressed my palms together, tipping forward in a reverent bow—

Clack clack clack clack clack

I jumped. The stones on my necklace clattered together, echoing in the hall. My stomach churned with embarrassment, and I was prepared to melt into the ground. Yet nobody batted an eye.

These were normal sounds, I realized: prayer beads jostling together; the soft rustle of cloth as worshippers shifted in their seats; the musical drone of prayers; and—to my chagrin—awkward teenagers making awkward noises at inopportune moments.

This was what normal looked like, and I felt . . . at peace.

This was it. This was my place in life, and everything that had happened thus far led up to this moment.

After the ceremony, Father ushered me forward to join the crowd waiting to meet the monk. The tiredness was obvious on Father's face, but he had an air of contentment as he took in the fruits of his labor: the elaborate setup, the excited chatter, the peals of laughter as children flocked outside to play games.

Wangmo was before us, dressed in all the finery her family had to offer. Her lips moved, but I couldn't hear her above the excited chatter. Then, she bowed her head. The lama snipped off a tuft of her hair and cast it into a little fire by his side. She looked up, bowing profusely in gratitude before stepping away with her family.

My eyes widened as I registered the little ritual. Wangmo had asked to become a nun, and the monk had granted her permission. Normally, there would be a special initiation ceremony for monastics, with elaborate rules and rituals passed down through the centuries. But lama visits were few and far between in rural areas, and serviceable temples were even rarer. So, it wasn't uncommon for worshippers to ask to join the monastic order at a prayer session like this. But I hadn't expected her to do so. She'd never mentioned her religious aspirations. She was a pragmatic girl, though, so she must've given it a lot of thought before committing her life to her faith. I could see her positively beaming, the flickering butter lamps giving her cheeks a warm golden glow. I wondered what other secrets she might be hiding, what other thoughts she kept to herself.

Before I could dwell on it too long, it was our turn to approach the lama.

Father offered the lama a pure white scarf, known as a khata. I bowed deeply as well, trying not to visibly wince as the stones around my neck clattered loudly again. The lama didn't seem to mind, graciously ignoring the noise in favor of greeting us in return.

"Thank you for your hospitality," he said.

"No, it was the least we could do," Father said. He seemed to stand a little taller. He put a hand on my shoulder and added, "This is my daughter Punjun."

I bowed again, not sure what to do as the monk laid his glinting brown eyes on me. I'd met monks before, but this was a high lama. Was I supposed to greet him in an extra-special way? Was I supposed to say something different? Was there some formal greeting?

My thoughts tangled together, until I blurted out the first thought I could.

"I'd like to become a nun."

The low chatter around us continued. But Father's and Uncle's silence was palpable. Behind me, someone cleared their throat awkwardly.

"I mean, please," I added hastily.

"Punjun," Father said evenly. "Perhaps we should speak more about this. At home."

For a moment, I almost felt guilty about my impulsiveness. Not only was I making a rash decision, I was putting my family on the spot in front of the whole village. There wasn't really a polite way to say *Absolutely not, Punjun* in front of a revered monk.

Father added, "You can join a nunnery when you're older. Maybe twenty, twenty-five."

I stiffened, muscles seized with frustration.

What? How could I possibly wait any longer when I could be married off at any moment? Father was a man of his word, but at that moment, I wasn't so sure. He'd been the one to bring up marriage in the first place, after all. I was fourteen. I'd have to wait six more years to turn twenty, and that was plenty of time for someone to change his mind. Maybe he was worried that I was being rash, that I was too young to know what I truly wanted. But he somehow thought I was old enough to get married. No, this had to happen now. At fourteen years old, I was running out of time. I did not have the luxury of growing up.

The truth was, I hadn't thought it through. Yet the pieces clicked together as I thought of a counterargument.

I was not an educated girl. I didn't know much about religious texts, or history, or even what was happening around me in the present. But joining a nunnery would be a starting point. I was painfully aware of the limits of my knowledge. If I became a nun, I could learn how to read for real. I'd learn more about my beliefs and my culture. And to top it all off, I would never have to worry about getting married ever again.

When Father said nothing, I bowed my head and repeated, "I want to become a nun." This time the words were measured, certain.

The anxiety of being denied ran rampant in me like startled livestock, skittish and jumpy. My heart thudded against my ribs, the rush of blood in my ears growing louder and louder. I almost missed the soft *snip* of scissors right above my head. Then, the sharp, acrid smell of burnt hair. My breath stuttered as reality began to settle over me.

"You'll need a new name," the lama said. He studied me carefully, a glint in his eyes as he considered the options. The possibilities. Ones that I'd barely dared to dream of, now about to become reality.

"Tsultrim Dolma," he finally said.

My eyes widened. To be named after the bodhisattva Jetsun Dolma, the goddess of compassion . . .

"Thank you. Thank you so much." My voice was small, cracked, disbelieving. Father and Uncle murmured the same before steering me home.

Mother pulled out a fine razor to shave my head as soon as we got home. Tufts of hair fell around me, itching my nose, getting in my mouth as I spoke softly with her.

"Being a nun is a serious responsibility, you know," she said. "It's not the same as praying with your father or saying a few mantras at the dinner table. Laypeople will look to you for prayers and guidance, and it's your job to help as many of them as you can, as best as you can."

"Like Great-Aunt Jampa," I said. She nodded.

"Tsultrim Dolma," Father muttered. I snuck a glance at him, where he'd been sitting in silence. He didn't seem mad, just lost in thought, like he was replaying the moment of my decision over and over in his mind. Finally, he smiled at me. "It's a good name."

I returned the smile. I mouthed the name again and again, wrapping my lips around the unfamiliar sounds until it was as though they'd always been there. Perhaps I was being vain, repeating my own name like that, but I had to make sure this was all real, that it wasn't just another idle daydream I'd conjured up.

Mother's hair swished softly as she cleaned up the final

strays on my head. Her hair was thick and dark, cascading all the way down to her waist. According to my mother, a woman's hair signified the longevity of her husband. So, for as long as I could remember, I'd never seen her cut her hair. They would grow old together in this little house, and I always thought I'd be here with them.

One moment, my new life wrapped around me like a cozy blanket, only for it to smother me in the next. I was excited, nervous, a little at a loss, not quite knowing what to do. I'd been knocked off balance, off the course that had been neatly charted out for me. Still, I didn't regret my decision for a single moment. No matter what lay ahead of me, this was who I was meant to be. I let that conviction seep into my bones, settle deep in my marrow.

And as I basked in that exhilarating, terrifying, comforting, disconcerting mess of emotions, I focused on something I knew: My name is Tsultrim Dolma, and I am a nun.

CHAPTER
TWELVE

For the next few weeks, I found myself running a hand over my shaved head in awe. I really was a nun. Mother delegated fewer tasks to me than before out of respect for my new status, but I still continued most of my chores, the most exciting of which was rebuilding the local monastery.

The project was a community effort. My friends and I mostly helped grab materials, leaving the actual building to the adults. We scoured the area for wood, hacking into the pieces with the same tools we'd used to collect firewood. This time, though, we were turning the pieces into wooden tiles for the monastery's roof. Mother would bring us yogurt during breaks, and I'd watch as the villagers laid the tiles onto the roof, carefully overlapping them to keep out the rain. Stone by stone, we restored the monastery to its former glory.

I contributed to that, I thought, chest filling with warmth. All those years ago, Pema and I had pulled books and prayer flags from the ground, right by this site. It was fulfilling to see the fruits of our labor, to build a concrete symbol of our culture in broad daylight.

Once we rebuilt the monastery, I had more time off than ever. At first, the abundance of free time was exciting, so full of possibilities. Would I learn more prayers? Or would I be able to visit a temple and listen to lectures from esteemed monks and nuns? Maybe I'd be able to go back to the cave where I'd found the smashed statues and meditate there like my predecessors had.

However, spring bled into summer, and the river thawed out. Insects crawled out of their eggs, and clusters of edelweiss unfurled their white petals. The only thing that stayed the same was me. Sure, Mother served me meals in our nicer bowls, and I got to sit on lusher cushions at the table. Though some boys still harassed me, most others learned to keep their distance when they saw my shaved head. Yet if I looked at my life from a bird's-eye view, it was painfully obvious that not much had actually changed. I was needed at home, and my newfound nunhood did not conjure up a functioning nunnery overnight.

Had Great-Aunt Jampa felt the same restlessness that plagued me now? Had she joined the nunnery in Lhasa not only to continue her education, but because Pelbar Dzong felt too small, too quiet? I could only speculate, and now I had plenty of time on my hands to do so.

Relief from the monotony came when a neighboring village asked for help to rebuild. Like most other towns in Tibet, the village had been terrorized during the Chinese invasion, its buildings ransacked and pillaged beyond recognition. Now some concessions had been made, and we were to restore the village's temple.

This time, I was more involved with the actual building process. It was backbreaking work, but it gave me a sense of purpose that I could cling to, at least until construction was over. Finally, something different. Something to *do*.

Every morning, I set out with a group of other youths, dutifully trudging along for an hour or more until we spotted the squat houses of the village. With the help of the locals, we laid down rock after rock, filling in the gaps with an adobe made of dirt and straw. The calluses on my palms grew thicker, protecting tender flesh from rough stone. I wore that sign of progress with satisfaction, knowing that I was making a tangible contribution. My skin tanned under the unrelenting sun, and I found out too late that my bare scalp was susceptible to sunburn too.

The days stretched longer as we approached midsummer.

"I wonder what Lhasa is like this time of year," Dawa mused.

We were on our way home, dragging our footsteps after an exhausting day of work. Behind us, the sun sank past the horizon, turning orange and purple, throwing long shadows at our feet.

Yongten—Wangmo's dharma name—piped up. "I'd like to see it someday. I heard there are dozens and dozens of temples there."

"It's beautiful," I said.

Their eyes turned to me, and I tried not to shirk under the intensity of their gazes.

"Tell us about it again, Tsultrim," Dawa said. "I want to hear about the people. And do their accents!"

My face flushed as I tripped over my poor imitation of a Lhasa accent, idly wondering if it was offensive. Still, I was more than happy to recount the adventure again: the crowds and sounds, the giant prayer wheels and incense burners. Statues that stood taller than my father, dogs that ran underfoot in the bustling markets. Dawa positively glowed with excitement. Yongten was instead more interested in the temples. They both listened with rapt attention, their eyes glittering with awe.

"And it's not just the Jokhang. There were dozens and dozens of temples and shrines, so many that I can't remember all the names." Bitterness seeped into my tone then, and I fought to keep my voice even. "A lot of them were destroyed."

Yongten frowned. "Can't they just rebuild them?"

"I don't know," I admitted, again frustrated at how little I knew of the world. There'd been so much Chinese military presence all across Lhasa, much more than in Pelbar Dzong. Their obvious distaste for local Tibetans soured the air.

I took a deep breath. I was in Kham, in a rural area where the military presence was not as strong. I was home. Somehow, that thought only made my stomach sink.

"Wow." Dawa had a wistful look on her face. "I wish I could've gone."

Her remark brought me out of my thoughts, and my frustration ebbed, just a bit. That was right. There were plenty of people who would never leave their hometowns. There were those who had been forced to flee. My life was fine. I should simply cherish my memories of Lhasa, be content with the privilege of having been to such a holy site.

"Maybe one day," Dawa said to the sky.

"Maybe one day," Yongten agreed.

I tuned out the sound of their chatter as we continued down the road, dirt crunching lightly under our feet.

"Let's go. To Lhasa."

I wasn't sure who said it. I wasn't even sure someone had said it at all. But all three of us slowed until we came to a halt. In the end, it didn't matter who said the words, because we'd all been thinking the same thing: *We need to go to Lhasa.*

"Do you still remember how to get there?" Dawa asked slowly.

"More or less, if I can ask for some directions here or there," I said. Then I took a deep breath and met their gazes head-on. I had to drive this point home. "But it's not just a hard journey, it's a dangerous one. Someone died on the way last time."

Although I hadn't thought of her in three years, I could still picture Lhakyi's face in my mind's eye. The way her steps had faltered, how her body began to swell up, the air of loss that permeated the damp little barn, her husband's silent grief. The way even the memory of her name seemed to fade in the village, never uttered between any of us as the years had gone by.

But she'd already been struggling prior to the journey. Dawa, Yongten, and I were healthy and well-fed. We'd built up the stamina needed for a long, arduous hike, especially in our adolescence. Since it was just the three of us, we might be able to hitchhike too.

"Let's say we get there," Yongten said. She was clearly as excited as we were, but as the eldest at around seventeen, she had to be the voice of reason. "And then what? Where would we stay?"

"We could sleep outside," Dawa offered. "We do that all the time here."

"No, no," I said hurriedly. "It's different there. Sleeping outside in Lhasa is . . ." I cringed at the memory of the officer who'd humiliated Father our first night in the city. Then the thought came to me like a thunderbolt. "Great-Aunt Jampa!" I exclaimed. "She joined a nunnery in Lhasa. We could go to her."

"And which nunnery is that?" Yongten pressed. "There are dozens there, you said so yourself."

"Chupzang," I said confidently.

"I know that, but which one is it?"

I faltered. "I could ask the locals."

"You? Shy little Tsultrim? You mean *I'll* ask the locals," she chided lightly, but she lessened the sting with a small smile.

"I have relatives in Lhasa," Dawa added. "I'll go to the nunnery with you first and ask around for them."

"Now that that's settled, we need to prepare for the actual journey."

I listed the items that I could remember. "Barley flour, butter . . . I think we brought some hard cheese as well."

"We made plenty of dried meat this past winter, I can bring some."

"Don't forget blankets."

"I bet it gets cold in Lhasa."

"Do you think they'll have books?"

We stacked our ideas one on top of another, building our futures from the ground up. And though I'd tread the same path home plenty of times—up the hill, up the steps, through the family room door—this time, I felt like I was actually moving forward at long last.

Over the next few weeks, we took turns borrowing supplies from our families. At first, I could barely keep from squirming with guilt whenever I snuck a pouch of flour and hid it in the livestock pen. It wasn't really stealing if I was just taking it from my own portion, right? Besides, we really were just borrowing. We'd return them. At some point maybe.

When the day came, I tried my best to look as normal as possible. Let the yak out, milk the dri, churn some butter. Then I lingered in the pen to collect the requisitioned supplies, praying that nobody would notice the extra bulk in my bag. Finally, it was time to leave the house. I wiped my sweaty palms against my trousers.

"I'm off to work on the temple." I tried to force my face into something casual. "It's almost done."

Mother looked up from where she was spinning some yarn. "And you'll be with your friends?"

"Yes. Dawa, Yongten, the usual."

"As long as you stay safe, Tsultrim."

I nodded, not trusting my voice not to waver.

My steps slowed on the way downhill, not because I was having second thoughts, but because I wanted to sear everything into my mind. Pelbar Dzong would always be my home, and I wouldn't be able to live with myself if I forgot anything about it. My eyes lingered on Sherab's little shack, but the old man was nowhere to be seen. When I reached the meeting place, Dawa and Yongten were already there.

We came to a fork in the road. Almost by instinct, I let my feet carry me left toward the neighboring village. I caught myself and slowed to a halt. Yongten looked at me, concerned eyes darting around my face, looking for any sign of illness or unease. Before she could ask what was wrong, I turned sharply to the right and put one foot in front of the other.

We stuck to the main road as much as we could. A truck approached, heading in the same direction as us.

"Let's try to hitchhike," Yongten said, and promptly began to wave her arms. Dawa and I joined in, jumping up and down and gesturing wildly. The truck neared, but the driver showed no sign of slowing down. I waved my arms even more furiously, my shoulders aching from the strain.

The next thing I knew, Yongten was throwing rocks at the truck and shouting obscenities. Carried away by the excitement, Dawa and I followed suit.

"You . . . you . . ." I faltered. I snuck a look at my friends, who were shouting indignantly and unabashedly. Then, I pulled my arm back and hurled the stone at the truck. "You *asshole*!"

The stone didn't land anywhere near the target, but I was too shocked at my audacity to care. I'd never raised my voice like that before, let alone cursed at someone. Then I bent down and picked up another stone.

"Yeah, that's right!"

"You tell him, Tsultrim!"

"Selfish bastard!"

"You're going to hell!"

Again and again, we yelled and threw rocks at the truck,

even after it zoomed past us and disappeared down the road. Then our yells dissolved into raucous laughter. Jumping up and down, not caring what other people thought, saying bad words . . . It felt thrilling. It felt *good*. I should've felt guilty. After all, I was on my way to Lhasa to become a nun! But as we continued down the road, joking and screaming and being teenagers, I simply felt free.

CHAPTER
THIRTEEN

Unlike my pilgrimage, the journey took only a few weeks this time, as a few kind strangers had agreed to drive us part of the way. We arrived at dusk, the sun painting Lhasa's whitewashed walls in purple and orange. After asking a passerby for instructions, we headed north toward Chupzang Nunnery. The nunnery is part of Sera Monastery, along with several other hermitages. One could think of Sera Monastery as a university in charge of different colleges and dormitories in the area. Though each hermitage operated separately day-to-day, they would hold joint lectures with guest speakers and celebrate major religious festivals together. Sera is one of the most important religious and educational institutions in Tibet, but that wasn't the only reason I wanted to be a part of it.

Great-Aunt Jampa had left Pelbar Dzong several years ago to live at Chupzang Nunnery, and I missed her dearly. She'd always been hesitant to speak about the education she'd received as a young nun, the same way the other village elders held on to their own secrets. But surely, Great-Aunt Jampa would be more comfortable sharing her knowledge here at a nunnery! I was almost bouncing with excitement, imagining all the time we'd be able to share together after so many years apart.

Dawa and Yongten, having never been to Lhasa, marveled at the view every step of the way. Though I'd visited the nunnery before, I hadn't been able to stop and gawk for long during our whirlwind pilgrimage. Now I drank in the view just as eagerly as they did.

The path to the nunnery took us up a hill covered in shrubs, tufts of green and brown covering the slope. My legs shook with the effort, the climb feeling much steeper than it actually was after weeks of travel on foot. Still, I rushed on, ignoring the protests of my achy joints and swollen feet. My body was exhausted, but my mind was buzzing so hard with anticipation, and a light tingle began to wash through my limbs as reality sank in. The girls were panting harshly beside me, but their eyes gleamed when a complex of buildings came into view.

In the dim light, we saw the blocky outlines of the main temple, its rigid lines softened by tapestries and curtains that fluttered in the wind. The temple was crumbling, having been partially destroyed, with stone remnants strewn around. The sounds of chanting, neat and orderly, drifted on the breeze with whiffs of burnt juniper. The doorframe and eaves were painted red, with floral accents in gold, green, and pink. We climbed the last few steps before knocking on the door and cracking it open.

Finally, we were here.

The head monk was summoned, and soon we were face-to-face with a stocky man with barely there brows. He was wearing standard monks' robes, threadbare but well loved. He listened quietly as we recounted our journey, sipping on a cup of steaming tea.

"And what of your parents?" he asked, not unkindly.

I hesitated. "They know Yongten and I are nuns, of course, although Dawa is just here on a pilgrimage."

"But?"

"But we didn't tell them we came. They would've stopped us." My throat tightened as I recalled the day I became a nun. Father had clearly been unhappy, but he hadn't argued with the high lama either. Perhaps . . .

No, it was obvious that he listened out of respect for an ordained monk. Had I asked him for permission directly, he would have refused. *It was the right choice,* I thought, and took a sip from my own cup. The tea was thinner than the brew back home, the taste of butter not as cloying. The hot liquid soothed me for a moment, until the memory of Father's preferred tea flooded my mouth.

A wispy voice broke me from my reverie, so light that it might have dissipated into thin air. "Punjun? Is that you?"

I looked up to see Great-Aunt Jampa toddling over with an expression of awe on her face.

"Do you know these girls?" the monk asked.

"Yes. Yes, of course!" Her voice was back to her usual, booming volume. "That's my great-niece and her friends." She took a moment to take in our appearances. Great-Aunt Jampa let out a hearty laugh as we reintroduced ourselves with our new names. Soon, though, the pleasantries turned back to the real matter at hand.

"So, your families don't know you're here?" the monk asked. We nodded, desperately hoping we wouldn't be sent back. We hadn't even prepared ourselves for the possibility. "And there are no nunneries nearer to your hometown?"

"They're all gone," I said. Great-Aunt Jampa seemed to tense for a second. She stared into the middle distance with blank, clouded eyes. I knew that she'd been educated near Pelbar Dzong, but by the time I'd been born, there wasn't a single nunnery left in the area. I wanted to press for information, but if she wasn't going to elaborate, then I'd keep my mouth shut out of respect.

The head monk studied us for a moment, brows furrowed in thought. I tried not to fidget under that searching gaze. The longer he stared, the more the panic began to bubble in my chest. What would we do if he turned us away? Would we have to turn back immediately? Surely, he'd allow us to stay a few days to restock for the return trip. But then, how would we even get new supplies? Oh, heavens, and how would my parents react? Or even worse, what if I died on the way back? I glanced at Yongten and

Dawa. They, too, were sitting stiffly. What if *they* died on the way back?

The thought made my stomach churn, and my jaw began to hurt with how hard I was clenching my teeth. I took deep breaths, imagining the air filling up my belly, spreading through my body in a steady stream, loosening up each joint. I focused on trusting that it would all work out, as long as we were honest and well-intentioned. Not quite praying, but something like it.

"Very well, you may stay. You deserve an education." The tension drained from my body, and I felt like a puppet with its strings suddenly snipped. He continued, "Pilgrims come and go between your region and Lhasa, so make sure to send word that you're okay."

I thanked the head monk and followed as Great-Aunt Jampa led us to our lodgings, up and down a series of stone steps to the first day of the rest of my life.

Dawa set off for the rest of her pilgrimage the next morning, and Yongten and I soon settled into our new life as nuns. As the newest initiates, we were assigned the more menial tasks. Since I was so used to taking care of my little siblings, I figured I'd help out in the kitchen. But the first time I'd tried to help cook, Great-Aunt Jampa had shooed me away with a tut and a flick of her hand.

"Out, out! It's much too crowded in here; you'll just get in the way. Go set up the altars," she'd said. The words had been blunt, but there had been a playful glint in her eye, as if she'd known how much I loved taking care of the shrines.

I woke when it was still dark, the early autumn chill cutting through the haze of sleep that lingered over me. The routine was almost reminiscent of the one I had at home.

My mind quieted as I focused on gathering and setting up the offerings. Seven goblets of fresh water, filled in a row from left to right, all with their own meanings so that all beings may know compassion and kindness. Paper flowers—since we didn't want to kill plants—mindfully arranged so that we might achieve enlightenment. Incense, symbolizing the fragrance of discipline. And there were, of course, the butter lamps. Though I was only lighting a few, there would eventually be hundreds, if not thousands, throughout the nunnery. They illuminated the chamber, bringing it to life.

The walls were painted with religious figures, a collage of stories told through bursts of blue and red and gold. I'd always take a moment to bask in their presence, imprint the many iterations of the Buddha into my mind. In time, I would learn what all of these murals meant, the history woven into the tapestries, the nuances of each word in a prayer book. Then the same thought would catch me by surprise every day, like the first tangy-sweet bite into a crisp apple: I would learn to read.

After a communal breakfast ("See? We do just fine without you!" Great-Aunt Jampa teased), we would gather in one of the temples to listen to lectures or pray together. Guest lecturers came and went, some local, some from places I'd never heard of. Regardless, I would sit with my fellow nuns on the floor, cross-legged, captivated by their every word. Every day, I followed along diligently with a prayer book in hand, tracing each symbol as the head monk recited the contents. I repeated after him, connecting sounds to symbols until they began to form sentences. Progress was slow, but phrases gradually came into focus. Every new word I learned filled me with such awe, uncovering ideas and concepts that I never could've imagined. Great-Aunt Jampa seemed equally delighted with my progress, and often kept me company when I practiced reading in the courtyard.

The clearing was full of foliage: flowers growing in pots, grass sprouting from the dirt, and thin, nimble trees lining the perimeter. Whenever I had a moment, I would sit under one such tree with a prayer book and practice reading until my vision blurred. Great-Aunt Jampa would join me, pointing out my errors and answering my questions. She even shared stories about her days in Pelbar Dzong, well before I was born.

Then, as the months wore on, the stories changed shape.

We were alone in the courtyard one evening, my lips moving slowly as I deciphered the words on the page. Like other sutras, the text was long and dense, packed full of the Buddha's wisdom, but I was determined to learn it. After all, the Sutra of the Golden Light was a text that ended suffering and violence, and if there was one thing the world needed, it was peace.

Maybe it was the subject of the sutra, or the encroaching darkness, or simply the weight of decades of secrets that prompted Great-Aunt Jampa that evening.

"The nunnery in Pelbar Dzong," she murmured, and my ears instantly perked up. She so rarely spoke this softly, so different from the strong, confident tone she normally used. She was silent for a while, and I was beginning to think I'd imagined her voice when she continued. "I was still inside when the Chinese bombed it."

My eyes widened in disbelief. I'd seen the nunnery from afar, just a hint of crumbling stone in a sea of trees, and I'd always known the Chinese government had destroyed it. What I hadn't realized until then was that people had been inside when it happened. Great-Aunt Jampa continued as I let that thought sink in.

"They did it at night. We were just praying. Just praying to relieve all this suffering in the world. And then out of nowhere, they bombed us. The ground shook so hard, I thought it would split open. They did it knowing some of the nuns were getting on in years. Imagine being so narrow-minded, so fearful of the power of faith that you'd attack a group of people sworn to keep the peace. We were lucky to even escape alive." Her voice was so soft and frail, like she was a scared young girl again.

I snuck a glance at her, afraid that looking directly would

break the spell and make her stop talking. She looked so fragile, like the slightest breeze could shatter her. Her expression was haunted, shrouded in a fog of fatigue that couldn't be dispersed. Yet underneath that, I could almost picture the young woman she'd once been, a novice nun desperately helping her elders flee a crumbling building. For a moment, Great-Aunt Jampa looked so old and so young at the same time.

"You know," she continued, "I've even heard that in some other monasteries, the monks and nuns took up weapons to defend themselves when the Chinese attacked. I don't think that counts as breaking their oaths of nonviolence." Suddenly, she shook her head, as if trying to rid herself of the memories. "Forgive the ramblings of an old woman, Tsultrim. I don't know what's gotten into me."

Then she rose, dusted off her robes, and headed inside.

Monks and nuns, taking up weapons in self-defense . . . Would I have had the courage to fight back like that? To break my oath to fight back? I shuddered, hoping I would never have to find out.

CHAPTER
FOURTEEN

I acclimated to life in the nunnery at a steady pace, but the one thing I couldn't quite get used to was asking for alms. Worshippers visited our nunnery and donated what they could. Many became regulars, but they couldn't sustain the nunnery when times were tough for everyone. When we ran out of resources, the younger nuns would go door to door and beg. Especially now that winter was on its way, we needed to secure as much kindling as possible.

It wasn't humiliating, per se—we were following our vows of living as simply as possible. But the girl who gleefully threw stones at truck drivers had disappeared. I was plain old Tsultrim again, hiding behind someone braver as she knocked on door after door.

Our begging took us all around Lhasa: the markets, the nicer residential area, the outskirts of the city. Our route today took us just outside of Lhasa, and I always appreciated the opportunity to see the farmland. Small flocks of yaks and sheep wandered around, under the watchful eye of their owners. They bleated and bickered, flicking their tails to ward off pests and lowering their snouts to munch on some hay. I smiled at the familiar sound.

My mind continued to drift as Yongten asked a woman for alms. It had been a year and a half since we'd left home and shed our old names. We were no longer little Wangmo and Punjun, playing make-believe by the river. We'd taken a chance on ourselves, running away to become Yongten and Tsultrim of Chupzang Nunnery.

But now that we'd reached our goal, I couldn't help but wonder what I was truly doing with my life. Every day, I prepared the altars and cleaned the temple. I learned to read bit by bit and participated in prayer sessions. I helped rebuild the nunnery and took care of my elders. These were all meaningful tasks similar to the ones I'd done in Pelbar Dzong. Should I have just stayed home instead? What was the point of coming all the way to Lhasa? What was my purpose?

That was it. I lacked purpose, a goal to keep me on track even when my resolve wavered.

My thoughts were interrupted when the woman came back with a bundle of firewood. "I'm sorry, but this is all we can offer right now."

"No, please don't worry. We're grateful for your generosity." We accepted the bundle with another bow, and returned to the nunnery, where I sought out Great-Aunt Jampa for counsel. Yet not even she could help me solve my dilemma. So instead, we visited Drepung Monastery to consult a high lama.

It wasn't uncommon for monastics to visit other hermitages for lectures. I'd been to quite a few, all over the city. But consulting a high lama was a different story. I sat next to Great-Aunt Jampa as we listened to the high lama's teachings, straining my ears for any advice that might guide me. But no matter how I tried, I couldn't find a way to apply his teachings to my conundrum. It wasn't my faith in my religion that faltered. It was my faith in myself.

Afterward, Great-Aunt Jampa and I headed toward the high lama's living quarters, hoping to receive an audience. But when we reached the top of the stairs, there wasn't a soul to be seen. We tried the door. It was locked.

I bit back a frustrated groan. It was unfair for me to act so impatient like this. I wasn't entitled to a meeting, especially with no prior notice. Every time I thought I'd found my answer, some miniscule reason to stay here in Lhasa, another voice in my head would list out all the reasons why it would make more sense to go home. I felt like I was scooping water out of a leaking boat.

"He's not in," said a passing monk. I recognized him as Lhamo, one of the monks who lived here. He was a meticulous man with an unreadable face, straight-backed and straightlaced. Every word he spoke was carefully considered and enunciated. He couldn't have been more than ten years older than me. "He's in high demand, of course, so it's incredibly hard to seek an audience with him."

"I see," Great-Aunt Jampa said. We'd expected as much. We weren't the only ones who needed help.

I turned to her, trying not to let my disappointment show too much. "What do we do?"

"What *can* we do?" She regarded me carefully, a look of pity in her eyes. She knew how much my doubt was eating me up inside.

"You're welcome to wait here," Lhamo continued. Despite his cool demeanor, he was always eager to extend a hand. "If not, I'll let the high lama know that you were hoping for an audience when I see him."

I wondered for a moment if he'd ever felt the same doubt I was feeling now. Lhamo was from Lhasa, born and raised. Did his hometown ever feel stifling to him, the same way Pelbar Dzong had to me? Or were things different for him as a man living in a busy city? Lhasa was, after all, the land of the gods; who would ever want to leave such a sacred place?

Me, apparently, I thought with a flash of guilt.

Great-Aunt Jampa let out a dejected sigh. "Let's try again some other time. Come, let's go back."

We were halfway down the flight of stairs when a voice rang out above us.

"Come, come," the high lama said, his soft voice carrying in the stairwell. "I have time for one more chat."

We thanked him profusely as he led us into his quarters. The high lama listened as I told him of my predicament.

"You should stay here," he said as soon as I finished. I barely stopped myself from gaping. How could he be so certain? "Why did you come to Lhasa in the first place?"

"Well, I wanted to become a nun, but there were no opportunities at home."

"And what if you'd stayed?"

"I would've gotten married and become a farmer." And at sixteen, I would have already given birth to a child or two. I fidgeted, the mere idea making me squeamish.

"Precisely. Now, let me ask you this." He looked me straight in the eye. "Do you want to be a farmer? Do you want to be a wife and a mother? There is no shame if you do; they are all noble, important roles. But is that what you really want to do with your life?"

The answer came to me immediately. "No."

He nodded and leaned back with a knowing smile. "Then stay here and learn as much as you can, Tsultrim. It's young people like you who will preserve the knowledge that has been passed down for so long. You will keep our tradition going."

I let his words sink in. When I was a little girl, all I'd wanted was an education. I wanted to know things and to better myself. Then I'd become jaded somewhere along the line. I was learning to read, I was learning about the world, but I couldn't figure out what to do with all this. Learning for learning's sake wasn't enough for me anymore.

Memories of dismembered statues came to me then. Words placed on a high shelf, never to be spoken. Stories and histories left to disappear as time went on. I knew my answer, my purpose.

"Yes, I'll stay," I said, feeling lighter than I'd ever been. "I'll stay in Lhasa. Thank you."

I began working twice as hard, staring so intently at my books that Great-Aunt Jampa joked that I would bore holes into them. I was still deathly shy, but I spoke to as many people as I could, not just monks and nuns, but the visiting worshippers, vendors at the market—anyone who would give me the time of day. They shared stories: historical anecdotes, regional folktales, stories about their unruly grandchildren, or that one time they visited a restaurant—I devoured every word. Before I knew it, I had made friends all over the city from all walks of life.

"I swear, it's like walking through a lake!"

I smiled into my cup of water as Phuntsok recounted his recent trip to India. Phuntsok was a businessman who loved to tell stories about his travels. His children were grown and lived outside the city, and hadn't been able to make it home, so he'd invited me to celebrate Losar with him, his wife Tashi, and a few other guests. Not for the first time, I wondered if the couple almost saw me as one of their own. He gesticulated wildly as he continued. "Maybe it's not so bad in other parts of India, but where I was? *Oof.* It was so humid, I swear I was breathing in water."

Back in Pelbar Dzong, the new year was an almost extravagant affair. But to my surprise, Phuntsok and his wife were fasting. For them, Losar was an opportunity to reflect and abstain in observance of such a holy occasion. It struck me then how varied and multifaceted Buddhism was. I knew there were different schools of thought, the intricacies of which I'd yet to learn. Yet even for believers with the same overarching philosophies, we still approached our traditions in different, personal ways, reflecting the histories of our different communities. My hosts offered me a simple cushion and some water, and I marveled at the breadth of our faiths as we bowed our heads together in prayer.

I continued to step out of my shell bit by bit, drumming up the courage to speak with strangers who piqued my interest. Yet there was always one group of people I never dared to approach. Westerners had started to visit Lhasa more frequently. I'd see their mops of blond, brown, even red hair in the crowd. Their skin was extremely pale, and their light-colored eyes scanned the markets, trying to make sense of the city's chaos. How would I even strike up a conversation? I had no idea what languages they spoke, and though I'd overheard some foreigners speak Tibetan, the prospect of speaking with someone from a distant land was much too intimidating.

However, a strange man approached me at the market

one day. His features were angular, his skin pale, his eyes deep set, and his hair a light, mousy brown. He carried a large backpack, as if he'd been on a hike. When he spoke, his accent was like nothing I'd ever heard from a Tibetan.

"For . . . you," he finally managed.

It was a photograph of an elderly man clad in gold and red robes, a pair of glasses sitting atop his nose. He had a long face, clean-shaven but for the thick eyebrows that framed his kind eyes. He had his palms raised in greeting, as if looking out onto a crowd of followers.

It was the Fourteenth Dalai Lama.

My heart squeezed and my hands shook as I accepted the photograph. It had been years since I'd last seen an image of the Dalai Lama, and in those years, I'd come to learn just how important he was. He was the last in a centuries-long succession of spiritual leaders, each a reincarnation of the bodhisattva Avalokiteśvara. He was a god-like figure in Tibetan Buddhism, a teacher of unparalleled wisdom. And he was dead.

He was dead, and the Chinese prevented us from searching for his next incarnation. A whole lineage, gone. The grief threatened to overwhelm me.

"Thank you," I whispered, bowing to the stranger. He bowed back, albeit a little unpracticed, and walked off in the direction of Jokhang Temple.

"Ani-la!" someone yelled, using the traditional address for nuns. I spun around to find a spritely, middle-aged woman rushing toward me with a big grin on her face.

Chodron sold produce around Jokhang Temple. Instead of having a stall, though, she wandered the square with a little cart, and I was always amazed at how she could keep her wares from tumbling on the ground. She had mountains of potatoes, whole pyramids of carrots. Every now and then, she would have tubs of yogurt and stacks of dried meat, all arranged into a delightfully chaotic display. She was an excitable woman, always bouncing on the balls of her feet, eager to chat with me.

Chodron glanced at the photo in my hands and said, "I see you got a picture of the Dalai Lama. Lucky you!" I nodded dumbly, aware that I should be more courteous yet unable to shake off my disbelief. "I suppose that was an American tourist. I hear about them from my customers all the time. They just walk up to monks and nuns and hand out pictures of the Dalai Lama, just like that! Now that I think of it, I've seen quite a few of them myself. A lot of them come here from India. I guess they're allowing more tourists into Tibet nowadays. The rules are always changing though, so meh, what do I know?"

My head swam. Phuntsok had talked about India, but he'd never mentioned Americans. What was an American? Was that an ethnic group in India, or perhaps some sort of religious sect?

"This picture is so new," I muttered, tracing the edges with my fingertips.

Chodron studied the photo over my shoulder. "Huh. Must be a recent one."

"But how?"

"What do you mean 'how'?"

"Well, he's, you know . . ." I trailed off, hoping she'd take the hint. I didn't want to say it out loud. She only looked more confused at my silence. "Passed," I finally mumbled.

She looked at me quizzically. "Ani-la," she said slowly, "with all due respect, you do know that His Holiness is still alive, don't you?"

"Excuse me?" Hope was blooming in my chest like a soft ache. "How do you know that?"

"The tourists," she explained, nodding toward the stranger's retreating back. "They come in with all sorts of gossip."

"Then where is he now?"

Chodron's beady eyes darted around then, before she leaned in. "He's in India, but he can't come home."

My blood ran hot and cold. Our leader was alive. He was alive, and there was hope for us all. I tucked that new piece of knowledge right next to my heart. I wanted to dig for more information. How was he? What was he doing? How could we help him come back? But I knew that grim look on Chodron's face. There were things even bold, talkative Chodron couldn't discuss in depth, out in the open like this. I could almost imagine the hard glare of a Chinese officer digging into the back of my skull.

There were things meant to be left unsaid, even in Lhasa with its gleaming architecture and religious displays, even with its foreign tourists and countless monastics. The capital of Tibet was, after all, full of Chinese occupiers slowly pushing out the Tibetans.

Then, everything came to a head on October 1, 1987.

CHAPTER
FIFTEEN

Not for the first time, I marveled at my good fortune as I walked past Jokhang Temple. It seemed like only yesterday when I first laid eyes on its grand facade, savored the ashy sweet scent of incense. Now I'd lived in Lhasa for just over two years and attuned myself to the city's rhythm.

I wandered the Barkhor, glancing at the vendors who'd set out their wares at the crack of dawn. Great-Aunt Jampa had sent me to the market to find her a thermos. Her insulated bottle was old and dented and could barely keep water hot. A chill had already begun to settle on the plateau, exacerbating her declining health.

This was home. All I needed to do was ignore the military presence that loomed over us. Ignore how more and more of the store owners selling incense and prayer wheels had no idea what it meant. Ignore the whispers about people disappearing for no reason.

Head down, eyes forward, I reminded myself. *You'll be fine.*

A loud bang ripped through the market chatter.

I whipped around, heart beating hard.

There, in the distance: a group of twenty or so monks. They walked across the square in a steady stream of red and gold robes. Passersby gawked from a distance as they approached, a mix of awe and terror and respect. They held up banners and makeshift signs, and from afar, I couldn't quite catch what they were saying.

"What are they talking about?" I asked, too wound up to even care that I was asking a complete stranger.

"They're protesting against the Chinese occupation," the stranger said. "On China Day, no less. Heavens, they've got to be incredibly brave or incredibly stupid, probably both. *Hey!* Where are you going?"

My feet carried me toward the procession in a daze. They were drawing closer to the temple now, and I could finally make out their shouts and screams.

"Let the Dalai Lama come back to Tibet!"

"Let him come home!"

"Tibet is not part of China! Tibet will *never* be a part of China!"

They marched toward us, some onlookers beginning to flock around them. A monk raised a large piece of cloth over his head. As I drew closer, I began to notice the details.

A golden sun sat in the middle of this flag, its rays alternating between red and blue. Underneath was a white triangle, where two green-maned snow lions held up multicolored jewels. A yellow border lined three sides of the flag.

It was a makeshift banner, as if it had been hastily thrown together with whatever material was at hand. Yet the fraying threads and small stains couldn't hide the majesty.

The Tibetan flag unfurled against a cloudless blue sky, and a knot of tension loosened in my stomach. Seeing my country's flag for the first time was a revelation.

Passersby looked on, some with palms pressed together in prayer, some urging the protesters to go home, lest they get arrested or worse. Others turned away, traumatized by memories of Chinese brutality. Soon, monastics from other hermitages and even Jokhang Temple joined the procession, making circuits around the Jokhang.

"Release the monks from Drepung Monastery!" they hollered, fists raised, referencing another protest I'd seen from a distance a few days prior.

"Free Tibet!"

"Long live the Dalai Lama!"

On and on and on. The protesters yelled all the things we were not supposed to even whisper. Their voices cracked, rasped, split. Nevertheless, they refused to stay silent. Monastics and laypeople mingled together, regardless of background or personal beliefs.

The Chinese government wasn't simply targeting Tibetan Buddhism. No, it knew religion was an integral part of Tibetan culture, regardless of how religious each individual was. These beliefs were entrenched, and to suppress the religion, the language, the culture was to suppress the

Tibetan people. Everyone, even the youngest of children, had their culture stripped from them. And it was unfair. It was wrong, and I was tired and angry and mourning and pained. But more than anything, I was tired of being silent. I was tired of being silenced.

I should go back, I thought dimly. Great-Aunt Jampa was still waiting for me. I needed to get her a thermos. There were meals to cook and laundry to do and shrines to clean. This wasn't the first protest I'd seen, nor would it be the last. But before I knew it, I was already half running toward the protesters.

How many times had I acted so impulsively like this? Blurting out questions, bringing home religious items on a whim. I'd relented so quickly whenever I was reprimanded. Yes, I'd stood my ground when I'd asked to become a nun; I'd run away to pursue an education. But if I continued to keep my head down and my mouth shut, if I kept ignoring the protests that sprung up more and more frequently, would I not simply be relenting again? What good was an education if I didn't use it?

My faith, my obligations as a nun—that was not something to take lightly. Mother had said so, hadn't she, on the day she'd shaved my head? My responsibility was to the people, not just my own family and friends. I was a nun, and I had to help as many souls as I could.

My feet slapped the gray flagstones, growing surer with each step. And then I screamed.

"Free Tibet!"

My voice was shaky, but as we continued our march around Jokhang Temple, my hoarse little voice folded into the crowd, until I only heard the singular cry of the people.

I didn't think I'd ever been that angry in my life. Or maybe I'd always been angry, but hadn't been allowed to acknowledge, let alone express it. The rage that fueled this protest had been building up for decades, passed on from generation to generation through hushed words and pained silence. I thought of Bhuti and Yeshe. I thought of Gelek. I thought of lush green forests that we'd never gotten to see, books that we would never read, stories we would never hear.

I took a deep breath and screamed again.

"Free Tibet!"

With each cry, I felt an extraordinary catharsis, some sort of bittersweet pride in the way we were fighting back. What a beautiful thing that was, to find joy even when the oppressor did its best to burn it to ash in the flames of fear.

The authorities came in jeeps and on foot, a flood of olive green armed with rifles and batons, covered in all sorts of protective gear. Officers began to disperse the gathering, brandishing their weapons mercilessly and indiscriminately.

"You're not allowed here," they barked.

But why?

"You can't say things like that."

But why?

"This is sedition."

But *why*?

All these years, and I still couldn't understand why the Chinese government chose to be so cruel. I couldn't understand how they'd forgotten our humanity, or why they decided to ignore it on purpose.

The police began grabbing people left and right. They wrenched the protesters forcefully, dragging them off to the police station. Perhaps the arrests were meant to be some sort of deterrent, an example of what would happen if we didn't behave. But it had the opposite effect. The crowd let out an enraged roar, and we converged on the police station, demanding their release.

The officers only increased their efforts. It was utter pandemonium.

A hand clawed at the back of my head, and I jerked away, too scared to look back. A baton struck me in the side, driving the air out of my lungs. I doubled over, the sharp pain fading into a dull throb. My ribs were tender and I swayed on my feet, but I couldn't let myself collapse. The police would swarm like vultures if I did. They were doing so as other protesters fell to the ground, landing blow after blow. Officers dragged monks across the square like deadweight. I blinked away the sweat stinging my eyes as I caught a flurry of movement to the side. *Those are police,* I thought dimly, my inner voice barely audible over the chaos. *They're wearing normal clothes to blend in with the crowd.*

There was a loud crash and a roar of vindication. At the edge of the crowd was an upturned police truck, belly up with its wheels spinning uselessly in the air. A man fumbled with something in his hands, flicking his wrist in sharp motions over and over. A box of matches, I realized. When the match finally caught, he dropped it onto the vehicle, which erupted into flames. Even though I was a ways away, the heat hit me like a solid wall.

Men wrestled guns away from the police, holding them above their heads and then smashing them onto the ground. Women and children began throwing rocks and other small debris, trying to drive the police away. I grabbed a stone the size of my fist to do the same. For a split second, I wondered if I'd be betraying my vows as a nun if I threw the rock.

I looked at the scene playing out around me as if in slow motion. Officers in green uniforms and plain clothes swung their fists. They threw around the women, beat up the men, roughed up the elderly, all for the grave sin of demanding a better life. Children screamed, separated from their parents or even getting attacked themselves. In between howls of pain, the crowd kept chanting: *Free Tibet! Free Tibet! Free Tibet!*

"Go home!" someone yelled at me. I whirled around, half expecting an officer to attack me. Instead, it was an ordinary man covered in sweat, blood, and bruises. His lip was cut and swelling. "You need to go now, before it gets any worse."

"I can't," I called back, fighting to be heard over the chaos. "I can't abandon them. *You* need to leave, sir. Please."

"You've done enough. You young people need to live on. Go, live and fight another day. Leave this one to us old folk who have nothing left to lose."

He wasn't even that old. He was around my parents' age at most. My heart shattered into even tinier pieces. He had everything to lose, if he hadn't already lost it all.

But me? I was a nun. I'd cast off my attachments. I didn't have children of my own, or other people who depended on me to survive. I had no earthly possessions, no land that could be taken from me. *I* had nothing to lose.

I understood why monks and nuns led the charge.

These were the people we'd sworn to care for. We prayed for peace and happiness for everyone; that did not mean standing idly by as the colonizers degraded us again and again. I didn't know the nuances of the politics or the intricacies of statehood. But I did know it was wrong for armed officers to attack peaceful demonstrators. With shaking hands, I hurled the stone toward a row of guards closing in. I didn't bother seeing where it landed. I just picked up another and threw it, the solid weight of the rocks grounding me to the moment.

The man gave me one last look of despair before turning away to approach another teenager.

Soon, another fire broke out, a mass of reds and oranges that twisted as if it were alive. The crowd answered it with a roar. Someone had set fire to the police station in order to break in and save the arrested demonstrators. A group of monks led the charge, breaking down the door and disappearing into the thick smoke. The crowd waited with bated breath, the tension growing thicker as the flames grew. Finally, after ten minutes, there was a flurry of movement at the doorway, and the group emerged triumphantly from the wreckage.

I recognized one of them as the Venerable Jampa Tenzin, the caretaker of Jokhang Temple. His skin was severely burnt and peeling off in large pieces, leaving behind angry blisters, but he charged on, getting the others to safety first. The crowd cheered and carried him on their shoulders, lifting him high as they celebrated his bravery and selflessness.

Then the gunshots started.

Perhaps I was naive, perhaps I was ignorant, but for the life of me, I could not see how shooting unarmed protesters could possibly be okay.

Another bang, and a protester next to me burst in a splatter of red, and suddenly my face was splashed in something warm and wet. I swiped my hand across my face, and it came away bright with blood. I watched in horror as he crumpled like a rag doll. His life, taken from him as if it was nothing.

This was so different from Lhakyi's death all those years

ago. Hers was a quiet passing, save for the sound of her husband praying by her side until the very end, butter candle flickering as she drew her last breath.

This was loud, too loud. It was violent. It was cruel. My ears rang from the gunshots and the screams. More gunshots rang out, the crowd ducking for cover as best they could as they screeched in horror and anger and fear, stepping over the man's lifeless body, taking care not to trample him.

The rest happened in a terrifying blur. Protesters pushed against one another in confusion as the bullets kept coming. My foot slipped on the flagstones, and I looked down to see a child, a river of blood flowing from his chest. With his body mangled, it was all too easy to imagine Bhuti in his place, or Yeshe, or any of the village children. It was easy to imagine myself in his place, lying in a pool of blood. Before I could properly mourn him, a large crash came from the Jokhang. Officers had begun throwing monks off the rooftops.

I did not want to die.

The police continued to assault the protesters and drag them away, thinning out the crowd. Some protesters began to leave, either out of fear or determination to live and fight another day. Taking advantage of the confusion, I slipped into a group of people running away, and I fled. I stumbled around in a daze, still not fully comprehending the sheer violence on display.

News of the commotion spread fast, and tension had already permeated the nunnery by the time I returned. My ears were still ringing when I ran into Great-Aunt Jampa in the kitchen.

"There you are!" she said. "You were gone longer than I thought." She sounded like she always did, cheerful and almost girlishly bubbly. She puttered around the kitchen, preparing some hot tea, and reached a hand out. "The thermos, please."

I blinked owlishly. "I . . . I forgot," I stammered. The mayhem had completely wiped the errand from my mind. Great-Aunt Jampa studied me for a moment, and I squirmed under that shrewd gaze. There was no annoyance in it, not a hint of judgment or condemnation. Yet as she took in my trembling, the way my eyes darted everywhere, understanding seemed to dawn on her.

"You make sure to stay out of trouble." Her voice was uncharacteristically soft, the same voice Father had used after my fistfight with Nyima. Maybe he'd learned it from her. "Whatever it is, it's not worth dying for."

The guilt of fleeing from the protest sank in as I tried to go about my routine for the rest of the day. How could I simply carry on like this, as if nothing had happened? For all my zeal and idealism, I'd still left those people to fend for themselves. Death was a part of life; it was nothing to fear, and yet I'd feared it all the same.

CHAPTER
SIXTEEN

The Chinese authorities ramped up surveillance. They dragged people out of their homes. They tore down Tibetan houses to make way for tall buildings, so that they could keep an eye on the crowds below. Trucks and tanks began rolling into Lhasa en masse, preparing for any possible sign of unrest. Chatting, shopping, existing—anything and everything was cause for suspicion.

Monastics began to protest in droves, some taking care to disguise themselves to not lead the police to their hermitages. Chinese officers showed up unannounced, arresting whoever looked suspicious. And it seemed being a devout Buddhist was an automatic red flag.

Despite the thick fog of unease and the disturbances, we continued to attend lectures, cleaned the temples, took care of our elders, and prayed for hours and hours, hoping against hope that those arrested would come home unscathed. But something within Great-Aunt Jampa seemed to have shifted since the protests started in earnest. She still taught scriptures with gusto and commanded the kitchen with the confidence of a seasoned chef. Yet in the moments between, her voice would drop to that low murmur she reserved for unearthing decades-long trauma.

"They made us harvest yartsa gunbu on those mountains," she said out of the blue one night. My eyes darted to her. Her expression was carefully neutral, as if she wasn't fully in the room with me as we prepared for bed. Her hands went through the motions of laying down our blankets as if on autopilot.

"I picked some once, when I was little," I offered, as if it were any consolation. I toyed with a corner of my blanket as she gave me a guarded look.

An odd little twig had peeked through the grass, a dull, light brown. When I'd dug it out, the bottom half was in mustard-yellow segments, as if it were a caterpillar. An animal and a plant at the same time. I'd rushed home in excitement, looking forward to sharing my incredible discovery with my family. "Mother got really, really angry with me."

"Because it's a sin to pick a sacred herb," Great-Aunt Jampa said softly. "And they made us do it. They made us dig up yartsa gunbu like it was a common weed."

I just hummed, not knowing what to say in response to such a violation of faith. I responded in the same way each time Great-Aunt Jampa recounted another horror story: monastics forced to renounce their vows and marry; people snitching on their own kin; families being kicked out of homes to make room for Chinese colonizers.

After all, what else could I do? I couldn't just attend protests whenever I wanted—what if I died? It wasn't just Great-Aunt Jampa; the elderly nuns at the monastery needed me. There would be one less nun to help them up the stairs or bring them food or gather firewood to keep them warm. I had an obligation to these women who had welcomed me with open arms.

But each time I saw demonstrators congregating at Jokhang Temple, I felt drawn to them, and before I knew it, I was in the crowd once more. I was still terrified each time I joined, my voice shaky and uncertain. But a complete stranger would shield me from a blow from the police. A monk would explain the origins of the Tibetan flag. I would see children hurling stones with their small fists to fend off assailants. Photographers snapped pictures from precarious locations, bearing witness even as smoke burned their lungs. Vendors handed out free bottles of water, and worshippers discreetly prayed for the protesters' safety.

The police would yell at us to register our complaints through "the proper channels," but that led nowhere. I could see it in the eyes of the other protesters, and they often said as much: That they'd tried, they'd negotiated, they'd pleaded, but the Chinese government simply did not care to listen. Protests and disruptions were the only things that forced the authorities to pay attention, even if they planned on shutting us up.

With each demonstration I attended, my confidence grew, and soon enough, I knew this was exactly where I belonged.

Several people began to shelter protesters whenever the authorities descended on us like vultures. Phuntsok and Tashi even allowed me to stay overnight and borrow their clothing so I could return to the nunnery undetected. After one especially chaotic demonstration though, they greeted me with grim looks.

"I hear the police got some photos of demonstrators from the last protest," Phuntsok said. I tugged a hat on to hide my shaved head. "Be careful, Tsultrim."

I froze. Before I could voice my concerns though, Tashi waved a hand in the air.

"Oh, hush. You're always welcome here. Don't you dare think otherwise." She handed me a parcel of food as she saw me to the front door. "We'll help you for as long as we can. Won't we?"

Phuntsok nodded. "You have our word."

With one last murmur of thanks, I stepped out onto the street, keeping my face hidden from the patrolling officers. I was putting this nice couple in more danger with each visit. Every shirt they loaned me, every drink of water they offered, they were painting a target on their backs. I pulled up the collar of my borrowed jacket higher, the fine material brushing my jaw. If they were willing to risk their lives for me, the least I could do was be as careful as possible.

"Wrong. Focus, Tsultrim." Great-Aunt Jampa cut me off as I attempted to recite a prayer from memory.

Nuns were required to memorize a wide array of prayers and sutras, and we took oral tests like this every few days. However, I read so much that I'd opted to have these small tests almost daily. Great-Aunt Jampa was more than happy to oblige, listening carefully in our shared quarters as I recounted everything I'd learned. I still couldn't write, but I was now able to read at a decent pace. It was exhilarating to see my collection of prayer books grow, tangible proof of my progress.

But today, my heart just wasn't in it, no matter how I tried.

Earlier that day, a group of officers had been circling Jokhang Temple counterclockwise. A part of me had wanted to give them the benefit of the doubt. Perhaps they were new, and didn't know that Tibetan Buddhists circumambulated clockwise. But they swaggered headlong into the stream of worshippers, their rifles and disrespect on full display. After my great-aunt's stories, it was all too clear that they weren't merely satisfied with silencing us. They wanted to spit in the face of our traditions, and they relished it.

I considered telling her what I'd seen. During my time here, she'd become a mentor to me, explaining passages with the utmost patience. She cracked jokes every now and then, trying to make me laugh. She cared deeply about my well-being, and would never judge me or my worries. But what would telling her about the officers accomplish?

Before I could make up my mind, a novice nun called for me. I had a visitor.

My stomach plummeted. Was it the police? Did they track me down? Which protest did they follow me from? When the man approached, he was wearing a simple shirt and trousers. A pilgrim, then. But why would a pilgrim ask to meet me? My blood thundered in my ears and almost drowned out that familiar accent. Similar to my own, but slightly crisper. The man was from my region.

"Are you Tsultrim Dolma from Pelbar Dzong?"

"Yes," I said, a little wary. The past few months had taught me that not even my own people could be trusted. The police could easily find civilians to do their work for them.

"Excuse me, ani-la. I have a message from your family. Everything is fine!" he rushed to add. The panic on my face must have been obvious. "Your father wants you to know that the family is doing well." Then he fished a little pouch out of his pocket. "I was asked to give you this as well." He placed it in my palm, and my eyes widened at the jingle of coins.

"How did he get all this?" Judging by the weight, there was enough to cover our meals for a month at least.

"He only said to hand it to you, ani-la. But he doesn't want you to worry about it. Says that everyone is fine and he hopes you're eating well."

"I am," I said, still staring at the pouch in disbelief. "Tell him . . ."

What was there to say? So much had happened since I'd left home, and really, all I wanted to know was how my family was doing. How had Father gotten the money? Did he get a new job somewhere? The Chinese had been expanding their factories to the plateau, so it wasn't entirely out of the question. Or maybe Bhuti and Yeshe were old enough to take on more demanding tasks. They must've been at least ten years old by now. And Mother? Was her hair still the deep raven black I remembered? Or had the stress of the last few years added white strands to the waist-length tresses? Was Gelek still living with our grandparents? Were they even still alive?

"Tell him thank you," I started, and cast my eyes around, trying to come up with something to add. Something that wasn't generic or hollow, something that told my family that I still cared, despite leaving them without so much as a whisper. My gaze landed on Great-Aunt Jampa. She sat cross-legged, leisurely sipping at a cup of tea as she waited for me to return to my test. Memories of weather-beaten hands flooded my mind. I could hear the delicate whisper of yellowed paper at dawn. The heavy taste of tea lingered just at the back of my tongue, laden with spoonful after spoonful of salty yak butter. I felt a slight twinge behind my eyes and swallowed down the memories. "And tell him that my reading has improved."

The man didn't question my request, only nodded and excused himself with a bow.

"Tsultrim?" Great-Aunt Jampa prompted, startling me from my thoughts.

"My apologies," I said, bowing sheepishly. "It was a visitor from home."

"Home, you say?" She regarded me carefully. After a moment, she cracked a smile, almost girlish in its naked enthusiasm. "That reminds me, I've been meaning to tell you a particularly funny incident when your father was your age. But first, let's finish this text."

Great-Aunt Jampa looked so content. She hummed happily as I continued reciting from memory, like spending time with her great-niece was all she'd ever wanted in life. Telling her what I'd seen at Jokhang Temple would probably just ruin her mood. Better to keep it to myself. I pushed away the memory of gun-brandishing officers and focused on my studies, at least for now.

CHAPTER
SEVENTEEN

*I stifled a yawn as I peeked under the lid of a simmer*ing pot. The kitchen was unbearably warm, but it was a welcome change from the late-winter cold outside. I took a slow sip of butter tea and rolled my shoulders, working out the tightness. I'd grown to enjoy the taste of the thinner brew in Lhasa, without the heavy weight of dairy gurgling in my stomach.

"Check the soup," Great-Aunt Jampa said. She was as energetic as ever, betraying nothing of the late nights we'd been sharing. Each night, her voice grew more haunted. Just last night, she even seemed to hallucinate.

"The Dalai Lama will be returning," she had said last night as we lay in our bedrolls. "Sometime during the full moon. That's what I heard." I could just barely make out the slow flutter of her crepey eyelids, drooping lower and lower in the dark. Her hand had twitched against my scalp as if on instinct. A shadow had flitted by then, a dark smudge across the silver moonlight streaming through the window.

"Is that him?" she'd murmured, lifting her head wearily. Then she'd dozed off and said nothing more.

Now, as she mixed a handful of barley flour with water, it was as if nothing had happened. I almost thought I'd imagined our late-night story time. It didn't help that talk of protests and politics was minimal in my nunnery. We shared only whispers about planned demonstrations, and spoke no more than we needed in order to coordinate.

Without cheerful Dawa to bind us together, Yongten and I had grown further apart during our time here. Yongten never said as much, but I knew she wasn't thrilled about my protesting. Not because she condoned state violence, but because she was terrified of the consequences. Always looking out for me, even now. I was surprised, then, when Yongten asked to speak with me out of the blue.

"I spoke to the head monk," Yongten started carefully. She smoothed a hand over her head, where her hair was getting a little too long. "I'm leaving. There's a construction job not far from here. Homes and shops and temples that got torn down when . . . well, you know."

"When will you be back?"

Yongten looked aside. "I'm leaving the nunnery," she said finally, "and I'm renouncing my nunhood."

"Oh."

"I'm just tired of feeling helpless," she said, her exasperation clear as day. "I could be out there, rebuilding homes, really helping people—not that you're not!" she added hastily. "You are, I know you are, the way you . . ." She twirled a hand in the air, encompassing all the things that couldn't be spoken, even now. "It's just that, all this . . ."

"It's just not for you anymore," I finished for her. Beliefs shifted as people changed. Yongten wasn't abandoning me; she was stepping away out of respect because she could no longer devote herself as fully as she'd thought. "We have different paths in life, different roles, different ways to help people." It was as much a reminder for myself as it was for her. A hint of sadness snuck into my gut. We'd taken the leap to become nuns together, and now she was moving on.

Yongten's shoulders sagged with relief when she realized I wasn't upset. It wasn't unheard of for monastics to return to their lives as before. It was a monumental decision, but it wasn't the end of the world either.

"I'll visit when I can," Yongten promised. She gave my hand a small squeeze with a smile, which I couldn't help but mirror. But her expression turned somber. "One last thing: Be careful of that nun." She spoke more softly now. "You know the one."

We all did. The nun was a newcomer. Despite the crackdown on monastics, a few initiates still joined monasteries and nunneries every now and then, and Chupzang was no exception. They came from all walks of life, all over the country. But there was something off about this nun.

At first, we'd thought that she'd come from a wealthy

family. Maybe she didn't do many chores and had to learn the basics first. Maybe her skin glowed because she'd been well-fed, her hands smooth because she'd never worked a day in her life before becoming a nun.

That was when we noticed her possessions.

Nuns were not forbidden from owning a few simple things: clothing, shoes, books, and the like. But the few times she'd brushed by me, her robes had flowed like water, silken and smooth. New. Expensive. While I had to scour the Barkhor for secondhand prayer books, hers were pristine, their spines uncracked. Her prayer beads shone, the lacquer intact and showing minimal signs of use. The way she arranged the beads around her neck reminded me of Chodron's wares: an announcement, a display that clamored for your attention. Then I learned that she had a room to herself, while the rest of us shared spaces. And as the days wore on, she kept to herself, barely speaking, only listening to conversations with an uncannily sharp look in her eye.

There was a very good chance that she was a spy for the Chinese authorities. It wouldn't be the first time the authorities sent their agents undercover in hermitages.

"Take care of yourself, Tsultrim," Yongten said.

"You too."

She gave my hand one last squeeze, and she went off to pack.

Though I missed Yongten dearly, I was comforted by the fact that I never lacked company. I continued to visit my friends in their homes, a routine that offered some semblance of normalcy as the unrest grew. Chodron was particularly enthusiastic.

"They're broadcasting a new television show tonight," she chirped one day. "Come by my house later. I think you'll love it."

Despite my reservations, I showed up right on time, clad in a plain shirt, pants, and a hat to hide my shaved head. Chodron ushered me in with a grin, and mercifully, there were only a few other guests, who seemed content to chatter among themselves after greeting me. A clock hung on the wall, its arms jerking as the minutes ticked by, until it was finally time for the broadcast.

Chodron fiddled with the television antenna one last time, stepping back when tinny music began blaring through the room. I frowned as the images began to dance on-screen.

"What's wrong?" she asked. "Do you not like it?"

"I do." I squinted harder at the screen. "It's just that I think I've seen this before. Not the exact same thing, but something like it."

One time, the officers in Pelbar Dzong had brought a movie about a monkey and a monk. Or at least, that's what I could glean from the flashing images. The entire movie had been in Mandarin Chinese. But now as I sat in Chodron's house, a giddy recognition began to wash over me. This show had been dubbed in Tibetan, the mismatched movement of the actors' mouths making them seem like puppets on the screen. This time, I finally understood the story.

It was the tale of a Chinese monk tasked with bringing back sacred sutras from India. As a holy man, his flesh was rumored to grant immortality to those who devoured it. As a result, demons hounded his every step, clamoring for a bite. In order to survive the harsh journey to the west, the monk was accompanied by a powerful monkey king and two other demons. Despite the dangers, they were able to retrieve the sutras and return home safe and sound.

"They say the monk was actually a real person," Chodron said as the credits began to roll. "Some sort of Chinese Buddhist from ancient times."

My jaw dropped. A real person walked all the way from China to India and back, with danger nipping at his heels? I simply had to learn every detail I could. I came back every week to catch the newest episode, always on the edge of my seat as the nights ended on cliff-hangers. Each week, the monkey king thwarted another attempt on the monk's life, and the travelers trudged on, one foot in front of the other, journeying through lush forests, barren deserts, lands dotted with lakes and swamps. Chodron was all too happy to host me each time, and we settled into a pleasant routine. We carved out a space for joy and excitement as violence mounted in the streets.

CHAPTER
EIGHTEEN

Great-Aunt Jampa continued to share her stories at night, as if it was her own little protest, just between the two of us. She stroked my head, fingers trembling.

"You know," she said out of the blue. "They used to make nuns and monks line up, facing each other, almost like a collective arranged marriage. We had to pretend to be lovers so we wouldn't be punished."

I didn't know what to say, wasn't even sure if I was meant to hear it. So, I kept my eyes closed, figuring she might just be speaking to herself.

"My brother broke out of prison."

I blinked the sleep out of my eyes, hard. Great-Aunt Jampa's brother . . . so that was one of Father's uncles, then. I didn't know much about him, but prison? Surely, I'd misheard.

"I don't know what he was doing there in the first place, but he escaped," she continued. "And then he came to me.

"When I opened the door, I could barely recognize him

after all those years. He'd become so skinny, and his clothes were in tatters. He kept glancing over his shoulder, sunken eyes darting everywhere, as if he was expecting his pursuers to leap out of the shadows. He said he had to kill some guards to escape. It scared me. *He* scared me. I couldn't be caught aiding a fugitive. Even just talking with him would cast suspicion on me, especially because we were family.

"I wanted to help him. I wanted to bring him inside and give him food and water. But when he asked, I said no." She paused as if she'd slipped into a trance. I thought she'd fallen asleep, when she continued quietly. "He was my own brother, and I said no. Instead, I gave him some tobacco and made him leave. Later on, I saw a plume of smoke in the mountains, and I knew. I knew that had to be him.

"The Chinese came for me the next day. They said, 'You have to find your brother, or else we will kill you too.' So what was I to do? I went into the mountains where I'd last seen that smoke. And I ran and ran and ran, trying to find him, almost like I was hunting him. I didn't know whether or not I wanted to find him at all.

"They found me collapsed by a river, on the brink of death. They brought me back and let me be. I suppose that meant that they got him."

The pain in her voice was almost tangible, scraping past her throat until it dropped between us with a heavy *thud*. I willed my heart to slow down, taking deep breaths and focusing on the rough-spun cotton under my cheek.

The authorities had come for her, even though she hadn't been involved in any suspicious activities herself. She'd sent her own brother away, but they still arrived at her door, threatening to kill her too. For a sickening moment, I thought of my own little brother.

"What was I to do?" she asked again. "What was I . . . What could I possibly have . . ."

I don't know, I wanted to say, but deep down, I knew the answer was *Nothing*.

But then a few nights later, I heard snippets of conversation in a secluded hallway of the nunnery.

"They're still holding the monks," one voice said.

"They're saying only a few people died at the last protest," said another.

A bitter taste flooded my mouth. I'd been there. I'd seen, along with dozens of other witnesses, just how many peaceful protesters had been killed. Yet the authorities were blatantly lying about what had happened. "So tomorrow morning, at Jokhang Temple?"

"Aren't you afraid?" I blurted, shocked by my own boldness. Five pairs of eyes snapped straight to me, glinting in the semidarkness. I recognized these nuns, but I hadn't spoken to them much before, especially not about politics.

"Of course I am," someone finally whispered. She was one of the newer initiates, around fourteen years old. She sucked in a shuddering breath, like she was already on the verge of tears. "I'm so, so scared, I can hardly think straight."

"I keep going back and forth," another nun added, one I'd glimpsed at previous protests. "I worry about getting the whole nunnery in trouble. But the occupiers won't rest until they've erased our culture and religion entirely, so standing idly by won't help the nunnery either."

So, they shared my fears. Of course. We were only human, after all. We weren't the unshakable heroes of old, important people who shaped history and fate. We were just six teenagers huddled in a hallway, whispering under the cover of night. But maybe we didn't need to be infallible. Maybe we didn't need miles-long credentials or influential families. Maybe it was enough for us to simply try to do the right thing.

"Then I want to join you." My voice came out surprisingly steady. If it was with my fellow nuns, then I could do it. I could put my life on the line and speak truth to power with my small voice.

The second nun nodded. "Wake early to complete your tasks first. We'll leave the nunnery separately and meet up in front of the Jokhang. If the police catch us . . ." Tense silence settled around us. There would only be six of us at this protest, not counting any passersby who might join in. We would be easy targets. "We keep our mouths shut and keep one another safe."

The night of April 15, 1988, I studied my great-aunt's face as I settled into my blankets. The morning of April 16, I woke up prepared to die.

My pockets were empty. My parents had sent me money to help offset living expenses over the years, and I'd saved as much as I could. Now I made sure to give it to the unhoused people I passed on my way to Jokhang Temple. There was a slight chill in the air. I shivered under my thin shirt, having left most of my clothing at the nunnery.

When we die, we leave behind all earthly possessions. There was no point in keeping my belongings when I was sure to die today. As determined as I was, though, I slowed my pace just a touch. Jokhang Temple was as majestic as ever in the morning light, its outlines softened by a thin shroud of fog. Lhasa was just beginning to wake, stretching and yawning as the sun peeked over the mountains.

I allowed myself to linger a little more by the book stall, the tree where Chodron took breaks between sales, the patch of flagstone tiling where I'd spent my first night in Lhasa, all those years ago.

I wondered if the officer who had harassed my family was still stationed in the city. I could almost see his face in the hundreds of other officers I'd seen these past few years.

Animals, he'd called us. Filthy animals from Kham. I'd felt humiliated then, confused why he'd spat out the name of my home like a curse. But now, a sense of pride settled within me, fortifying my bones and calming my nerves.

My ancestors had fought against Chinese occupation decades ago, despite the overwhelming odds. Chushi Gangdruk, they'd been called, named after the four rivers and six mountains of eastern Tibet. Though I didn't possess their martial prowess, nor did I wish to, it was time for me to carry on their spirit. Those rivers flowed within me, alongside my Khampa blood, and the Chinese settlers could never dam them up.

The other nuns began to arrive, slipping into the growing crowd.

We made circuits with the crowd of worshippers. I reached out to spin the giant prayer wheels one last time.

Then, the protest began.

"Free the monks!" one nun yelled, and we followed her like an echo. "Free Tibet!"

"Let the Dalai Lama come back!"

A crowd began to gather, as they did at other demonstrations. They followed us as we continued around the temple, adding their own slogans to the cacophony.

"No more occupation!"

"Tibet is an independent country!"

And again, there were onlookers urging us to go home, to save ourselves. But I could almost hear my mother's voice: *You have a responsibility to help other people.* I thought of her and yelled even louder, screamed all the words she couldn't herself.

The officers arrived in jeeps, brandishing batons and guns, merciless as always. They, too, began to yell as they rained blows down on unarmed protesters: This wasn't allowed, this wasn't sanctioned, this was hateful.

Except I didn't hate the Chinese government, and I certainly didn't hate the Chinese people. After all, they too faced harsh censorship and suppression from their own government. I didn't want revenge, I wanted justice. All I wanted was for them to leave us in peace. But what is peace, if it is on the terms of the oppressor? What is liberty, if it can be torn away at the whims of the powerful?

A whole swarm of officers descended on us because there was nothing more threatening to them than someone telling the truth. They twisted our arms, fingers digging into our skin as they dragged us across the flagstones. They tossed us into jeeps like luggage, packing us together tightly like livestock. The metallic tang of blood mixed with the sour scent of sweat. The engine roared to life and the vehicle began to move in rough jerks. Outside, the crowd demanded our release, even though they had to know it was useless as they drove us out of Lhasa.

If imprisonment was the price for freedom, I would gladly pay it. If my death was the price for life, I would pay it twenty times over.

We looked at one another wordlessly, faces swollen and lips cut, knowing that we were not alone. The last I saw of the crowd was a banner—a flash of blue and red, bordered by a brilliant yellow.

What a beautiful thing, to look at your people's flag and know that they will raise it over their heads no matter how many times it's torn down.

CHAPTER
NINETEEN

The guards shoved us off the trucks toward a huge gate, keeping our heads down with sharp jabs and punches. The high walls enclosed a field that reminded me of the vast farmlands I'd seen, so many of them that they blurred together in my memory. But I didn't think I'd ever forget that field because I had never seen a garden so stunning, so full of life.

There was an apple tree, or maybe it was a peach tree. Some sort of tree that would begin to bear fruit as spring turned into summer. Dirt crunched beneath our feet, the grayish brown feeding the little flowers that dotted the lush expanse of foliage. Viridian, emerald, hunter green, jade, with splashes of wildflowers in every color imaginable, like the dresses at home. Our footfalls joined the humming of the bugs that danced from blossom to blossom under a clear sky that stretched for miles, so close to the heavens. The prospect of being thrown into jail didn't seem so bad then, if Gutsa Detention Center was home to such beauty.

But as we traversed the clearing, ankles tickled by long tendrils of grass, I began to make out two large forms, like careless blotches of dark paint. Prison blocks. We stumbled through a smaller gate that led to the women's prison, marking the end of the sprawling greenery.

Cold, dead concrete propped up the buildings that towered over us, relentless shadows cutting sharp angles into the golden spring sun. It lined a long, long hallway, windowless and damp. It blocked our view of the sky as we entered a world far different than the one that had greeted us. Walking sent shock waves up my exhausted legs; the guards herded us farther into the complex like animals.

We were marched to a dark, dank office, where more masked soldiers stripped us of our belts and shoelaces, anything that we could've used to harm ourselves or our captors. None of us dared make a sound as they yelled at us in accented Tibetan. Traumatized by the ruthless violence at the protest, some of the girls did their best to hide their soft whimpers when the guards made sudden movements. I peeked at my fellow nuns. Tears and snot ran down their grime-covered faces, along with streaks of blood. Open wounds scattered across their clean-shaven heads, black bruises creeping down their necks and arms, disappearing under their roughspun shirts. There was still defiance in their eyes, standing steadfast and proud, but they were terrified. I probably looked the same.

I wiped a hand across my face, already tender and

swollen, and it came away with blood. I didn't even know whose blood that was. The man from my first protest sprung into my mind's eye, and I saw him collapse over and over again, a spurt of red arcing through the air. The coppery tang in the air still lingered at the back of my tongue.

Then some chatter floated in from the hallway. I strained my ears, struggling to make out the words, but I knew that accent. It was Tibetan. A Tibetan was outside. The door flew open and I couldn't help but sneak a glance at the newcomer. "Eyes down!" a guard barked. I winced, heart hammering away in my chest. A short Tibetan woman hobbled toward us, her face bare and her form hunched over as she took slow, careful steps. Wrinkles lined her weathered face, and there were crow's-feet around her rich brown eyes. She could've been any of the elders in my village.

Relief flooded through me so suddenly I could've cried. *She's here to help us,* I thought. I was so certain that she was here to bail us out, to make everything okay the way Mother would.

"Hi, how are you?" I said in a small voice, chancing a smile. No response. Mustering all the hope and fight in me, I added, "Free Tibet!"

The woman barely registered my words, didn't even smile at the voice of a compatriot. But her features shifted ever so slightly, as if trying to suppress a reaction, so I pressed on, determined to appeal to her kindness. "What's the problem here? We've only been telling the truth about Tibet. What's wrong with that?"

And she slapped me hard across the face, the blood on my cheek smearing across her palm.

"Don't release them," the woman commanded with a gruff voice, her crow's-feet deepening from her glare. "They're being held for reeducation."

My heart crumpled in on itself.

Reeducation, for a girl who never had the chance to receive a formal education in her little village. The village, where my parents still lived, worried sick over their runaway daughter in Lhasa. My life in Lhasa, rebuilding temples destroyed by the Chinese government and gathering firewood for the older nuns. The nuns, who took me in and urged me to keep my head down to stay safe.

But how could I when my people were suffering? When my parents spent their lives working on land seized by the Chinese? When my neighbors spoke of their homeland in hushed tones, as if Tibet were a shameful secret? When countless nuns, monks, and laypeople had been arrested, brutalized, killed for our freedom?

I regretted nothing even as I was shoved down the hallway, tossed and beaten by long lines of faceless guards.

Who would've thought they'd throw us into separate cells? The detention center must have held quite a few prisoners, so surely it would've been more economical to cram as many of us into one space as possible. I'd never had a room all to myself before.

Night had fallen, but the cellblock was eerily quiet, all of us too beaten and worn to make a sound. All I heard was the faint whisper of ragged breaths as I lay on the bare ground. My friends were alive. I'd caught a few glimpses of them on the way here, barely recognizable from the angry welts on their faces. But beyond that metal grate, they were breathing. They were alive. The thought calmed me a little until another squeezed my heart. I missed them. I missed the nunnery. I missed my friends and the river and Sherab's inexhaustible silence. I missed my family. I missed Tibet.

I *was* in Tibet, of course, not far from Lhasa, but this was not the Tibet from my memories. Sleeping under the stars with a mountain of blankets. Sneaking into the schoolhouse. Banging on pots for my baby siblings. Hiding a cringe while sipping my father's bitter tea. Innocent. Simple. Free. Or at least, a poor facsimile of *free*. I buried my face into the crook of my elbow, nose barely brushing the ground. Funny how I could miss a Tibet that had yet to come.

Crisp footfalls rang through the silence, accompanied by the methodical jangling of keys on a belt. They stopped at my cell.

"Dinner." A masked guard placed a metal dog bowl on

the floor, filled to the brim with brown water. I was famished, my stomach a heavy knot of hunger. The last time I'd eaten was this morning before the protest, but I sat up and just stared at the lumps of raw vegetables. "What? You never seen soup before?" She promptly landed a few blows on my head for her trouble.

Another guard joined her, handing me a tin cup of water and a small white pill through the prison bars before leaving with a sharp salute. "It's a painkiller. Take it," said the first guard, eyes never leaving mine. I stayed silent and did as I was told, slipping the tablet under my tongue and emptying the cup in a single gulp, just like I'd seen in some movies. After how they'd treated me, I didn't trust them to actually give me any medicine. If anything, it was probably some sort of drug to disorient or hurt me, to make it easier to extract information that I did not have. As soon as she left, I spit the pill into the slop bucket in the corner.

Picking up my meager meal, I settled into what I'd designated as my rest area, the little patch of concrete right under a tiny, barred window. My breath whistled faintly, joining the soft chorus of labored lungs in our block of cells. Some light sniffling drifted down the hall, along with a few hiccups and muffled sobs that soon died down. We were too tired to even cry. I blinked rapidly, hoping to clear the blur of fatigue from my vision. I needed to know everyone was okay. Thankfully, the metal bars that allowed the guards to keep an eye on me also let me catch glimpses of my friends in their own cells. As I poked at my food, I couldn't help but imagine the hunched forms of other prisoners, now also in their own cells. I thought of them moving slowly, gingerly, mindful of their wounds as they tried to find a comfortable position on unrelenting concrete. I wished I could help dress their wounds. I wished I could lay a reassuring hand on their shoulders, the same way Great-Aunt Jampa would. I wished I could patch up their tattered clothes like Mother. I wished I could talk to my friends.

    Oh. So that was why we were in separate cells.

CHAPTER
TWENTY

Only a frail beam of light snuck through the high window in the room. I wasn't sure how long I'd been standing here, hands cuffed behind my back, but it must've been hours, judging by the orange glow. My knees buckled. I nearly crashed onto the floor face-first, but managed to catch myself in time.

"Tired already?" The soldier's tone was cloyingly sweet with mock concern. He checked his wristwatch. "But you just got here."

Unlike the soldiers who had brought me in, he left his face uncovered. The red patches on his collar stood stark against the olive green of his uniform, whereas the previous guards had worn faded uniforms. This man spoke Tibetan, but with a distinctly Chinese accent. Not a grunt, then, but a ranked Chinese officer of some sort. Another unmasked officer stood to one side.

The air was so still I could smell the stale sweat on their

skin. I tried to adjust my hands to get some relief for my aching shoulders, muscles locked in place for far too long. My thighs shook hard as I strained to stay upright, and my knees felt like bone grinding on bone. The first officer noticed and pressed his lips into a razor-thin smile.

"You know what to do to make this go away. We just want a little chat, that's all. Now," he said as he settled against a table. "Who sent you?"

My eyes drifted over to the table, a dozen tools strewn across its dull metal surface. A few I recognized: batons, pliers, chains. I furrowed my brows at a red plastic stick the length of my forearm, two metallic prongs jutting out of one end. It was hard to think through the mental fog, but I could've sworn I'd seen that before.

"Let me narrow it down for you: the Americans. Where are they located now? I know you must have a place to report to."

What an absurd series of questions. He couldn't seem to fathom how Tibetans could possibly rise up of their own volition, with pacifist monks and nuns leading the charge. Did he think that we would simply lie down and accept Chinese oppression, just because we were peace-loving Buddhists? Did he think that our vows to help all living beings were just empty words?

My legs finally gave out and the world turned sideways as I crumpled to the floor, head hitting the concrete with a sickening crack. Impeccably shined black boots clacked into view, accompanied by a bright bark of laughter. "Get up." I couldn't. "I said, get up, filth!"

His hand shot out, gripping the front of my shirt and hauling me to my feet. My eyes watered from the pain as he jostled every aching bone in my body, but I somehow found my footing, trembling like a leaf. This close, I could see the way his eyelashes tapered into a soft brown in the waning light. His eyes, though. The spark of mirth was gone. "Who."

But before I could get a word out, a sharp blow forced the air out of my lungs.

I doubled over from the pain, blinking hard as I willed my vision back into focus. Then everything went white and I couldn't breathe. Something powdery filled my eyes, my nose, my mouth. My entire body heaved, trying to dislodge the dense powder clogging my weakened lungs. There was something covering my head. Was this it? Was I of no use anymore? Were they finally going to suffocate me after days of fruitless attempts to gain info? My nails dug sharp crescents into my palms. Another series of coughs wracked through me, so violent that for a moment, my stomach threatened to empty itself of nothing.

Suddenly the covering was ripped away from me. The world was sideways again. I was curled up on the floor now, the concrete a cool relief against my swollen face. The second officer came into focus, now towering over me with a roughspun sack in his hand. Flour. Then I registered the stink. Rancid flour. I never thought they'd use this as a torture method. A cloud of powder floated around me still, but I continued to gasp for air even though the coughs made my whole body burn. Then a steel-toed boot kicked my stomach, making me groan as my lungs screamed for oxygen. Then a blow to my neck. And another to my head.

Someone hauled me up and slammed me face-first against the wall, a puff of flour rising from my clothes, arms still twisted painfully behind me. I shoved against the gruff hands holding me down even though a part of me knew it was useless. Then for a split second, the hands disappeared. They'd let me go. Before I could push off the wall though, my muscles suddenly seized up. Then came a pain I'd never thought possible.

I must've been screaming, but all I felt was the sharp pain twisting into a relentless burn, crashing from my hands down to my feet. Every cell was vibrating, every nerve singed as I stood frozen in agony. A thousand wasps swarmed under my skin, piercing every inch of my face. It was so hot I almost felt numb despite the excruciating pain. I couldn't move a finger.

They must've cut my arms off. A faraway part of me registered my writhing and wheezing and shrieking, the way I dug my face into the wall as if I could hide from the agony. They'd cut my arms off. That was the only explanation for this pain. They cut my arms off. They cut my arms off they cut my arms off they cut my arms off they—

They uncuffed me, and my arms swung down to my

sides, like the lifeless limbs of a rag doll. I slid down the wall to crumple on the ground, the acute blaze of pain cooling into slow-burning embers. Slowly, I turned to face my tormentors, my eyes out of focus. I could make out the vague shape of the officer, and in his hand was the red stick that had been on the table. He'd used an electric baton on me. No, it was an electric cattle prod. For animals. I'd seen farmers use them around Lhasa. It crackled and hummed, like an invisible nest of angry hornets ready to strike again at the slightest disturbance. I almost giggled at the absurdity of it all. I hadn't had electricity growing up, but here I was, goodness knows how much raw power tearing through muscle and bone and sinew like a mad hive.

"You will die here," the first officer spat in my face. I barely batted an eyelid. The glum room had darkened, the sun having set. Then the dark continued to deepen several shades, beckoning to me, and I gladly answered.

I gasped, waking with a start when ice-cold water hit my face, lurching me from the blessed, inky depths of unconsciousness. And then I gasped again, this time from a rib-shattering kick with that steel-toed boot once more.

I thought I'd gotten used to my little cell these first few days, memorized every little quirk in between interrogation sessions. But that night, the single lightbulb shorted and flickered back to life with a soft hum. My hands spasmed. My breath stuttered. My new life had only just begun.

The sun was cold on my eyelids the next morning, forcing

me awake despite the bone-deep fatigue. I'd managed to sleep through the night despite the throbbing all over my body, curled on the concrete like a child. Feeling marginally better, I stretched a bit, wincing as my muscles pulled and my bones protested. The weak lightbulb had been turned off, or perhaps it had just given out, worn and battered like everything else in this cell. Slowly, I got to my feet, careful not to reopen any of my scabs. My hands still tingled from the baton, so I gently flexed them as I got a good look at the view from my window.

View might've been too generous a word. The neighboring prison block took up most of my field of vision, the dull gray interrupted by cracks and missing chunks of concrete. Rusty water stains streaked down the building, just a few shades lighter than the reddish brown under my broken fingernails. Below sat a patch of mottled grass, more brown than green, lit by the meager sunlight that managed to slip between the walls.

The blades shivered in the wind, a piece of the larger world outside. I would've loved to see how far that world went. Mine had been so small, just the few square miles of Pelbar Dzong and the promise of an arranged marriage. And now that I'd finally become a nun, my world shrank even smaller than before. All those miles under my thin-soled shoes, and for what?

A slight breeze washed across my face, and I took a deep breath with my eyes closed. I perched my arms on the narrow windowsill, and rested my forehead against a forearm. No one else seemed to be awake yet. It was . . . almost peaceful.

My thoughts drifted as I watched the shadows outside grow shorter, the sun inching toward its peak. Then a pair of feet shuffled outside the window. I snapped my head up and stepped away, wary of any patrols. But I was never one to rein in my curiosity. I angled my head for a better look as the rustling grew closer. It was an old man, clad in a threadbare shirt, ambling along with a slight limp. I realized belatedly that he was headed my way.

"Good morning, sir." My voice came out mangled. He was probably fifty or sixty, crowned with a shock of white hair that might've been black when he'd first been jailed. He grunted and reached a sun-spotted hand through the window bars. A sad gray lump sat on his palm. I just stared.

"Take it." He brandished the lump after a beat. "The men's block gets better food."

Accepting it with a thank-you, I studied it. This close, I could see it was a lump of bread, more of a dull beige than a true gray, covered in dirt and heavens knows what else. But the old man was right: This bread was better than the watery soup we got twice a day. I brushed off the dirt, careful not to break off any precious crumbs. I wolfed down the bread, trying to savor it at the same time.

Then the thought hit me, unbidden, and I swallowed around the lump in my throat. The old man had the same white hair as Sherab. He had the same heavy footsteps. He'd made the same wordless offer, expecting nothing in return. And just like with Sherab, I would never get the chance to hear this stranger's story. I would never learn how he found the kindness to share his own precious food in a desolate place like this, or why he'd been arrested in the first place. I would never hear tales of his youth, of the sights he'd seen and the people he'd met. This man was yet another voice that had been stifled by the Chinese authorities. I would never even know his name. When I looked up, he was already gone.

There wasn't much I could do, trapped in here as I was. But when the guards fetched me for my next interrogation, I envisioned his retreating silhouette, over and over again. I swore to hold on to the memory of his generosity, for however long I had left to live.

CHAPTER
TWENTY-ONE

We kept our mouths shut as we trudged through the yard, buckets in hand. Summer was in full swing, giving the stench of human waste an almost corporeal quality. Clouds of dirt swirled around our ankles as we dragged ourselves to the faucets in a neat line. I tilted my face up to drink in as much sunlight as I could.

There was no rhyme or reason to the guards' orders. If I looked down, they'd bark at me to watch where I was going. If I looked up, they'd scream to keep my eyes down with a baton to the gut for good measure. What I could count on, though, was that talking brought consequences.

The only times we could talk to one another was back in our cells when the guards were away. Once they locked us back in our cells and left our block, our furtive glances at one another were replaced by a comforting mess of voices.

"How are you?" someone yelled, a few cells down from me.

"I'm okay!" came the response, followed by a coughing fit.

I scooched toward the bars to catch the casual conversation.

We didn't talk about Tibet, didn't even talk about ourselves that much. We knew by unspoken agreement that the less we knew, the better. Yet the banality of our conversation tethered me, reminding me that there was life beyond Gutsa's horrors, that Gutsa would not become all that I was. The shouts coalesced into a cacophony of mundane talk, echoing throughout the cellblock.

"The weather was nice today!"

"I think it rained last night though. The ground got a bit muddy."

"No, that was water from the hose."

"Breakfast was especially bad this morning."

"Yes, the tsampa was like rock. We could do better with less at home."

Plain and pedestrian, like we were just girls. On and on went the idle chitchat, until a tense hush rippled down the hall, with murmured warnings of the incoming guards.

Jangling keys, sharp footfalls, the panicked breaths of dozens of girls. The screech of a gate grinding open. Tiny whimpers echoing between concrete walls. Then heavy thuds, followed by screams of terror.

"Please stop!" the girl begged, but the guards continued to rain down blow after blow.

It wasn't long before masked figures came for me next.

A pair of guards flanked me and watched me stagger

down the hallway. With nobody to distract me, the physical aches and pains resurfaced with a vengeance. My head was pounding, the rhythm speeding up with each labored step. My eyes were throbbing in tandem too, which I hadn't even realized was possible. I was dragging my feet, each step sending a shock of pain up my legs. The soft whisper of my slippers was grating. My jaw was clenched, so I opened my mouth a little to try to relieve some tension, splitting my chapped lips. Without a belt to hold it up, my trousers hung loose and sloppy. My skin felt ten times too big for me, coated in a layer of flour over a film of goodness-knows-what filth. I flexed my hands a little, making my knuckles crack as I got my circulation going. They were still numb from the cattle prod, but if I concentrated hard enough, I could feel phantom prayer beads slipping between my fingers as I recited mantra after mantra.

The guards shoved me into a room that looked like all the others. The same line of questioning roared in my ears: *Who sent you?*

Nobody. Nobody sent us. Nothing but the love for our people, our country, and the nagging, bone-deep feeling that this is not right. If anyone had planted the idea of dissidence in my head, it was the Chinese authorities who persecuted us without mercy.

But the guards who screamed at me were Tibetan. From what I could tell, almost half of the guards were locals, like the woman who'd slapped me on my first day in Gutsa.

Their voices should've brought me some modicum of comfort among a sea of Mandarin and stilted Tibetan. But they didn't, not really.

They hadn't been beaten and dragged through the prison gates as we had been. They'd brutalized us, helping the Chinese officers and landing a few blows themselves. Yet as I watched the men receive their orders with a tidy salute, I wondered how much of a choice they actually had. Would they have been in the cells like us if they'd refused to work for the Chinese? I didn't have the time or energy to ponder.

Time didn't seem to work the same in interrogation rooms. Despite the meager wisps of sunlight that shifted throughout the day, every moment shrank and spread into a nauseating blur of little infinities. Every blow, every insult melted into a haze. By the time I regained some of my senses, an unmasked officer had entered, staring down at my slumped form. The two guards hauled me to my feet with a rough jerk.

"You know you're asking for these beatings," the officer said, taking a seat. "You're asking for these beatings by protesting in the streets. Why were you demonstrating that day? Who sent you?"

My whole body trembled violently and my breath rattled in my chest, still reeling from the day before. "You claim that we have freedom of religion," I started. "But you keep arresting monastics and laypeople." My ribs protested as I drew in a deep breath. "Tibet belongs to the Tibetans!"

The officer leapt to his feet, infuriated, grabbing an electric rod and slamming it into my chest. I buckled, unable to get to my feet despite the commands and threats. As if to punish me for wounds they'd inflicted, a guard pulled down my trousers, and the officer shoved the rod between my legs, inside of me.

There were no words to describe the pain and the horror.

As the officers continued to torture me, my mind began to drift through the all-encompassing agony until it settled on a rare little herb in Tibet. The insect-like fungus yartsa gunbu that was sacred to us and fetched a pretty penny to those who didn't care.

"You forced them to sin!" I shrieked suddenly. Each syllable ripped through my parched throat, but I couldn't stop. The pain that radiated between my legs was a reminder of what they'd taken from me. My autonomy. My nunhood. My future. "You jailed them, the monks, the nuns. You made them harvest the herb, you know that's a sin!"

They weren't satisfied with taking our land, our homes. They took our beliefs, our religion too. They took our people, they took our history. They took my voice, now foreign to my own ears.

But I would forge a new one, and another, and another, as many times as it would take until my people were free.

The rusty water stain outside my little window spread as the months passed, like some sort of crude, morbid clock. The old man continued to sneak me pieces of stale bread with a nod and a grunt. I got a cellmate, who was released not long after. The gentle breezes grew warmer. The grass outside my window traded brown for green.

Lying in my cell, I fiddled with the hem of my filthy shirt to distract myself from the distant screams floating down the hall. Would I have begged so desperately to become a nun if I'd known what would happen?

I ran a hand through my grown-out hair, strangely familiar even after years of keeping it shaved. The slow drag of a razor against my scalp. My mother, running a hand over my head, checking for uneven patches as best as she could, murmuring softly in my ear as she watched remnants of her daughter's old life scatter across the floor.

What was it she said to me, the day she first shaved my head?

Before I could remember, the door to my cell screeched as a guard wrenched it open. I steeled myself, phantom prayer beads slipping through my fingers by habit, each prayer a little act of resistance. Like the little girl pelting yak dung at a Chinese officer, all those years ago.

But instead of an interrogation room, I was pushed down a corridor I hadn't seen in months, alongside dozens of other women. I fixed my eyes on my feet, despite how desperately I wanted to make eye contact with my companions, to glean the slightest morsel of information as to what was happening.

I heard the groan of a gate opening and then a bright light seared my eyes. I recoiled, squeezing them shut as colors burst behind my eyelids. Slowly they receded, and I blinked my eyes open gingerly.

We were back in the garden. Sunlight, like bucketfuls of gold pouring from a clear blue sky. Summer plants flourished, the spring flowers long wilted. Insects called out to their mates, and the tree had borne fruit. A breeze swept past, carrying away the sour stench of unwashed bodies, bringing with it the smell of greenery and life.

A fleet of trucks sat waiting, plumes of exhaust billowing lazily in the air. A few dozen male prisoners stood in neat lines on the opposite side of the garden. One by one, the guards loaded the prisoners onto the trucks like nothing more than yaks awaiting slaughter.

But the women stayed put. No push toward another truck, no prod of a baton. Just a stream of gaunt faces paraded before us, and the merciless roar of the engines as the vehicles pulled out of the detention center.

"Out," a guard barked. Hundreds of heads looked up for what seemed like the first time in eons, tentatively, expecting punishment for following the guard's directions.

The prison gate was wide open, the lush garden of Gutsa fading into a dirt road.

We were being released.

Dozens of cars lined the road—reds, greens, blues, all dulled with a layer of dirt. Supporters had driven to the detention center, waiting to usher us to relative safety. Hundreds of us filed out the gate after months of despair. The buzz of conversation, anticipation, relief, and even cautious joy grew in the air, almost a tangible wave that carried us to the awaiting vehicles.

The crowd thinned as people helped the prisoners—*former* prisoners—onto their vehicles, spiriting them away to safety. Then, by some miracle, I spotted the five girls I'd protested with on April 16. They emerged from the chaos one by one, all looking as haggard and worn as I felt, forced to age decades in the span of four months.

I want to say that I called out to them, forcing the words out of my parched throat, or that I waved my tired arms above my head to catch their attention. I want to describe a tearful reunion where we exchanged stories, or an emotional embrace where we collapsed in relief. But the truth is, I don't remember the details. The only thing I do remember is the fear rushing out of my chest, leaving it hollow for a split second until the joy came flooding in. The sensation was so overwhelming that I felt it like a physical blow. They were alive. We were all alive.

We made our way down the road, looking for someone to take us home. Dirt swirled around my ankles as a truck lumbered past. I had no idea how long it would take for us to reach Lhasa. Truth be told, I wasn't even sure we were headed in the right direction. All I wanted was to stretch my legs after so long in captivity.

"Wait," I said abruptly, stopping in my tracks. My lips curled into a wobbly smile. "Let's walk. It'll be a celebration."

The girls looked at me like I'd grown another head. My feet felt like lead, weighed down by months of torture. My back hurt, carrying the thoughts of prisoners left behind that fortified metal gate. My vision still swam a little, and my eyes watered after months of very little sunlight. Then there was the throbbing headache and the tension in my neck and the soreness in my arms. The idea of sitting in a truck and letting it ferry me to safety sounded heavenly. But I wanted to feel my body, this time without hands holding me down or eyes glaring daggers at me. After a moment, my friends nodded. After all, each sting and strain was a reminder that we were alive, against all odds.

And so we walked, free at last, leaving behind the cells, the screams, and that beautiful, beautiful garden.

CHAPTER
TWENTY-TWO

The walk back to the nunnery was a blur. My eyes were stinging from the sunlight, and I could feel a migraine forming just behind my temples. I barely felt the crunch of dirt under my thin soles. As cars drove past, bearing released prisoners toward Lhasa, the whirring machinery sounded oddly muted, as if my ears had been stuffed full of cotton. Though I should've been alarmed at my hearing loss, I found it bizarrely peaceful. No more guards hurling abuse, or the sickening thud of fists, or the terrified screeches of my fellow inmates. Just a blanket of quiet that wrapped around me as we returned to the nunnery.

There was a ceremony going on, or maybe a sermon or prayer session. I could've sworn I'd seen this in a dream the previous night: a voice droning from large speakers, a congregation dressed in their finest, Great-Aunt Jampa sitting at the front by the head monk. For a dreadful moment, I thought I'd hallucinated our release from prison. Perhaps I was still dreaming, and it had all been a cruel trick my mind played on itself.

But then Great-Aunt Jampa looked up, and her eyes met mine. Her face crumpled into a mixture of horror and desperation and fragile hope. I saw her lips form my name, and before I knew it, I was pushing through the crowd. The congregation showered us with supportive words and gentle touches, guiding us toward the front when our limbs began to fail. Finally, I collapsed into her arms, trembling and weak but so very real.

"Oh, oh, Tsultrim," she whispered shakily as she petted my head. "It's okay now, you're alive. Oh, my dear Tsultrim. You're here now." She continued to mutter in disbelief, as if reminding herself that I really was back in the flesh. I let myself sink into the embrace, feeling her frantic breaths against the top of my head.

We were brought food and drink as soon as we arrived, and the scent of incense and butter candles was as comforting as ever. But now that we were safe at home, I felt the adrenaline bleeding out of me, and the aches and pains began to really clamor for my attention. It was as if my body decided it could finally be vulnerable after four long months.

I could barely even sit up, and as thirsty as I was, I could only take a few sips of water before my stomach started cramping. My head was swimming, and the faces around me began to blur together, just a smudge of color and warmth.

"I thought of you every single day. We all did. We prayed and prayed for your safety, and here you are at long last." She was thinner than I remembered, not quite haggard but definitely worse for wear. "Now, your only job is to rest up. Leave the rest to us."

A few days later, a Tibetan man came to the nunnery, asking to see the six nuns who'd just been released.

"There's a foreign journalist here, looking for people to interview," he explained.

I sat up straighter, the hope in my chest sharp as a knife. "As in a reporter? They want to show what's happening in Tibet?"

"Yes. They snuck into the country, and now they're making a documentary in secret. And after hearing about what happened to you, they want to hear your stories."

"I'll do it," I said immediately. It was a no-brainer. Somehow, I'd survived, and I couldn't just take this for granted. Gutsa Detention Center had stolen four months of my life—there was no changing that, no taking back the time I'd lost or reversing the damage they'd done. But what I could do was bear witness, to tell the truth and spread the word. The guards had been obsessed with this place called America, absolutely convinced that we'd received foreign orders. Surely that meant the Chinese occupation didn't just affect Tibetans, and I was determined to shed light on our plight. If the international community didn't know, then I would make them know. If they didn't care, then I'd make them care.

In the end, four of us agreed to meet with the journalist. The other two were still too weak to even entertain the idea. We followed their instructions, taking care not to be followed as we meandered through muddy alleyways until we reached an old, decrepit building.

A Tibetan man peeked out from a window and waved us over urgently. He was part of a group of informants that arranged travel and interviews for the foreign journalist.

"Come in, hurry," he said. "Did you get here okay?"

We nodded and stepped into the little room, where more people were waiting. A slim woman with dark brown hair wore Tibetan clothing. From a distance, I might have mistaken her for Tibetan. But as we got closer, the sharp slope of her nose became more prominent, her eyes deep set under strong brows. She had a serious look about her, but when she saw us, her expression softened.

With the help of an interpreter, the woman introduced herself as Vanya Kewley, a journalist for a British company called Channel 4. With her limited resources, she had to be careful choosing who to film. So today, she wanted to get to know us first.

"Thank you for meeting with us," she said, after we'd settled in. "I understand that six of you from Chupzang Nunnery were arrested during a protest, correct?"

"Yes," I said softly. At the mention of prison, I felt like I was beginning to float away from my body, while the images replayed over and over in my mind's eye. *Like a movie*, I mused. Something that had happened to someone else. But the more I spoke, the more I settled back into my body. The feeling came back to my fingers, and I heard my own voice more clearly with each second. Then the tears began to flow as I relived every horrifying moment.

One by one, we began recounting the horrors we'd endured: the beatings, the torture, the interrogations, and assault. Kewley listened closely, her eye contact firm and level. Satisfied with the veracity of our statements, she explained our next steps.

"We'll film your stories in a few days' time, at another location. We can disguise your voices and faces, but even then, we cannot guarantee your safety if you choose to be in this documentary. I wish I could, but I cannot."

"We understand," one of the girls said. "And we're willing to take the risk."

"You also need to promise that you will not tell the authorities about us if you get caught."

"Of course."

"I don't mind if you show my face," I said. Maybe if more people saw our faces, they would finally acknowledge our humanity. Besides, there was no real point in hiding my identity. The Chinese authorities already knew who I was;

one interview would hardly make my life any harder than it already was. "You can also use my real voice."

"I'm sure you know how dangerous that would be."

Of course I did. I'd already gotten caught once; I couldn't imagine the Chinese government would be thrilled to learn I was talking again. According to my faith, I could no longer be a nun after having been sexually assaulted. It was a bitter thought, to have been robbed of my nunhood. It had been my life's purpose. It was what motivated me to protest in the first place. But even though I could never be a nun in name again, I could still be one at heart and continue fighting.

I'd been confused when I was younger. After all, the Chinese had offered concessions over the decades: pilgrimages, festivals, the reconstruction of buildings. But you can't demand laurels for returning what you'd stolen in the first place. You can't demand thanks for healing a wound you willingly inflicted, especially when you're still causing harm.

I now knew without a shadow of doubt, not just as a nun or a Buddhist, but simply as a human being with a conscience, that everything the Chinese occupiers had done was wrong.

"Yes. I can't speak for everyone else, but we will all die someday. And if I die for my country, for my people, it would be a worthwhile sacrifice."

The girls murmured their assent. We were in this together. We might not live to see a better future, but we would fight like hell for it.

A few days later, we met again, this time in a different safehouse. The journalist's team milled about the room, studying the light hitting the faded walls. Soon, they had us sit together by a wall as the foreign man fiddled with his camera, angling it this way and that. I could feel the soft press of my friends' bodies against mine as we huddled close. The touch was grounding, keeping me tethered to my own body as I steeled myself. They were warm and alive, thighs and shoulders against mine. We were alive, and we were going to make every second count.

The woman held our gazes, firm yet kind, as she directed one last question to us. "Are you absolutely certain you want to show your faces?"

"Yes."

She studied our faces for a moment, quiet and intense. As if she was burning our images into her mind, so that she could remember us as we were, in the flesh and not on film. "You have my word that we will take care of the footage. I can't promise that it'll make it out of Tibet, but we will do all we can to keep your stories safe."

The foreign man pressed a button on the camera, and we began to speak once more.

The days passed, and I felt worse than ever. Something was seriously wrong with my stomach. I'd gone so long without food that I kept throwing up whenever I tried to eat. I could barely keep water down and was now extremely dehydrated.

It became clear then, what the officials at Gutsa meant when they said I was free: free to die wherever I'd like, with bile in my mouth and blood in my lungs. The Chinese controlled the hospital, so it was all but impossible for me to go seek treatment. Plus, I was persona non grata, someone unwelcome. To associate with me was to invite scrutiny and trouble.

Eventually, the nuns snuck me into a hospital with the help of some sympathetic doctors. My intestines had ruptured. I lay in a bed for days, hooked to an IV, only catching bits of conversation as I drifted in and out of sleep for a whole month.

After I was discharged in secret, a group of visitors came knocking at the nunnery. I stumbled to the waiting room in a haze. I'd recovered enough to leave the hospital, but eating remained a challenge, and it left me weak. It took considerable effort not to collapse after just a few steps. I braced myself in the doorway to catch my breath. Then I looked up and froze, suddenly wide-awake. It was a group of around seven people, but my eyes zeroed in on the man sitting on the floor.

He was in his early forties, his wrinkled skin dotted with sunspots. His leather shoes were homemade, mended over and over again. He sipped at a mug of tea that was far too thin for him, but he was too polite to ask for extra butter. His voice was soft and gravelly, and I would have gladly listened to that voice for hours as it whispered prayers at dawn.

For a moment, I wondered if I was actually still in the hospital, hallucinating.

"Tsultrim?"

Father said my name, and I finally fell apart.

One moment I was staring in disbelief. The next, my father gathered me into his lap like a baby, stroking my head as I sobbed. The onlookers sniffled as they watched in silence.

We simply clung to each other, sobbing and wheezing as if we couldn't believe the other was really there. For the first time in a long while, I felt safe enough to let my guard down and give in to my emotions. This was my father, the man who'd scolded me and cared for me and worried himself sick over me. This was my father, who loved me no matter what, and whom I loved in return.

When Father pulled away to speak, his eyes were swollen and red-rimmed. "Officers came to our house, told us to come fetch you."

I stared vacantly, not quite wrapping my head around what he was saying. Maybe it was a warning: *You're responsible for your daughter, so come get her.* Maybe it was a threat:

We know who your family is and where they live. Maybe it was some unexpected display of leniency. Either way, it didn't matter. "Fetch me?" I asked.

"I'm taking you home," Father said gently.

"Home," I muttered.

"Yes, Tsultrim." He smoothed a hand over my forehead, a tiny smile on his lips. "We're going home."

CHAPTER
TWENTY-THREE

I was home again.

The same house, the same stove, the same livestock pen, minus the family horse Father had sold to send me money. It was eerie, the way nothing had changed much on the surface.

When I arrived, I visited every family in the village in a sort of welcome home tour. They greeted me enthusiastically, heaped snacks and delicacies onto my plate, refilled my cup over and over as they asked how I was. All I offered was a smile and a few murmured words. Nobody said anything about how emaciated I looked or how I was barely nibbling the treats they offered me. Then, I was promptly put on house arrest, stuck in my childhood home day after day.

Everyone was acting like nothing had changed. As if all I'd done was return after a few years away. But I knew better now: It was an attempt to hang on to whatever scrap of normalcy they had left. I also let myself indulge in the simple gestures of domesticity for a while. Now that I was no longer a nun, I resumed my household chores.

"Give me a hand," I said to my younger brother. Bhuti was around twelve or thirteen now, all awkward angles and lanky limbs. He'd grown so much in the three and a half years I'd been away, and now he sounded a little like a honking goose when he talked.

He sat on an overturned bucket and began milking a dri as I tended to another. He hummed while he worked, soothing the dri with a few words when she got antsy.

"A bunch of old people were crying about you the other day. Some kid even thought you were dead," he said nonchalantly. I froze, anxiety making my blood run cold. I tried to laugh it off, hoping my reaction didn't betray my panic. By the time I was his age, I'd already sensed something amiss with the village. As I watched him adjust his long legs, trying to get comfortable on the tiny bucket, I understood more keenly than before why our parents had tried so hard to keep me from asking questions as a child.

I looked up at the tree line to quell my anxiety, slowly counting each yak and cow I could see. Then I spotted a thin trail of smoke wafting from the mountain and thought of Great-Aunt Jampa's brother. I thought of her as a young woman, staggering through a forest to find him at an officer's orders, collapsing on the ground from exhaustion. If Bhuti learned the details of my situation, if the police came after him, thinking him a coconspirator . . .

When I met his eyes, though, he looked at me, thoroughly unimpressed. "It's so stupid. Why would you just drop dead? But I guess he is just a little kid," he continued. "Are you having trouble with that one?"

"What?" He nodded to where my hands had frozen on the dri's teat. "Oh. Um."

"I'll show you how it's done. Move over and watch closely."

Bhuti nudged me aside and began elaborating on the finer points of dri milking.

I nodded along, even though I already knew all of that, content to just watch him work. He looked so proud of himself, so confident as he showed off everything he knew, his eyebrows lifting and furrowing animatedly as he described the temperaments of our livestock.

"You're really good at this," I said, just as he was finishing up.

He beamed. I would've done anything to keep that grin on his ruddy face. "I sure am! Whenever someone's missing a cow or something, they usually send me to go find them."

"Well, since you've got this under control, I'll go see if our grandparents need any help."

In truth, our grandparents' house was one of the few places I could go freely. Nobody would suspect me of anything if I was just visiting family. The villagers greeted me along the way, but their smiles were strained as they scurried past me with a cursory glance. I couldn't blame them.

Although nobody knew the details of my detainment, the Chinese authorities had made it abundantly clear that I was in trouble.

The stray dogs began barking, and I saw a strange man trying to shoo them away from his door.

"Damn curs," he muttered, and settled onto a low chair with a grunt, a cigarette between his lips.

The man had arrived just weeks before my return. Nobody knew where he came from or who he was, and while the villagers wouldn't normally mind, the man spoke in a fake Kham accent. Instead of simply keeping to himself and existing in the background like Sherab, this stranger was actively hiding who he was. Suddenly, he fixed me with an intense stare. A spy maybe, dressed as a civilian to keep an eye on me. He wasn't a very good one though, with the way he didn't even bother to blend in properly. I tried not to fidget as I walked past him. It wasn't his being a spy that bothered me; I'd seen officers dressed in plain clothes, posing as protesters before. Rather, there was a sharpness to his gaze that pushed me off-kilter. Unlike the covert glances of the officers, his was a gaze with a very clear message: *I'm watching your every move.*

I only relaxed when our grandparents' house was in sight.

Gelek and his wife were outside, tending to the barley field. Even though he'd gotten married and moved in with his in-laws, he still came around to take care of our grandparents. He called out in greeting and I headed inside.

My friend Thubten was sitting on a cushion, a bunch of raw wool lying forgotten as she made funny faces at Gelek's children. Thubten's health hadn't improved while I was away, so she continued to help with domestic tasks like babysitting while the other adults worked outside. Hearing my footsteps, she twisted around to greet me.

My heart did a little swoop when the baby girl giggled at me. Her laughter was clear and clean, like snow melting off a tree at the end of a hard winter.

"Hi," I cooed, bending down to sweep my niece into my arms. She babbled at me, curling her chubby hands into fists as she reached for my face. I leaned in to let her squeeze my nose, and she giggled even more, delighted at something so small and silly.

I couldn't help but giggle along, pleasantly surprised by the lightness in my chest. I still had no interest in getting married, even if someone was willing to take me as a wife. I didn't want children of my own, either. But there was something comforting about the way babies fit perfectly in the crook of my arm.

Babies didn't have secrets or ulterior motives. They expressed themselves freely: laughing with their whole body, crying with their whole soul. It took some guesswork to figure out what exactly they wanted, but their demands were always straightforward, unlike adults, who said one thing while meaning another.

And no matter how much these babies cried, their voices never gave out. I didn't want to let the world force a legacy of silence onto these children. But it seemed almost inevitable.

I imagined watching my niece and nephew grow up, supporting them the same way my uncle Tenzin had supported me. They would pick up chores when they got old enough, learn how to survive off the land as we had for centuries. And then what? School was out of the question, and hermitages were under strict surveillance. Would they even learn Tibetan, if they could go? Would they learn about their culture, or just some watered-down version that glorified the occupiers?

After prison, I didn't know how I could possibly fight back against the overwhelming might of the Chinese government anymore. But at the very least, I could stay and watch over my niece and nephew. I could change their diapers, burp them after meals, lull them to sleep after a long day. I could sneak stories to them as they grew older, like Great-Aunt Jampa had, little crumbs of truth that they could pass to their own children.

I could be happy here, I thought. *I am happy here.*

Gelek ducked his head through the door then. "Tsultrim, give us a hand out here," he said, mopping up the sweat on his brow with a rag. "We need water for the crops."

I lightly pinched my niece's chubby cheek before passing her to Thubten and heading outside. My body still felt a little creaky, so my sister-in-law helped strap a bucket on my back, and we headed for the river. I took a few sips as I waited for the buckets to fill up. The water here had a slightly tangier taste than in Lhasa, and I realized with a start that I'd missed it. It flowed down my throat, smooth as silk, pooling into my stomach with a pleasant chill.

I stood up to haul my bucket back to the house, but a stabbing pain lanced through my abdomen. I stumbled with a cry, curling myself into a little ball on the ground. For a split second, I was back in that awful prison, wheezing as a man stood over me, kicking me in the stomach over and over and over—

"Are you okay?" Gelek asked. He was crouched over me, eyes wide with concern.

I picked up the bucket as slowly as I could, trying not to spill too much water. It splashed against my clothes, making me shiver, but the cold was grounding, forcing me into the present. "Yes. I can handle it."

"I know you can, but that doesn't mean you should."

"I'll handle it," I said again, firmly. "This is nothing compared to—" I clamped my mouth shut. Even though I'd left, that prison still had its claws in me, tainting these moments of peace with reminders of cattle prods and steel-toed boots. Even now, it was determined to take and take and take.

Gelek grabbed the bucket from my hand, and his wife slung my arm around her shoulders, tugging me back to reality. "Next time," he said. "Next time."

The early autumn air filled my lungs, crisp and grassy. I wrapped my jacket more tightly around me. I really could live like this: wrapped in Mother's handmade clothes, passing the time with good, honest work.

The sound of cowbells drifted across the clearing, echoing in the open air. I squinted. Though my eyesight was nowhere near as clear as it had been before due to the beatings, it had been steadily improving. It wasn't rare for other households to let their livestock out on the same patch of grass. But as she drew closer, I recognized the springy step of the cowherd, the gentle lilt of her voice even as she hollered at a cow wandering away from the herd.

Pema wandered over, her hair in neat braids.

"You're back," she said.

"I'm back." We'd seen each other when I visited her family, but we hadn't exchanged words then. Now, surrounded by nothing but browning grass, seemed as good a time as any.

Pema hummed. We sat on the ground, keeping an eye on our livestock until she finally broke the silence.

"How are you?"

"Good. You?"

"Good."

"I'm glad."

I knew I was killing the conversation, but I didn't know what else to say. She pressed on with renewed vigor, determined to chatter like when we were children.

"My cousin married a girl in Lhasa," Pema tried again. "He moved there a few months ago."

"That's good."

"I also got married."

"Congratulations."

"Thanks, he's a good man." A beat. "What about you?"

"I'm not exactly wife material, am I?" I was a disgraced former nun currently under surveillance. Nobody in their right mind would want to marry a woman who had the authorities breathing down her neck.

Pema looked back at the animals, lips pressed into a tight smile. We sat in tense silence as the sun inched across the sky. Pema stood after a moment, patting off the dirt stuck to her clothes. I expected her to say her goodbyes and gather her flock. Instead, she took a deep breath and screamed.

"Free Tibet!"

I jumped to my feet, my joints protesting the sudden movement. I pulled on her sleeve. "You can't, Pema. Are you trying to get caught?" I hissed, but there was no heat behind the words, only a resigned frustration. The Pema I knew would never do anything like this. The Pema I knew was polite and delicate, a girl who didn't care much for religion or politics. But then again, she wasn't a girl any longer.

She jerked away with a roughness I'd never seen in her before. "There's nobody listening to us," she muttered. "No one ever does." She turned back toward the mountains and wailed. Every word that tore through her throat was raw with despair.

"This is wrong! *Everything* is wrong! What did we ever do to deserve this? We did nothing wrong! Give us back our country! Give it all back!"

"What is wrong with you?" I asked, but she ignored me, opting to continue screaming at the distant mountains instead. She was a sobbing mess, her cheeks gone blotchy and wet with tears.

The truth was that there was nothing wrong with Pema. This was a normal reaction to an abnormal situation, a natural response to living under occupation for two decades and not seeing an end in sight.

She was right. Nobody ever listened to us. Why would they? We were nothing. We were Tibetan—less than nothing. Her screams seemed to reverberate in my chest even as they dissipated in the wide-open plains. I took a deep breath and started screaming with her.

The cows and yaks continued to graze, sparing us only a few lazy, curious glances. The distant mountains took in our every word but said nothing back. We emptied our lungs and sucked in harsh, grating breaths to scream again until there was nothing left. Patches of greenery were missing like bald patches, and it felt almost inevitable that those snow-capped summits would soon melt to nothing too. Everything was broken, and we didn't know how to fix it.

"I still think you made a big mistake, Punjun." Pema's voice was so soft and hoarse, I almost missed the words. I wondered if that was how she still saw me: Punjun, the quiet little girl who trailed after her, who didn't speak unless spoken to. Her eyes wandered up and down my figure, as if she could see the half-formed bruises and badly healed ribs under my clothing. "You're right. It's not fair that we're treated so poorly. But you should've just kept your mouth shut."

CHAPTER
TWENTY-FOUR

I was bringing in firewood from the yard when an offi-cer trudged up the hill to our house.

"Tsultrim Dolma? You're being summoned to the town hall for a struggle session."

"Got it." I deposited the wood by the door and dusted off my hands. After I returned to Pelbar Dzong, I learned that the public shaming sessions I'd witnessed as a child had a special name: "struggle sessions." They were an almost daily occurrence now. Best to just get it over with.

Father caught me by the elbow as I turned to leave.

"Remember, just stay quiet. Don't speak unless spoken to," he murmured.

"I won't. I promise."

"And you should change your clothes."

I frowned and looked down at my shirt. "What's wrong with what I'm wearing?"

"It's red, Tsultrim, like a nun's robes. They'll think you're wearing it to provoke them." I could see his point, but I doubted my choice of clothing would really make that much of a difference. It was just a color. My skepticism must've been obvious, because he added in a pained voice, "Please."

I relented and went inside the house to change into a black shirt. When I emerged, Father nodded in approval, but I could still see the worry in his eyes, following me as I set off for the town hall.

It was just as I remembered as a child: plain, with only the most basic furniture and a raised platform at the far end of the room. The officers nudged me toward the platform, where a blackboard had been propped against the wall.

"Don't think we've forgotten your crimes," one sneered, never mind that I'd never been on trial or charged with any crimes.

Then he hung the blackboard around my neck. I tipped forward from the weight. I was still recovering from my ordeal in prison, and the board was wider than my torso, the rope digging into the delicate skin at the back of my neck. Large Chinese characters had been scrawled across the surface, with smudges of old chalk underneath like the ghosts of past victims. I was not the first to wear this board, nor would I be the last.

The man beckoned to another officer. "Go round them up."

Soon, the soft patter of footsteps approached, and the villagers began to file into the town hall, their expressions grim and resigned. The hall was deathly silent. There was just enough light from the open door that I could make out individual faces. Father, Mother, my siblings. Thubten swayed on her feet, a look of sorrow on her face. Pema looked somewhere past my shoulder, her lips pressed in a line. Nyima stared straight at me, her expression unreadable.

Once everyone had entered the room—the elderly, the children, the sick and the poor—the officer began the meeting.

"Tsultrim Dolma was caught inciting violence in Lhasa," he said in a booming voice. "Countless innocent civilians were caught in the crossfire due to her recklessness."

That was probably what the message on the blackboard said. It was so bizarre that they'd chosen to write it in Chinese when nobody could read it.

"The Chinese government came to Tibet to liberate you from the clutches of your backward traditions. We've built hospitals and roads, we've created jobs and boosted agriculture. And how do these insurgents repay us for our generosity?" He spat on the floor right next to me.

"The Dalai Lama and his clique choose to disturb the peace just to further their own rancid agenda. They choose to sow chaos and split the motherland, turn her children against one another." He grabbed me by the collar, shaking me like a rag doll. "This is the face of someone who would harm you just to advance her own ideals! They're everywhere, hiding in your communities, and we must work together to weed them out.

"Tibet *is* free, and China is the one who freed Tibet! You have the freedom of religion." He gestured to the cluster of monastics in the crowd. "You have new roads so you can go wherever you want. We cleared the land so you can grow more food."

He went on and on, repeating the same talking points. Perhaps this gathering wasn't just to humiliate me and serve as a warning to the others. It was also an attempt at hammering these untruths into our minds. But as I looked out over the sea of faces, I could see that they heard the truth behind his words loud and clear.

Freedom of religion—to profit from us and entertain tourists.

Clearing the land—and sending valuable timber eastward, leaving nothing for us.

Planting wheat—even though the crop couldn't survive here and had caused devastating famine.

Paving roads—to China so they could take our resources and colonize our land more easily.

Creating jobs—for Chinese settlers, who were the only ones capable of meeting the absurd and unreasonable qualifications they set themselves.

Building schools—to teach Mandarin Chinese and erase Tibetan language from the face of the earth.

Opening hospitals—to give Tibetans subpar health care and forcibly sterilize women.

"There are legitimate ways to file complaints. If you have

grievances, you come to us. You talk to *us,* so we can help you help yourselves. *Peacefully*. Protests achieve nothing but violence."

He could ramble all he wanted, but he could never make us forget the things we knew.

My joints creaked and my vertebrae popped at an alarming volume. Dusk was falling as I waited for my bucket to fill up at the stream. I stretched my neck this way and that, trying to work out the kinks and knots. The struggle sessions weren't helping my recovery, but my health was improving, slowly but surely. Besides, I had all the time in the world now that I'd settled down.

Then the dogs started barking, and a gruff voice cursed before calling out. "You."

I kept my gaze forward. It was the strange man who'd been keeping an eye on me. He called out to me again. "Tsultrim Dolma. Come here."

I gritted my teeth and faced him.

"You need to leave."

That . . . was not what I was expecting. I couldn't imagine a spy for the Chinese government wanting me to run free. Was this some sort of trap? An attempt to lure me into escaping, just to snatch me up again?

"Your family is in danger, girl," he growled. "There are spies everywhere. The Chinese are paying them five hundred yuan each just to keep an eye on you, maybe sniff out some coconspirators while they're at it. That's five hundred *per day*. They're out to get you, and they won't stop until they do." There was a desperation in his voice, hidden under that gruff tone. His words came out rushed and urgent, like he was running out of time. "As long as you're here, your family will get harassed, and it'll only get worse every day."

His eyes bored into mine, the same piercing look that he'd fixed on me since I returned to the village. And I believed him. Perhaps it was foolish of me to trust the word of a stranger, especially one that I'd suspected was a spy. But truth be told, he was just saying what I'd always known but was too afraid to acknowledge: There was no place for me here, not anymore. I couldn't keep deluding myself like this. The authorities would hound me until I died, possibly at their hands. Pelbar Dzong had more Chinese officers than ever before, and the whole village felt the tension. Anyone close to me would get roped into this mess, just like Great-Aunt Jampa when her brother had run away.

The bone-deep exhaustion I felt had now buried right into the marrow. I let my head fall back and gazed at the emerging stars, as if the little pinpricks of light held some secret solution.

The stranger was right. I had to leave. Not because I was ashamed, nor because I was admitting guilt or defeat. And yet . . .

"Where am I supposed to go?" I asked, almost pleading.

Just when I thought I'd found some semblance of stability, it was wrenched from me yet again. Even now, they were determined to take and take and take.

The man scoffed. "How would I know? Go hide in the mountains or leave the country or whatever. You just can't stay here."

It came to me then: Great-Aunt Jampa at Chupzang Nunnery. The Chinese had tightened up restrictions on monastics ever since the protests. But even if I couldn't stay at the nunnery, I could at least get some guidance from her. She would know what to do.

"Whatever you do, don't tell another soul," he continued. "It's you they want, so you better not get anyone else caught in this."

I kept my plans to myself. I didn't even approach the strange man again to ask for advice. But one day, as I was running through the details of my escape, Nyima approached me.

"So, you're running away to Lhasa. Again," she said unceremoniously. "I'm going with you." Not a question, not an offer, but a simple demand.

It seemed like yesterday when Nyima and I were exchanging blows over a pair of earrings. As precious as they were, they couldn't compare to the weight of other lives, now sitting in the palm of my hand.

"How do you even . . . ?" I started incredulously.

"Because I know you," she replied, voice flat.

"Then you know I'm not someone you want to be caught with."

"What's the plan?" she said, bulldozing over me. It was so very Nyima that I almost laughed.

"We walk."

"And then?" She narrowed her eyes at me when I didn't answer. "That's it?"

"Yes. We'll try to hitchhike along the way as well."

"Is that what you did last time?" I nodded, and she pinched the bridge of her nose, a deep frown on her face. She hadn't asked me why I was leaving, so I would do her the same courtesy. Whatever her reason, it was important enough to risk a dangerous trek with a dissident like me.

"Fine," she said. "I'm in."

We agreed to meet in a couple of weeks and parted ways to make our final preparations. I hid a bag in the barn, just as I had done so many years ago, and began setting aside some flour in secret. This time, I took extra care in being discreet, taking only the absolute bare minimum—it wouldn't do for my parents to catch on, not with the stakes so high. The officers were sure to notice my disappearance; my parents needed plausible deniability.

The bag filled up bit by bit, until one day, I weighed the satchel in my hand. I had enough flour now. I had the blanket, the metal bowl, the thick woolen dress Mother made for me—all I needed to leave home. All that was left was to do it.

"Tsultrim?" Mother looked up from where she'd been bent over her needlework. I drank in the sight: We'd just finished dinner, and the room was bathed in the warm orange glow of the woodfire stove. Mother's long hair had started to go gray, her soft brown eyes now lined with crepey wrinkles.

"I'm just going outside for a bit. I need some fresh air."

Concern immediately came across her face. "Are you feeling unwell? Would you like some tea? Maybe I can whip something up—"

"No, no," I said quickly. The last thing I wanted was for her to work herself into a frenzy. I didn't want her last memory of me to be fraught with anxiety. I wanted to see Mother smile, just one last time. "I'm okay, I promise. I just want to clear my head."

She eyed me suspiciously for a moment before returning to her needlework.

I walked down the front steps, listening to the wood creak under my weight one last time. The livestock snorted as they began to settle down for the night.

The black-haired dzomo bumped her snout against me. I stroked her head with a sad smile. Like me, she'd always stuck out—not a dri or a cow, but something else entirely. Unlike me, she'd get to live out the rest of her life here. Then, I left my childhood home for the last time.

When I reached our meeting place, Nyima wasn't the only one waiting.

"Thubten?"

"I want to go too," she said. "On a pilgrimage."

"But your health—"

"I promise I won't slow you down," she said quickly, but that was the least of my worries. Memories of my first trip to Lhasa flashed in my mind: a barn, a lamp, and a lifeless body. "Who knows when my next chance will be? I want to see Lhasa, even just once."

"You did say we'd try to hitchhike," Nyima said. "It's not like we're walking the entire way."

I could see the devotion burning bright in Thubten's eyes. I'd been so lucky to not only see Lhasa, but live there. I wanted her to experience it for herself too. Thubten knew her body and her limits better than anyone else. It would be condescending for me to deny her the chance just because I thought it would be too dangerous.

"You promise you'll tell us if you're struggling?" I said.

"I promise."

"And you'll make sure not to push yourself too hard?"

"I will."

"Good heavens, are you done?" Nyima moaned. "Start walking. Now."

We decided to rest for the night when we reached the monastery we'd rebuilt so long ago. The monk there greeted us like family, ushering us inside and offering us steaming cups of butter tea. My distress must have been apparent, because he kept his small talk to a minimum, and I was relieved when he left us to rest.

Then he came waddling back in, his brow furrowed.

"There's a man coming," he said.

I poked my head out of the doorway, and my breath caught in the beginnings of a sob. I could recognize that gait anywhere, from any distance, even in the dim starlight. After all, I'd made sure to hold on to the sight lest I forget.

"It's my father," I croaked. "Please, you need to send him away."

"You don't wish to see him?"

Of course I did. I wanted to see him so badly. My conflicting emotions must've shown on my face, because the monk ushered us into the next room without another word and closed the door firmly. I pressed my ear against the wood just in time to hear an exchange of greetings.

"Have you seen my child? She's eighteen, about this tall, skinny with a sharp chin and red nose. My wife said she left for a walk and never returned."

I stifled a gasp and squeezed my eyes shut. Father's gravelly baritone seemed to reach into my chest, squeezing hard until my heart ached. How was it possible to feel so much all at once? But I couldn't bear to cover my ears, not when it could be the last time I'd ever hear my father's voice.

"I'm afraid I must ask you to leave," the monk said, neither confirming nor denying. But Father had always been a shrewd man.

"Could you at least tell me where she's headed? When you saw her . . . was she okay? Did she look well?"

In the silence that followed, I could hear Father's heavy breath as he let reality sink in: I was leaving for good.

"Have faith and pray for her," the monk said softly.

"I will." Father took in a shaky breath; I let one out to keep from crying. "I will."

For a moment, I imagined throwing the door open. I'd apologize and beg for forgiveness and try to explain why I'd run away. Father would sag with relief upon seeing me, and then promptly berate me for my impulsiveness.

"Her mother and I both—we'll pray for her, morning and night. Her siblings too. We'll pray for her. We'll always pray for her, all of us." He cleared his throat. "Thank you for your help. I'll be off then. Sorry to have disturbed you."

Then, the sound of receding footsteps.

I could catch up easily if I went after him now. My fingers grazed the rough wood, and I could feel the girls' gazes, heavy with sympathy. A million thoughts tangled in my head until it felt ready to burst. I just didn't know anymore. So, I listed the things I *did* know.

My family was in danger. The Chinese government was keeping an eye on me, and innocent people would be caught in this mess. The very building I was standing in had been painstakingly rebuilt after being destroyed; the government surely wouldn't hesitate to decimate it again, if given an excuse. I didn't fear death anymore, but I feared my family's death. I needed to leave. If I saw Father's face now, I wasn't sure I could find the resolve to leave home again.

So, I resisted the urge to sneak a peek at Father's retreating silhouette, and we didn't step out until the monk told us he had gone.

CHAPTER
TWENTY-FIVE

To my relief, we had much better luck hitchhiking than the last time I'd left for Lhasa. We had nothing to offer, but many drivers slowed down, tires crunching over unpaved stretches of dirt. Miraculously, nobody questioned why three young girls would be so far from home. They probably thought we were pilgrims, and we didn't bother correcting them. Besides, it *was* partially true, at least for Thubten. I pulled my jacket up to my ears though; I could never be too careful. When we couldn't flag down a vehicle, we simply kept walking along the main road, stopping at bare-bones way stations for the occasional break.

When we reached Lhasa three weeks later, the green hills were just as lush as I remembered under the midday sun. Hermitages still dotted the landscape, and I recalled the first time I'd greeted the sight—the anticipation bubbling in my gut, the slight spring in my step, the awe that threatened to take my breath away.

Now I simply felt tired. Regiments of soldiers cut a swath through the crowds, boots hitting the ground in unison. Buildings had been demolished to make way for tanks, civilians dragged from their houses as they looked on in despair. Once again, that hopelessness dug into my chest, like a rock stuck in a shoe. These cruelties couldn't be changed by a Good Samaritan or two. What we needed was wholesale change: to tear down the system and rebuild it, brick by brick. Yet being a fugitive, I was terrified that getting involved would only endanger these movements.

Eventually, we needed to pause by the side of the street. Thubten hadn't made so much as a peep during the trip, but the travel was clearly wearing her down.

"I hope my family isn't too worried. Or even mad." Thubten shuddered. My stomach dropped, and I tasted the guilt in my mouth like bile.

That was right. Thubten would probably return home, one way or another. But me? I'd abandoned my family entirely. I pulled the collar of my jacket up, even though it could go no higher.

There was no use dwelling on the past. Father, Mother, and Gelek would understand, even if they somehow resented me for leaving without a word. Bhuti and Yeshe would too, once they were old enough. As for Gelek's children . . . I ached at the thought that they wouldn't remember my face.

Nyima must have sensed my souring mood. She snuck a glance at an officer coming down the street, then trained her eyes on me.

"Time to find a place to stay," she said. "You're going to Chupzang Nunnery?"

I nodded. "Just to speak with Great-Aunt Jampa for a bit and figure out where to go from here."

"I guess this is where we say goodbye, then." Nyima regarded me for a moment, taking in my hunched shoulders and lowered face. She leaned closer and said under her breath, "Listen, I don't know how much trouble you're actually in, but . . ."

"I get it," I said. "It's safer this way."

Nyima looked at me for another long moment. She still retained that sharp stubbornness that she always had, but it was now dulled by grief. We never spoke about what happened after I'd left all those years ago, yet it was clear that the years had not been kind to her, either. She'd been uncharacteristically quiet throughout the journey, whereas the old Nyima would've chattered away to her heart's content. When she did speak, she was curt and dismissive. But when she spoke this time, I knew she meant every word. "Whatever it is that you're doing," she said, "I hope you stay safe."

"Thank you."

"Take care of yourself."

"You too."

Nyima helped Thubten onto her feet, and I didn't even

dare watch them blend into the crowd. Later, I would occasionally catch a glimpse of them among the pilgrims that swarmed Lhasa, but I never let my eyes linger. It was safer this way.

The incline seemed so much steeper than the first time I'd climbed the hill to Chupzang Nunnery. Yet night was falling, and I needed a roof over my head. *One step at a time, I told myself,* lungs burning. *A little longer and you'll see Great-Aunt Jampa again.*

I thought of her arms around me, when I'd first been released from prison. By the time I reached the nunnery, I felt ready to collapse into her embrace.

Chupzang Nunnery was quiet as always, except for the steady stream of chanting that drifted from the main temple.

"Excuse me," I said to a nearby nun. "Is the nun Jampa around? I'd like to speak with her."

She eyed me warily, a stark contrast to the welcome we'd received when we first stepped foot here. Her eyes were red-rimmed and swollen. "May I ask who you are?"

"Tsultrim Dolma, I used to be a nun here."

She seemed to soften somewhat. "Ah, yes. She used to talk about you." Her eyes darted around, and she bit her lip hesitantly. Finally, she said, "Let me fetch someone."

When she scurried back though, it was not with Great-Aunt Jampa at her side. Instead, she was accompanied by a monk I'd never met before. We exchanged bows, and the monk looked at me with a sympathetic expression.

"I'm afraid Jampa is no longer with us."

"Do you know where she went?" I asked, growing nauseated by the second. Surely, he couldn't mean . . .

"She passed away just a few weeks ago."

My stomach lurched and my voice sounded distant to my own ears. "Oh," I said numbly. "Okay."

I stared blankly at him for a few more seconds, taking in the dark circles and deep frown lines. I wasn't exactly surprised. Great-Aunt Jampa was no spring chicken, and her health had been deteriorating. I was well aware that death was a natural part of life and had come to terms with that fact.

I just thought we'd have more time. Together. I had so much I still wanted to tell her. Even if I couldn't talk about the details of my arrest, I wanted to at least bring her news of home. I wanted to hear her bark of laughter as I described Bhuti's honking voice. I wanted to hear her tell me that everything would turn out okay, just one last time.

Her voice seemed to echo in my ears, growing dimmer and dimmer with each repetition. I strained my ears, as if I could hold on to the sound just a bit longer.

The monk coughed, his mouth and brows pulled into taut lines. He opened his mouth, and I already knew what he was going to say. I closed my eyes and took a deep, even breath.

"We cannot allow you to stay here."

I'd braced myself for the words, but it was a massive blow nonetheless. I wondered if this was how Great-Aunt Jampa's brother had felt when she turned him away with some water and a hushed apology. I had to believe that the monk felt the same guilt Great-Aunt Jampa had felt, or else I would break. I had to believe that he wanted to help, but simply couldn't, or else I would disappear into a void of loneliness.

"Please, may I at least rest a moment here? I traveled all this way..."

"We can spare some food, but you need to leave. It's safer this way," he said softly. He was looking past my shoulder instead of meeting my pleading gaze directly.

My lip wobbled as I dragged myself down the hill. I'd slept rough before. I could do it again. He was right. It was safer this way. Taking me in would have put the whole nunnery at risk.

I repeated his words as I looked for a secluded alleyway to spend the night. I pulled the collar of my woolen dress all the way over my head, just in case an officer walked by. With the cloth pressed to my nose, I could smell a trace of the soap Mother had used to wash it. I could smell home, if only a little.

It's safer this way.

I could hardly believe my luck when I bumped into an old acquaintance in the market a few days later. My heart soared, and I felt the lightest I'd felt since arriving. Then, the monk's nervous reaction flashed in my mind, and my spirits came crashing down. I scurried away, hoping to slip into the crowd of shoppers. A hand squeezed my shoulder, and I jumped. When I looked up, Phuntsok was studying me with a sad smile on his face. He took in my disheveled state, the dark circles, and gaunt cheeks. And without missing a beat, he said under his breath, "You can stay at our place for a few days."

A few days. Not a single sleepless night, or a few hours to hide from the rain. Not a quick sip of water before spending the night by the road. Still . . .

"It's not safe. I appreciate the offer, Phuntsok, I really do. But it's not safe for you."

He dismissed my concerns with a wave of his hand. "Oh, please. It wouldn't be the first time. We will always be here to help you."

I bit my lip. "I can't offer you any compensation."

"I know. That's why I'm offering."

"And what about Tashi? Is she okay with me staying?"

"She's out of town at the moment, but she would love to have you, I know it."

I had no doubt that Tashi would welcome me. After all, she'd been the first to shelter me. Though they weren't exorbitantly wealthy, an extra mouth to feed wouldn't put a big dent in their resources, especially with their adult children having moved out. I could get my bearings, sort out my next steps without having to worry too much about safety . . .

"Thank you," I whispered. "I can't thank you enough."

"Don't mention it," he said. "You know where the house is?"

"Of course."

"I'll head back now. Give me a few minutes, and then come over."

By the time I arrived, Phuntsok had already made some tea for me. The house was just as I remembered: The television, the clock on the wall, even the smell was nostalgic—an earthy blend of spices that smelled like stability, like trust. This was where the couple had sheltered me after protests, given me clothing so I could slip back to the nunnery unnoticed.

"Here's some clothing. It'll be too big, but it'll have to do," he said, and handed me a clean white shirt and pants. "I'll get you some food as well."

Dinner was a simple affair: some tsampa and a modest vegetable soup. We ate in comfortable silence until Phuntsok finally spoke up.

"Tell me what happened," he said. I looked away and kept my mouth shut. He leaned forward, voice soft as he urged me on. "You can trust me, Tsultrim." Still, I stared resolutely at my teacup until he said in a sad voice, "You're in trouble, aren't you?"

I was never a good liar. "Yes." My voice only trembled a little, but he clearly heard it, his eyes melting in sympathy. "That's all I can say. Please, don't ask me anything else."

He nodded then and kept conversation to a minimum.

When he prepared to turn in for the night though, he gave me one last lingering look, his gaze going up and down my figure. "We will figure this out, Tsultrim. Sleep well."

"Thank you so much," I whispered. I didn't know what Phuntsok could possibly do. Sure, his family was better off financially, but he was still Tibetan. Maybe he could pull a few strings here and there with his connections. Despite my concerns, the hope ballooned behind my rib cage. His words had been so reassuring. He'd been the first to tell me things would work out, and I wanted to believe him. I closed my eyes, a sense of safety washing over me. Finally, a respite. Finally, some rest.

I'd barely fallen asleep when a heavy weight fell on my chest. There was an odd pressure at my crotch. Then a hand snaked under the blanket and tugged on the waistband of my trousers.

With a horrified screech, I realized that it was not a dream. I struck out wildly, hand landing on what felt like someone's face in the dark. That someone swore loudly.

"You ungrateful wench!"

In the dim light, I could just about make out Phuntsok's silhouette. One hand covered his nose, while the other still grabbed at me. I shoved at him as hard as I could, trying to get some distance between us.

"I gave you food! I gave you clothes! Who else do you think would take you in? You didn't really expect me to take all these risks for you for free, did you?"

"I . . . I don't have money." Everything about this felt surreal. "I already told you."

"Exactly," he snarled, and came at me again. He clawed at my clothes, fingers digging into my flesh. I dug my nails into his hands until he let go with a yelp.

"You're married!" I screamed. "You have a wife and children, for goodness' sake!" I grabbed whatever I could and flung it at him: a cup, a half-burnt candle, whatever ornament that was within reach. Anything to keep him away from me until I could make my escape. Clutching my little bag to my chest, I lunged for the door, crashing through it into the cool night air.

My cheeks burned with fury. Adrenaline coursed through my veins, keeping me going even after so many days with little food or sleep. Every inch of my body felt on fire, burning with an intensity that kept me moving. It wasn't fear. I'd known fear in its purest form, inside four concrete walls and a single barred window. What I felt was unbridled rage.

How dare he? *How dare he?*

I ran until I was sure he wasn't following and ducked into a deserted alley. I could finally process what had happened. A friend—if he could still be called that—had tried to rape me while I slept. He'd dangled an offer of support in front of me like a carrot. When I accepted it gratefully, he held up a stick and swung at me. We were supposed to be on the same side, weren't we? Yet maybe that was why Phuntsok knew he could get away with it. He knew that I was a fugitive, that I'd have no recourse. The authorities could not care less if a young Tibetan woman was assaulted, especially not when she was on the run.

Even if I weren't a wanted woman, I doubt I would've reported him. I knew that the Chinese authorities would punish him more harshly, as he was Tibetan. I buried my face in my hands, frustrated at my impulse to shield him despite what he'd attempted. I didn't want him to get in trouble with the authorities, but it angered me that protecting him meant keeping my mouth shut, after I'd vowed to speak up against injustice. I had to choose between protecting him or protecting myself, and the unfairness of the situation burned me inside.

Ultimately though, I was a penniless teenage girl fleeing from authorities. He was a family man who owned a house. Once again, the odds were stacked against me, leaving me without much of a choice at all. With nowhere else to go, I curled into a ball near Jokhang Temple, prepared for yet another long, sleepless night.

CHAPTER
TWENTY-SIX

I was reaching my limit. My entire plan had hinged upon getting advice from Great-Aunt Jampa. Not only that, it seemed like I couldn't trust anyone at all. I couldn't even visit temples or monasteries to clear my mind, not when guards roamed the grounds. The streets were no place to collect my bearings, to figure out what on earth I was supposed to do next. I used to know Barkhor Square like the back of my hand. I had friends here, people who greeted me with smiles and open arms. Now every corner seemed foreign, every shadow a stranger out to get me. Every day, more and more uniform-clad officers were swarming the city, armed with not just guns, but with cameras too.

Every single one of my nerves was pulled taut, ready to snap at the slightest pressure. When I heard a voice call my name, I practically jumped out of my skin. I looked down by instinct. The voice called again, closer this time. I tamped down on the urge to run. The commotion would only make things worse. Taking a deep breath, I looked up and was greeted by a familiar face.

"Lhamo," I said by way of greeting.

The poised, clean-cut Lhamo I'd known from Drepung Monastery was gone. He was no longer clad in a monk's robes and his hair had grown past his earlobes. He even had a hint of stubble, and he no longer held himself ramrod straight, straining under the weight of his large backpack.

"I'm not a monk anymore, no," he said ruefully, as if reading my thoughts. I flushed, embarrassed at being caught staring. He didn't seem to mind though, and we took our conversation to a secluded alleyway, away from prying eyes.

Here, the street was mostly mud, heavy and sticky under my soles. The only people around us were unhoused and unemployed Tibetans, ordinary people who'd been driven from their livelihoods, evicted from their homes to make way for Chinese occupiers.

"It's good to see you," Lhamo said when we settled in a corner. Instead of the level, mild tone I remembered, there was now a cynical edge to his voice. The shadows made the lines on his face more pronounced, and he seemed to have aged eons since we'd last met. "We heard that you were sent home after Gutsa."

I nodded. The silence stretched on, solid and unyielding. What was I supposed to say? *How are you?* His gaze was distant, as if he stared right through me. That was enough of an answer for me. So instead, I asked, "What are you doing now?"

"Odd jobs. Hauling cargo for merchants, repairing roads and the like. I'm leaving, so I need to save up as much as I can."

My ears perked up. "Leaving?"

Lhamo scanned the alleyway for eavesdroppers before leaning back in. "A handful of us found a guide to take us out of the country."

I could hardly believe my ears. "You're leaving Tibet?"

"There's nothing left for us here, not anymore. No jobs, no homes, no *life*." He cleared his throat with a loud cough, eyes bright and watery behind cracked glasses. Lhamo was from Lhasa. He'd grown up here, watching as the landscape changed into something almost unrecognizable. He'd been here as protests increased, and more of his comrades were thrown into jail and murdered. He managed a small smile. "We're going to India to see His Holiness the Dalai Lama. I need to see with my own eyes that not all is lost, not as long as he is alive."

"When do you leave?" Hope bloomed in my chest. It was one thing to hear vague stories about people making the journey to India; it was another to know someone with a concrete plan. And not just to leave Tibet for a short jaunt, but to relocate entirely and receive guidance from a godlike figure like the Dalai Lama.

"Next week."

"Can I go with you?" I blurted out.

I still wasn't entirely sure where India was, but I knew it was outside of Tibet. And if it was outside of Tibet, then the Chinese government wouldn't be able to get their hands on me. No more looking over my shoulder, no more hiding in shadows and street corners. If Lhamo could make it there, so could I.

Then he asked, "Do you have savings?"

Oh. The heartbreak on my face must've been obvious, because he looked away and pinched the bridge of his nose. "It's incredibly expensive, Tsultrim. I had to sell everything I own, on top of working the skin off my bones."

My insides went numb. I wasn't sure how long the journey would take, but the fee must be enormous. I forced the question out anyway. "How much?"

"Two hundred yuan."

That was twice the annual income of an average Tibetan farmer.

I should have known. Travel was only for the wealthy and the well-connected. The rest had to sacrifice everything, like Lhamo, just for the chance to somehow, maybe, miraculously make the journey alive. The only people I knew who'd successfully gone abroad were Phuntsok and Tashi, people who had official permits to leave. The mere thought of that man made my skin crawl, so I pushed him aside to focus on my current problem. There was no way I could scrounge up that kind of money on short notice, if ever.

But what other choice did I have? Sneak around Lhasa until I got caught? Get sent home and bring more trouble to my family? Get imprisoned again? The answer was clear: to bite the bullet and start saving, no matter how long it would take.

I began searching for work all over the city. Some employers were less than scrupulous, simply looking for the cheapest labor possible, not caring where it came from. Others were sincere in their attempts to help, offering as much as they could.

I took on whatever small jobs I could, hauling cargo, herding livestock—anything I could get my hands on. I slept on the streets, careful to keep my face hidden as much as possible. Even when someone offered to house me, I didn't dare stay for too long, lest my host get in trouble or try to take advantage of me as Phuntsok had.

The one constant in my life was Jokhang Temple. It anchored me as I drifted along aimlessly, a beacon that helped me reorient myself. There was always a massive crowd of worshippers circling the temple, despite the increased police surveillance. As the nights grew longer, I had to hurry over even though my body protested after a day of work. Prayer was safe for me during the day, when there were plenty of people around to keep me anonymous.

I'd follow the crowd of worshippers, prostrating as I walked around Jokhang Temple lap after lap. Now that I no longer owned prayer beads to help me count each mantra, I had to keep track of them in my mind.

Even then, there was a constant buzz at the back of my mind, telling me to watch out, to check every corner and doorway I passed, making it difficult to truly sink into the serenity that prayer would normally bring. The ritual was almost like an achingly sweet overripe fruit, the constant need for vigilance spoiling it with a bitter aftertaste that lingered with each bite.

Vendors cried out to the crowd, selling everything from incense to clothing. I spared a few yuan on incense and sandalwood, tossing the offering into the large stone burners, letting the fragrant smoke fill my lungs. Then, among the voices clamoring for attention, came a hawkish bark.

"Cabbage! Potatoes! I have carrots for the best price!"

Even in a massive crowd, Chodron commanded attention, her colorful piles of produce vibrant as gems in the sunlight. I could almost hear the wheels of her cart clattering across the flagstones. I started toward her by instinct but caught myself. I should leave her be. She had a family to feed. She looked right in her element, striking up conversations with would-be customers as if she'd always known them.

I was about to walk away when Chodron's bright gaze met mine. Her face split into an even wider grin, and my eyes began to sting with tears. When was the last time someone had lit up like that, delighting in my presence? Every encounter had been strained, every reunion tainted and heavy with anxiety.

She pulled her cart toward me and regarded me carefully. Then, her smile warmed, not with pity, but with care. "Let me buy you a meal."

"You look great," Chodron said, and I couldn't help but giggle a little. Her remark might've come off as rude, but her smile was every bit as genuine as I remembered. There were new streaks of gray at her temples, and her cheeks looked a touch sallower. Yet she was just as boisterous as I remembered, refreshingly candid and kind.

We sat in a secluded restaurant with only a handful of patrons. The air was thick with the savory scent of stews.

"You're a growing girl," she said, "so eat up."

I did as told, resisting the urge to wolf down everything in sight. After so many days with barely any food, I doubted I could stomach anything richer than thin tsampa and water.

"A customer told me there's a group headed west in a truck. They're bringing medicine to Mount Kailash," she murmured after a moment. My heart skipped a beat. Mount Kailash was a sacred mountain in Buddhist tradition. Setting foot on the mountain itself was prohibited, but performing kora around it was a major pilgrimage route. "You know where it is, right?"

"Somewhere out in the Himalayas?"

"Exactly," she said, eyes glinting. "It's in the west, near the border with Nepal. You could leave Tibet that way."

"I tried already, Chodron. There was a group of monastics heading to India, but the trip cost two hundred yuan. *Two hundred!* They had to sell everything they had to scrounge up funds. I have nothing. I'm working all the time and I barely have anything to show for it." Tears were welling in my eyes, and it took everything I had not to let my lip wobble.

"But this group isn't going all the way to India. Mount Kailash is in Tibet. They're just headed for the camp there, and they'll take you there for twenty-five yuan. It's crossing into Nepal that takes so much money. You can at least get closer to the border and then figure things out from there."

"And how am I going to earn the money to cross the border?"

"You can work at the camp. It isn't just pilgrims—tourists go there all the time too. They're not used to the high altitude like we are, so they hire Tibetans to carry their luggage for them." Her concern was clear as day as she studied me. Then her face hardened, and she pulled me closer. "Here. Take it." With her hand hidden in her shirtsleeve, she slipped a wad of paper into my hand. I smoothed out the crinkled paper under the table. They were banknotes. And though I wasn't sure of the exact amount, the color of the notes told me there was more than twenty yuan. I barely stifled a gasp. Before I could protest, she repeated in a firm voice, "Take it."

My initial reaction was to shove the money back at her. Chodron was a merchant, but she wasn't rich the same way Phuntsok was. How many hours had she spent on her feet, roaming the Barkhor to save up this money? How many days had she yelled herself hoarse?

But I needed it. I needed help. I had to trust her judgment, because at the end of the day, all we had was each other.

Sniffling just a little, I folded the money with sweaty palms and slipped it into my pocket. "Thank you, Chodron," I said, voice cracking.

When I looked up, Chodron's eyes were bright and watery.

"Come by my house. I can't guarantee anything since I live with my family, but I'll let you stay as often as I can."

Now she was offering me shelter? "I can't, you've already—"

"Yes, you can."

She stood to leave the restaurant and after waiting a few minutes, so did I.

We were to meet on the outskirts of Lhasa. A crowd of roughly ten people waited beside a rickety truck. Blotches of rust covered the vehicle like half-healed scabs, and I wasn't entirely sure it would make the three-day drive in one piece. Still, we had no other options.

"I know you," a voice said, deep and uncertain. A young man of around twenty was looking at me with a cautious gaze. I tried not to shirk away. Did he recognize me from a protest? A wanted poster? I'd hoped to blend in with the many pilgrims who ventured to Mount Kailash. He continued, words thick with a Khampa accent. "Have you done any construction work out east by any chance?"

I blinked. There was something familiar in his somber expression, the flat line of his mouth. I pictured him a few years younger. A fuzzy memory resurfaced: Dawa, Wangmo, and I waking at dawn to trudge down a dirt path, the sun beating down on my freshly shaved head, hauling rocks and stones to rebuild a temple. "Yes. Yes, you're from a village near Pelbar Dzong, aren't you?"

His face dawned with recognition, and he seemed to almost sigh with relief. "That's right. It's nice to see someone from home. Or somewhere close, at least."

We'd never talked before, but now that we had a long journey ahead of us, we had plenty of opportunities to fill the silence. The man's name was Lobsang, and he was on a religious pilgrimage out west. At least, that was what I assumed, and he most likely assumed the same of me. By unspoken agreement, we talked about everything but the trip.

The battered truck took us west, over paved roads and dirt paths. We drove for days, stopping only for brief breaks and sleeping outside overnight. The group was silent, too on edge to make small talk. It was early morning when we approached the swath of tents. Tibetans milled about with foreigners. Finally, *finally*, we were at the camp at Mount Kailash.

CHAPTER
TWENTY-SEVEN

This was the farthest I'd ever been from home, and I had no idea what to do next. My goal was to leave the country, but I didn't know how. There would be checkpoints at the border, manned by the Chinese army. I had no papers, no resources, no money to tempt soldiers into looking the other way. There was no way the authorities would let me pass alive.

So, for the time being, I focused on saving up money, tamping down the macabre thoughts as much as possible. Whatever was next for me, it would no doubt cost me a hefty amount of cash. Someone at the camp was kind enough to share their tent with me, which solved my housing problem. We were offered food from locals who believed us to be pilgrims. That meant that I was able to save most of the money I earned. Chodron had been right, there really were opportunities here.

Mount Kailash was not only popular with pilgrims. It attracted foreign tourists from across the world. Some came for the challenge; some came for the scenery. The one thing they had in common was altitude sickness. Though I wasn't in the best shape, I was still faring better than the foreigners. Their chests heaved with every step, breaths coming out in white puffs as they spoke with their tour guides. One such guide approached me one day as I sat on the gravel, nibbling on a piece of dried meat.

"The foreigners are going to do the kora around Mount Kailash, and they want to hire porters." He studied me carefully, sizing me up. "You seem strong enough. I can't guarantee how much they'll pay, but—"

"Yes!" I exclaimed, leaping to my feet. It didn't matter how much the pay was; something was better than nothing.

He raised an eyebrow but carried on. "Like I was saying, I can't guarantee how much they'll pay. It could be anywhere between twenty to a hundred yuan for each circuit. Each circuit takes around three days."

He brought me over to a group of tourists. Other Tibetans were already waiting, including Lobsang. The guide then rattled off introductions, interpreting between the two groups.

"Be prepared to camp out in the open. Tell me immediately if you start feeling sick or dizzy, and we'll stop." He pulled out a map and traced out our route, clockwise. "And to reiterate, we are *not* going on Mount Kailash—it's too sacred to be sullied like that."

We set out almost right away. The porters had all traveled

light anyway; we didn't have much to pack beyond the basics. A blond woman handed me her royal-blue backpack with a smile and a small bow. I almost staggered from the unexpected weight. The pack had to weigh at least sixty pounds. I slung it over my shoulders with my own bag with a huff and followed the guide out of camp.

I'd expected more security due to the high traffic, but to my relief, even after hours of walking, the scenery around us was unmarred. There were no tall buildings decked out with cameras, no guards breathing down my neck. Just a sense of serenity that I'd missed sorely.

Stones and gravel crunched under my feet as we climbed a gentle slope. According to the guide, Mount Kailash was sacred not just to Buddhism, but to many other religions like Hinduism and another Tibetan religion called Bön. Travelers of different faiths and ethnicities had been taking this route for centuries. Each individual step might not have done much, but altogether, they'd carved out the path that I was now walking on.

I gazed at Mount Kailash. The main peak stood at twenty-one thousand feet, already capped in snow though winter was still months away. At dawn, the sunlight hit the summit, bathing it in golden pink light. Mount Kailash looked like a jewel then, bright and shimmering like a beacon. No wonder so many religions believed it to be the home of deities. The sight was almost enough to calm my anxiety over what was to come.

I was only a fleck in the universe, a pebble at the foot of a mountain. I was small, miniscule, and the thought was comforting. There was something bigger than the pain roiling inside me. It was even bigger than the clear blue above, where vultures searched for another sky burial to feast on and return our mortal bodies to the earth.

With a renewed sense of purpose, I trudged on.

As I went about my days, I heard whispers of guides who smuggled pilgrims past the border to Nepal. It wasn't exactly a secret, but I was still hesitant to approach them. It was one thing to ask a stranger for a little food; it was another to ask them to take me straight past legions of armed border guards.

We were gathered around a small fire a few weeks later, halfway through a circuit of Mount Kailash, when Lobsang spoke up. His eyes darted around, making sure nobody was eavesdropping. Then he directed his steady gaze at me and muttered, "There's a guide who can take us across the border next month." He looked around again, checking that the coast was clear. "I talked to him back at the base camp. Seemed like a knowledgeable fellow."

"How much is he asking for?" I said, bracing myself for the exorbitant cost.

Lobsang looked grim. "Five hundred yuan."

A wave of nausea hit me. *Five hundred.*

That was more than twice what Lhamo had been charged for his journey all the way to India. Maybe he, like Phuntsok, had already had some sort of permit that allowed him to cross the border officially. But that was simply not feasible for me and most other Tibetans. Applying for official papers was expensive and time-consuming, never mind the fact that I was now a fugitive. The only way forward was to pay a guide to take me across the border illegally.

The smallest fee I'd received so far was twenty-five. If every trip was like that, I would have to do the kora twenty times. Each trip was three days. Even if I took jobs every day, back-to-back with no rest, that would take at least sixty days. It was late spring now, so at my current work pace, I could probably save up the money by early fall. But by then, it would be too cold and too dangerous to begin venturing through the mountains to cross the border. I'd have to wait for next summer when it was warmer and safer to travel.

I perked up at the thought. That was right: Summer was coming, and with the weather warming up, more travelers would come to Mount Kailash in the next few months, which meant more opportunities to earn money.

Besides, I'd also received large tips before; it could happen again. There was no point in catastrophizing. Even if the worst were to happen, I didn't have any alternative plans. All I could do was focus on what I could control.

I picked up the pace after that trip, taking job after job.

The soles of my feet began to go numb after several trips, until I could barely feel the cold through my secondhand shoes. Within a few weeks, I was able to scrape together the funds for the guide. The money burned a hole in my pocket. I'd never seen, much less owned, so much money in my life. I stayed vigilant, never leaving the money unattended until the night we met the guide.

We met him a few nights before we were set to depart. He was a stout man, with an even voice that commanded respect.

"I take Tibetans on pilgrimage," he said. "As you know, there are many holy places in Nepal and India, and I want to guide as many people on their spiritual journeys as possible."

I shifted, feeling a little guilty pretending to be a pilgrim. But nobody had actually asked why I wanted to leave Tibet. I wasn't technically lying. Besides, there were around ten people in this group. I suspected that at least a few others had to hide their real motives like me. The guide went around the group to collect his fee in a little pouch, and I was relieved to hand it over.

"It'll get warmer once we get past the Himalayas, so make sure to wear layers of thin clothing, instead of just a thick jacket," he continued. "We'll be crossing through all sorts of harsh environments, not to mention the possible guards along the way. This trip is not for the faint of heart."

The group was silent. The air was thick with tension but also with rugged determination. We had all resolved to see this through.

"May we all make it through unscathed."

The day of departure was here. We arrived at the edge of camp, as agreed. The moon was a mere sliver overhead, and the tents fluttered in the cool spring breeze.

Soon, I would be on my way out of Tibet, so even though I was jumpy with nerves, I sat as patiently as I could and waited.

And waited.

And waited.

The sun was peeking over the mountains when Lobsang finally said what we'd all been thinking through the night.

"We've been scammed."

Five hundred yuan, gone in the blink of an eye.

Maybe the man really needed the money, I told myself, my desperation bordering on delusion. *Maybe he had a sick relative. Maybe he needed to repair his home or feed his family.*

But the fact of the matter was, I needed the money too, and so did the other travelers who'd been conned by this man. Perhaps we were naive to hand over the money in full, but we were desperate for a path out of Tibet, whatever our reasons. It was beyond cruel for the man to take advantage of that and dangle the promise of freedom only to snatch it away for his own gain.

Still, I'd earned five hundred yuan in just a few weeks. I could do it again. I went straight back to work. There was no time to dawdle or feel sorry for myself. I would reach Nepal if it was the last thing I did. There was no looking back.

CHAPTER
TWENTY-EIGHT

A few more weeks passed, and slowly but surely, I recouped some of what I had lost. Lobsang had found us another guide to take us to Nepal. Though I was hesitant after our aborted attempt to escape, what choice did I really have? Winter was looming over us, a dark cloud that threatened to derail my plans even further. Between waiting for next year and getting scammed again, I would rather take my chances with the latter.

I took stock of my possessions, ready to leave at a moment's notice. I had a small metal bowl, dented but still usable. A fire striker so I could cook and stay warm. The pouch of barley flour would last me a few days. Three hundred yuan, tucked safely into my pocket until I could hand it to our new guide.

Last, there was the woolen dress that I'd brought from home. My chest tightened as I gazed at the bright colors and detailed embroidery, my mother's fine craftsmanship evident in every stitch. It was almost six months since I'd left Pelbar Dzong. The adults had to know that I would not be coming home this time. Gelek would be busy with his own family, but he'd feel the loss of an extra pair of hands. Maybe Mother would accidentally make an extra portion of food for someone who was no longer there. I thought of Father, praying alone in the morning.

With the sun high in the sky, Bhuti would have finished with the livestock. Maybe he was taking a break and making funny faces at our nieces and nephews. Would they remember me? Surely, they must've retained some fuzzy memories. Perhaps I was like a smudge of paint on a family portrait, just a contour with a general idea of eyes, nose, and mouth.

Tears stung my eyes as I recalled their faces, one by one, but I couldn't bear the thought of forgetting them.

Please watch over them, I prayed. I hadn't read a prayer book in a long while and had forgotten a lot of the verses I'd painstakingly memorized at the nunnery. But surely, the gods would listen if I were sincere.

The days dragged on. A few more pilgrims trickled in here and there, braving the cold to pay their respects at the holy site. Not every newcomer had brought their own tent, so some of them milled about, asking for shelter. I ignored them, determined to mind my own business as much as possible. The fewer people associated with me, the better.

It would be dangerous for them otherwise. Then I heard a tremulous voice.

"Excuse me," she said. "My friend and I are looking for somewhere to stay for the night. Do you have any room to spare?"

I looked up, the sight taking the breath from my lungs—a round, flushed face and bright brown eyes.

"Dawa?" I said incredulously. I hadn't seen her since we'd first run away to Lhasa together, almost five years ago.

"Tsultrim," she said, taken aback. "I didn't recognize you. I didn't expect to see you here."

"I wish it were under different circumstances, but it's still nice to see a friendly face." I'd gone breathless with excitement. The people at Mount Kailash were kind and cordial, but they didn't know me, not in any significant way.

But Dawa knew the person I'd been before prison. Dawa didn't just see a quiet young woman who kept to herself. She saw a girl who enjoyed listening in silence. I could see myself reflected in her brown eyes. What a joy it was to be known, to be seen in all one's complexity.

Then she averted her gaze. She kept shooting me furtive glances, as if hoping I would just leave her alone. The realization dawned on me. Dawa had caught wind of my arrest and didn't want to be associated with me.

"I need to go find a tent," she finally said, and walked away.

For the next few days, I would see her around camp. but we never interacted, save for a few glances here and there. It broke my heart. We wouldn't have been able to speak much about our struggles, but we could've at least shared each other's company.

I was making last-minute checks before we set off when I heard a commotion outside the tent. I lifted the flap and stepped outside, following the crowd's gaze and squinting into the distance.

Figures were coming in from the direction of Nepal. They stumbled toward us, silhouetted in long shadows as the sun began to set. They were limping heavily, falling forward and barely catching themselves before they hit the ground. As they drew nearer, we could see them huffing out labored breaths, uneven clouds of white bursting from their mouths. I frowned in confusion. They were barefoot, but they were clutching their shoes in their hands.

A man collapsed when he reached camp, and people scurried off to bring food and water. He was covered in grime after days on the road. He had an air of defeat and shrank into himself, his gaze unfocused and cloudy. I spotted Dawa in the crowd of spectators, wearing an expression of horror that surely mirrored my own.

"What happened?" someone asked.

The man's face was blank, his voice devoid of emotion

as he said, "We got caught. We were so, so close, but they found us near the border." Tears began to flow down his cheeks, slicing through the grime and dirt.

I steeled myself as I finally looked down at his feet. Bile rose in my throat.

His feet were a bloody mess, two slabs of flesh that were barely recognizable. Discharge oozed from cuts and scrapes that could've easily been treated. Patches of raw skin were visible under a thick layer of dirt, blisters covering his heels and toes. On the ground beside him was a pair of secondhand army boots, old but perfectly functional.

His voice stayed steady and stoic as he continued. "They made us take our shoes off, and then they had us march back. They rode in jeeps, with their guns pointed at us the entire time."

Anger boiled in my stomach. The guards had no reason to demand they walk barefoot, other than pure, unadulterated cruelty. They could've thrown the escapees into their jeeps and spirited them away to prison. But they made them march back to camp. This wasn't just a punishment. The army intended to make an example out of them.

This is what happens, the warning said. *There is no escape.*

"I'm giving up. I'm going home."

By the look on his face, the prospect of returning to the village was hardly a consolation. After all, nobody would risk their lives to leave their home, not unless home had become hell itself.

The man never explained why he'd tried to cross into Nepal in the first place. He could've been on a pilgrimage, or he might've been escaping from the occupation. But the reason didn't matter. He'd been caught leaving. Whether he went back to his hometown or a different city entirely, his life would not be easy, no matter how sympathetic his neighbors might be. Chinese authorities would see to that.

I wished I could offer him advice, some tricks to help him survive the humiliation and punishment that was sure to come. Some tricks to survive, period. But the words never came. Instead, I retreated to the tent.

Wherever the man ended up going, I hoped he would find even a modicum of peace.

The atmosphere had grown somber. The consequences of getting caught were much more real now.

Still, a dozen people showed up on departure day with looks of grim determination. Trekking blindly over mountains and through forests, sleeping rough and starving—that was preferable to whatever fate awaited them at home.

Our new guide was a lama, a spiritual teacher who hadn't taken monastic vows and was accompanied by his young wife. I couldn't tell if he was Tibetan or Nepali—to my ears, the accents around these parts sounded equally foreign. His oval face and full cheeks gave him an almost boyish look, but he had to be in his fifties at least. When he spoke, though, he emanated the fatigue of a thousand lifetimes. His wife, on the other hand, looked about thirty. They were no strangers to guiding travelers across the border, and only charged a nominal fee to offset the cost of supplies.

"We've been to Nepal several times," he said. "The path will take us through the Himalayas first, so be prepared for lots of snow. Once we get to the border, my wife and I will go through the checkpoint since we have official papers. However, the rest of you will have to sneak past them instead.

"There are two main routes to get past the checkpoint: one over a bridge and another through the mountains. The bridge is safer from the elements, but you're more likely to get caught by guards. The mountain route will take longer and will be harder to traverse, but there will be fewer guards along the way."

We all agreed. Getting caught meant certain death, or at least a few months of torture in prison. Better to die in a ditch than to be shot on sight.

"After we cross the border is a desert. From there it's a few more days' walk to the refugee camp in Kathmandu, the capital of Nepal."

After he outlined the route, we set off at a brisk pace with the rising sun at our backs.

Dawa was in the group and kept to herself. This was the most time she and I had been near each other ever since she arrived. I couldn't really blame her. The loneliness cut into my chest, deeper than I'd expected.

Then, as the two of us lagged slightly behind the main group, she finally spoke.

"I want to have a family." She was addressing the open air. "And I can't let my children grow up like we did, with all this . . ." She gestured vaguely, but I knew. The struggle sessions and censorship, the encroaching occupiers, the dwindling resources, and cultural erasure. The possibility of imprisonment and death over the slightest infringement.

Dawa wanted her future child to grow up with all the world had to offer. She wanted to raise a child immersed in Tibetan culture, but she'd have to do so outside of Tibet. What a spectacular contradiction.

Each step I took brought me farther away from home than I'd ever been. Yet I was surprised to find that I wasn't all that scared. The Chinese government had already made an example of me multiple times. Threats to my life no longer worked. If anything, my determination had been bolstered by the repeated displays of cruelty.

They couldn't keep getting away with this.

A wave surged within me, and I felt a little taller.

I felt full, sturdy. I felt powerful.

The Chinese government was scared of me. Why else would they keep a scrawny, malnourished eighteen-year-old girl under house arrest? They were scared I would speak out. They made escape next to impossible because they knew Tibetans who fled the country would expose their human rights abuses. They knew their deeds could not stay hidden forever. They knew the only way to shut me up for good was to kill me.

There is no escape.

Fine. Then I would force my way out or die trying.

CHAPTER
TWENTY-NINE

The route made the trip between Pelbar Dzong and Lhasa seem like a walk in the park. Whenever we neared any settlements, we had to stumble through the night to pass unnoticed. The lama and his wife were the only ones who could safely enter towns with their papers. As we inched toward the border, the rest of us were too wary of getting found out.

The journey through the Himalayas was a blur of cold and starvation. Sun reflected off the snow, the light stinging our eyes and limiting our vision. I gasped for breath, each ice-cold inhale scraping against my throat and lungs until my chest felt freezing and on fire at the same time. Compared to my companions, though, I was having a much easier time.

The lama's gentle face didn't betray much for the first few days, but as the climb began to grow severe, he couldn't hide the strain it put on his body. His wife kept an arm around him as we climbed, a firm grip at his waist lest he slip. But even an able-bodied woman had her limits under these harsh conditions. Aside from the brutal temperatures, the footing was treacherous and unreliable. Starting our journey in the summer helped us avoid the worst of the cold, but the snow was melting into slush. Each step we took was a game of roulette no matter how much we tested the ground with our weight. Yet the couple was determined to see this journey through. It was their duty, they'd explained. They knew the way, and if people were desperate enough to risk death to reach Nepal, then they had a responsibility to guide them as safely as possible.

The one who struggled the most was Dawa. We were descending the last mountain when Dawa cried out and crumpled onto the ground, hands clutching desperately at her stomach. I rushed over, barely stopping myself from asking her if she was okay. Of course she wasn't. Sweat was beading on her brow despite the cold, and her face scrunched up as she groaned. We had no idea what was wrong with Dawa. There was nothing we could do other than set up camp for the night.

Camp was perhaps too generous a word. We had no tents, no means of sheltering ourselves as the wind whipped furiously around us. The only options were to lie on a wet patch of earth or a slightly less wet patch. We helped bundle up Dawa as much as possible, but I could see her tremors even though she was on the other side of our loose circle.

I averted my gaze to avoid retching from the stress.

Suddenly, I was a child again, watching helplessly as a frail woman trudged through treacherous terrain. Except this time, it was my childhood friend. This was a young woman I'd known my whole life, and yet all I could do was . . . what, exactly? Give her words of encouragement? Stay quiet so as not to disturb her rest? We didn't even know what was happening for sure, but I couldn't help but imagine all the ways things could go wrong. It was as if I were poking at an open sore, knowing it would hurt yet unable to resist the urge to feel.

It almost hurt more to hope, to curl around a little flicker as the winds whipped at us relentlessly. But what was faith for, if not to help us stoke a spark into a flame, a flame into a bonfire?

I wrapped my mother's dress around me and bowed my head to pray.

We walked. Each second blurred together into an indecipherable mess until we finally began to descend from the mountains. Dawa's cramps seemed to have subsided, though she was still pale and clammy, lips pressed into a thin line. My knees were barely able to handle the pressure of hiking downhill, but it was preferable to the unrelenting cold. We eventually reached an open, muddy plain. It was a relief to walk on flat land. Weeks of relentless ascents and descents had all but ruined my knees. The trees began to thicken as we pressed on. We began to see cucumbers growing abundantly in the wild, providing us with a food source. Then, the sounds of human activity began to waft over, making our guts twist as if we were inhaling noxious fumes.

We were at the border crossing.

From our vantage point, we could see jeeps and trucks lining the road. Some officers even had massive dogs with them, sitting obediently at their feet, flicking their ears this way and that to catch even the slightest noise.

We gathered around a small campfire as the lama explained our next steps. As the climate was getting hotter, we didn't need the fire for warmth, but it was comforting to hold a steaming cup of tea to my wind-burnt face. I took small sips through cracked lips, trying to wash away the taste of cucumbers in my mouth. We'd been eating nothing but cucumbers for days now.

"It's a new moon tonight, so the odds are in our favor. But in the unfortunate event that soldiers do come, you run. Go in different directions, make it harder for them to catch you. Just run and keep running, it doesn't matter where. Better to die in the wilderness than to get caught." The group murmured our assent, the memory of the stranger's bloody feet still fresh in our minds.

"My wife and I will go through the checkpoint with our passports. As for the rest of you . . . You'll have to go around." The lama sounded almost apologetic. He began giving us rudimentary instructions: *Turn at this tree. Cross this stream. If you see this rock, then turn back, you've gone too far.*

I repeated his instructions ad nauseum as we waited for night to descend. The mind could play tricks on you and go blank at the most crucial moments, so I tried my best to sear the route into my mind until it became instinct. I picked at my bowl of boiled cucumbers. I was grateful to have food, but I was so, *so* sick of them. Still, I begrudgingly shoved a spoonful in my mouth, grimacing at the texture. I needed every bit of energy I could get. It was then when Lobsang approached me with a somber look.

"We're turning back," he said unceremoniously.

I almost choked at the sudden declaration. We'd been traveling for weeks now. We'd even crossed the mountains and weathered the cold, and he hadn't breathed a word about giving up.

"It's not just me either." He jerked his head toward a few of the other travelers. There were around five people with their packs in hand. "It's not worth it. Maybe if we had official permits, but . . ."

They were far too expensive. The lama had explained that passports could easily cost several thousand yuan per person.

I had a feeling that some who embarked on the journey would turn back, but I hadn't expected Lobsang to be one of them. Lobsang had been the one to seek out a guide for us in the first place, after all. He noticed me gaping at him and gave me a sad smile. "To be frank, I'm scared. I'm scared that I won't survive the attempt. I hope you don't think too poorly of me." A dog howled in the darkness, as if emphasizing his point.

I couldn't fully understand why he'd decided to turn back. I was determined to leave or die trying. But Lobsang knew his circumstances better than anyone else. People had their own reasons for leaving, and they had their own reasons for staying too. It wasn't my place to judge them either way.

We didn't say much then. We'd barely exchanged any words since we'd left Mount Kailash, and if we started now, it would sound too much like a eulogy.

"Good luck, Tsultrim," Lobsang said, and I barely had time to wish him the same when he turned on his heel. Maybe he thought he'd lose his resolve if he stayed a moment longer. Maybe going home was just as unknown as moving forward.

I pulled out the woolen dress from my bag. It had already lost the scent of home, but I pressed my face into it regardless, breathing in deep. On the far side of our makeshift camp, Dawa had her eyes fixed on her own meager meal, her face expressionless. She seemed to have mostly recovered from whatever had ailed her in the Himalayas, but she'd become even more reserved than before.

She wasn't the starry-eyed girl I'd once known, the one who'd helped me carry a confiscated statue down a mountain and jumped at the chance to travel to Lhasa. Now Dawa seemed so much older than her eighteen or so years.

I imagined sidling up to her to offer my company, to share the weight of whatever she was carrying, but I couldn't help shoulder her burden if she wasn't willing to share it.

Night fell, and we began tiptoeing through the dense foliage, lit only by a speck of starlight. We could barely see the person right in front of us, let alone the terrain under our feet. I could only hear the squelch of mud and grunts of exertion. There was no sign of the army. Surely we would see their flashlights coming from a mile away.

Then animals called to one another. They sounded nothing like dogs, but my mind conjured up images of ferocious canines, trained by the army to track down fugitives. They would snap their jaws, fangs glinting as they salivated at the scent of their prey. Next to them would be their human minders, hungering for their own targets too.

We're out in the wild, I thought, *so of course there are animals. Animals belong in nature, and they make sounds. They're just animals. We've seen yak and horses and goats everywhere.*

Another traitorous voice whispered, *But none of those are nocturnal.*

The night stayed miraculously, eerily still. There were no errant footsteps, no humming engines, no warnings shouted.

"Stop, stop," someone whispered urgently, and pointed toward their feet.

The ground broke off into a cliff. A gap yawned wide before us.

I couldn't tell if the drop led to a river or an endless chasm that led to nowhere. I was a child on a mountain again, a large basket of firewood on my back, frozen with fear as I faced a ledge. Except this time, there was no one on the other side to give me a hand. This time, I could barely see a thing. Death awaited me at the bottom. Death awaited me to my left and right, if I were to veer off course. Death awaited me from above if soldiers decided to rain bullets down on us. Death awaited me behind. Death probably awaited ahead of me too.

Everything went darker than I'd thought possible, my eyes wide open but unseeing with fear. I couldn't even see the faint outlines of my own hands under starlight now. The only sounds left were my raspy, frantic breaths, and the desperate pounding of my heart, warning me with each pump: *You'll die, you'll die, you'll die.*

I lifted my head, or bowed it, or maybe tilted it from side to side. I closed my eyes, I opened them, or maybe I was squinting uselessly in the dark. It didn't matter. I'd lost all sense of direction. Then, across the gap, for a split second, I could have sworn someone was beckoning me over. Maybe it was just my imagination, or perhaps I was hallucinating. But I hung on to that nebulous figure on the far end. I had to believe that someone was rooting for me on the other side.

In my mind's eye, that someone gestured to our surroundings, as if I were missing the obvious. They had just jumped across the opening with ease, and now they were urging me to do the same. The figure waved their hand, urging me to look at them, rather than down or up or sideways toward my death.

You can do it, Punjun.

Drawing in a shaky breath, I stepped back a few paces to give myself a running start. I clenched my eyes shut as my feet left the ground. And then I opened them.

I was flying.

The sharp bite of sticks and stones forced me back to the present.

I climbed to my feet, imagining a pair of hands grabbing my shoulders to haul me upright. I imagined them shoving me deeper into the woods, leading me away from danger. I conjured up a familiar silhouette in my mind's eye and followed it until the checkpoint was far behind us.

I flew, Gelek. I flew all the way to Nepal.

CHAPTER
THIRTY

The foliage began to thin, and we soon came across an open plain flanked by towering cliffs. A desert, high up by the Himalayas. The cliff faces were dotted with caves like dozens of eyes looking at us from above. The thought should've made me quiver, but instead my breath caught, and I couldn't help but gape in awe. Having grown up surrounded by mountains, I'd never seen anything like it.

Though it was ostensibly just a field of dirt and sand, the ashy brown stretched on for miles, meeting the cerulean-blue sky at the horizon. The vast plain was punctuated by shrubs and a few sparse, twisting trees, windbeaten yet sprouting stubbornly in the cold, dry climate. Hills lined the horizon, gentle and rolling compared to the towering peaks we'd climbed. A river slithered through the dirt, the sun glinting off the surface of the water. Herds of kiang, midsize animals that looked like donkeys, lingered by the water.

I was still looking over my shoulder in Nepal, as we'd

heard stories of the Chinese army crossing the border to snatch refugees. Yet there was something about the desert that inspired a sense of calm. Perhaps it was the sheer vastness, the openness. The way I could see for miles, not from atop a mountain, but simply on the ground. The way the sky looked so light and buoyant while being anchored by firm, flat earth.

We saw more villages as we pressed on, and we were even able to visit some of them. When we approached one particular town, the lama slowed to a halt, savoring the view with a soft smile.

"This is my hometown," the lama explained.

How long had he been away from home? How did he keep moving, knowing anytime could be the last time he saw his family? My throat felt tight at the thought of my own family. There was nothing I could do now, other than survive this journey. There was no point in dwelling on the past.

He brought us to his house, where his nephew greeted us at the front door. The house was large and blocky, made with some kind of pale stone or brick. Bundles of firewood had been stacked on top of the flat roof. Prayer flags fluttered cheerfully in the breeze, beckoning me forward like an old friend.

The nephew was also a lama, an animated young man whose eyes crinkled when he smiled. He was practically glowing, eagerly ushering us through a door painted rusty red.

"Here, please," the nephew said, setting out tea and a light meal.

I almost recoiled. Cucumbers. Again. I was grateful for the food, truly, but I couldn't help it. I never wanted to see one ever again.

It wasn't that they were bland. I could handle bland. They tasted like stale water, with a weird green aftertaste that made me scrunch my nose with every bite. The seeds stuck in my mouth, mushy and sticky. I swallowed the mush with a grimace, imagining cucumbers sprouting from my stomach with how much I'd eaten.

The old lama stood with a grunt. "If you'd like, let me lead us in prayer."

I perked right up. Now that I thought of it, I hadn't prayed with other people in quite a while. I expected the lama to begin right there at the table. Instead, he led us to a dedicated prayer room with a modest shrine. A sense of familiarity settled deep and warm within me. There were some minor differences of course—this was a different place and the lama followed a different Buddhist tradition. But for the most part, the layout was the same: brass cups of water lined neatly in front of a statue of a deity. The deity sat serenely at the altar, hands poised and legs crossed. Clusters of small wildflowers had been arranged on the altar, their fragrance just noticeable under the rich scent of butter lamps.

I hadn't realized just how much I missed the communal aspect of prayer. The last few months, I could only muster the energy to say a few prayers here and there. Always rushing, always alone. Though the kora around Mount Kailash had been a life-changing experience, it wasn't the same as sitting cross-legged on the floor, head bowed with fellow worshippers.

The nephew and another guest pulled out a pair of gyalings, a type of Tibetan woodwind instrument. When they played the first notes, I could have cried. The drone of the gyalings was a balm to my frayed nerves. They held a single, long note before fluttering just a little, like a mother humming to a baby in her arms. This close, I could almost feel the instruments vibrate. Low chanting filled my ears, buzzed under my skin, until my mind cleared and my chest expanded, wide and loose yet more connected to the earth than ever.

Afterward, the nephew brought out a small bottle of barley wine. He poured us generous servings—though I abstained—and I stared in fascination as the older lama threw back cup after cup. Never had I seen a lama drink alcohol. I didn't understand the appeal, but a sense of awe bloomed in my chest, spreading all the way to my fingertips. Why should it matter if our customs were different? They brought joy and peace to their worshippers, and that was good enough for me.

A few days later, I was running low on food. We were reaching the edge of the desert, but there were still a few days left until we would reach the refugee camp.

I bit my lip. I could go through my bag, see what I could sell or barter away, but I already knew there was only one item I could spare. I was in Nepal now, and according to Phuntsok's stories, India was hot and humid. There was no practical reason to hang on to my thick dress. So, when we passed through a modest village, I straightened out the wrinkles as best as I could. Then I roamed around to find potential buyers.

The material felt warm under my fingers, and I kept petting it like a docile animal. Mother had sewn it together, stitch by painstaking stitch, with the winters of east Tibet in mind. With me in mind. It was the last sentimental item I had, and even though I knew it was silly and unreasonable, I wanted to stuff it back into my bag and keep a piece of home with me.

It didn't take long to find a family that was willing to trade some flour for the dress. It was stunning, after all. But as I handed it to them, for a moment, I wasn't sure if I could let go.

It's okay, I reminded myself. *It's just an object. A material thing. Transient and impermanent. It's wasteful to keep it when someone else could put it to good use.* The thought helped to dull the ache in my chest. Just a little.

The girl beamed as she pulled the dress on, wrapping it around her slender frame. It looked lovely on her. She spun in circles excitedly, showing off her new clothing, and I couldn't help but smile with her. The blue accents flashed among the folds. The thick wool would protect her when winter came. The hem touched the ground, but the girl was still young. She had all the time in the world to grow.

As we left the village, I hoped that the dress would bring her as much comfort as it had me.

The warmth was a welcome change, but the increasing humidity made me feel like I was walking through a swamp of sweat. Stalks of bamboo shot straight out of the earth. Sunlight filtered through their sparse leaves, dappling the ground with little gold patterns that morphed like a kaleidoscope. But there was something off. Something unsettling. I knew that nobody could hide among the bamboo stalks, skinny as they were, but I still had the uncanny feeling of being watched. I looked around us, and sure enough, there was nobody in sight.

Then something rustled overhead. I looked up to see a gray mass jumping from stalk to stalk. It vaguely resembled a human, but it had a tail and was covered in ashy gray fur. Soon, more of them gathered nearby and stared daggers at me, as if I'd committed some unspeakable crime against them. They unnerved me, and I stayed far away from the strange animals as we continued through the bamboo. But something about the creatures seemed familiar, teasing the edge of my memory.

The lama caught me staring and chuckled. "You've never seen a monkey before?"

Aha!

"No, but I did see a movie about the monkey king." I chanced another peek at them, but immediately turned away, my back rigid. "I didn't expect them to be so . . . angry."

"You know, there's actually a temple in the Nepali capital that is home to holy monkeys."

I imagined a group of monkeys, all eyeing me suspiciously as I tried to do circuits around the temple. I doubted I could ever concentrate on my prayers under that sharp stare. But I couldn't know for certain if I didn't try, right? Settling into a new country would take time, but I'd eventually have the chance to try it, surely.

Ahead of us, I could already see the sprawl of Kathmandu, the capital city of Nepal.

CHAPTER
THIRTY-ONE

"*Name?*"

"Tsultrim Dolma."

"Where are you from?"

"Tibet."

The beefy man behind the desk looked at me over his glasses. "Obviously. I mean, where in Tibet? East? West? What region?"

"The east. Kham, to be exact," I added hastily.

"And what brings you here?"

I bit back my reply. My patience was wearing thin. This was a refugee center. I was obviously a refugee. I said calmly, "I had to leave home because I was arrested for protesting. My family would be in danger if I stayed any longer."

The man narrowed his eyes at me. Then he tilted his head, leaned back in his seat, and leaned forward again, as if studying me from all angles.

"You've been here before," he declared after a moment.

"Excuse me?" My brain was foggy. I must've misheard him. Or maybe it was his accent that was confusing me. He spoke Tibetan fluently, but I'd never heard such an accent before and couldn't tell if he was Nepali or Tibetan.

"I know for a fact that I've seen you before, girl—no point in denying it."

"No," I said slowly, enunciating every word to make sure they sank in. "I just got here. You can ask the group I came with."

"Sure, but this is your second time in Kathmandu." He planted his elbows on his desk, and something about the gesture was beginning to grate on me. Maybe it was the fact that he was sitting leisurely, while I was swaying on my feet from exhaustion. "I recognize your voice as well, so there's no use hiding it," he continued. "I can't help you if you insist on lying to me."

My thinly veiled annoyance was riling him up further, but I was tired of strangers making accusations without proof. I'd had enough of that in Gutsa Detention Center. All I wanted was to lie down and eat something other than cucumbers. "I have absolutely no idea what you're talking about, sir," I said flatly. "I'm from a tiny village in east Tibet. How could I have possibly visited Nepal twice?"

"You were a nun in Lhasa, no? Thrown in prison for a few months?"

I froze. I hadn't told him about that. How could he have known? My fingers began to tremble. Numbness spread through my limbs. He was going to send me back. He would send me back, and I would either perish on the return trip, or doom my family to a life of surveillance if I survived.

I was jolted from my thoughts when he banged his fist on the table triumphantly.

"*Aha!*" He was grinning ear to ear now. "I know you, you're that nun from the documentary."

It took my brain a few seconds to catch up. "Documentary?"

"Yeah, you and a few other nuns. You were arrested for protesting and thrown in jail. They did horrible things to you." He'd lowered his voice, the grin on his face smoothing out into a gentler expression.

Realization dawned on me. Vanya Kewley and her crew had completed the documentary. They'd successfully snuck out of Tibet, and now the film was being broadcast everywhere. Finally, people overseas would hear our cries and reach out a hand. I huffed, still a little disbelieving. "Yes, that's me." I didn't regret doing the interview, but I hadn't really thought about how odd it would feel to have strangers recognize me.

The man let out a hearty laugh. "My bad then!" His voice softened. "I think you're quite the hero if you ask me." Was I supposed to thank him? Would he think me immodest for accepting such high praise? Thankfully, he continued before I could whip myself into a frenzy. "Well then, now that that's settled, the worker will show you your room."

The only people who were allowed private rooms were couples, so I was assigned to a shared room. There wasn't much inside. Really, it was just a floor and four walls, strewn with piles of bedding and various personal belongings. Regardless, it was luxurious compared to the wilderness I'd endured for months. After exchanging a few greetings with my new roommates, I laid my own blanket on the floor and finally, blissfully, fell asleep.

Not much happened.

I woke up. I stared at nothing. I went to bed. Maybe it was the shock of the past year finally catching up with me. My limbs felt leaden, my head was foggy, and I was too sluggish to venture outside. The only times I would leave the room were to relieve myself or to clean up, and to share meals with the rest of the camp.

Workers dutifully ladled soup and rice into our containers. The meals were simple but filling; the fact that I could have three meals a day was nothing short of a miracle. The refugee camp was under-resourced, understaffed, and packed to the brim with desperate refugees. Nothing could compare to the cruelty of Gutsa, but it almost felt like I was in prison again: stagnant, overcrowded, aimless.

"How are you settling in?"

I turned to see Chokyi, the man who had spoken with me that first day in camp. Though we'd gotten off to a rocky start, he'd taken to checking in on me every now and then.

"Okay," I said. He nodded at me encouragingly, as if expecting me to say more. "It's different here," I added vaguely, "but I'm getting used to it."

"That's good. That's normal. It always takes a while to adjust to life here." I felt a touch better knowing that it wasn't entirely my own fault for being miserable. "Listen, there are actually a few journalists visiting camp," he said, "and the higher-ups want you to speak with them."

"Okay."

"I understand if you don't want to rehash everything ad nauseam."

"It's okay."

"If you're sure."

I was. Anything to fill the gaping hole in my chest that was expanding every day. So every now and then, I'd be summoned to the office, answering the same questions over and over again.

How are conditions in Tibet?

What happened in Lhasa?

What happened in prison?

What unspeakable things did they do to you?

How much have you suffered?

I knew that sharing my story was important. Change would never come if nobody knew the truth. But speaking only about pain was like taking a shovel to that hole in my chest and digging even deeper. It was like picking at a scab until it bled again, just to show other people that yes, the wound really did exist. Because maybe if they saw how it festered, how it rotted and ate away at my flesh, they would finally do something about it.

I kept at it despite the pain because there was nobody else that I could speak with, no safe space for me to process my thoughts externally. The only way for me to put my experience into words was to invite strangers to look at all the carnage. And if that space didn't allow for joy or comfort... Well, then, we all had sacrifices to make, didn't we?

Now that we were no longer traveling together, Dawa and I only saw each other at mealtimes. Our conversations remained stilted and shallow, but I grasped on to them as much as I could. She was my last real link to my home, and that was probably what kept us together. I was surprised when she approached me one day with an invitation.

"I'm meeting with ... a friend," she said, suddenly shy. "He works at a restaurant just outside of camp. Why don't you come with me?"

Dawa had been leaving the refugee camp more often lately to meet with her new friend Norbu, a cook at a restaurant in a Tibetan settlement nearby. The routine was good for Dawa: Color had returned to her cheeks, and her figure had filled out more too.

I, on the other hand, hadn't really left the refugee camp at all since I arrived. So, gingerly, I trailed after Dawa as she led us out of the refugee camp and into the streets of Kathmandu.

Pedestrians fought for space with rickshaws and automobiles. Red brick buildings stood proud, and passersby sheltered from the sun under the flared roofs. We passed small temples guarded by statues of what looked like lions, where worshippers lit candles and incense. The sweet smoke mingled with the bitter exhaust of mopeds, and pigeons flocked around a large square, pecking at crumbs on the ground. Vendors laid out their goods on bright red cloth. They sold everything from children's bicycles and plush toys to prayer beads and Buddha sculptures in every color imaginable.

We didn't go far before we spotted the restaurant. It was a modest place nestled in a narrow street. Prayer flags had been hung between the buildings, crisscrossing and forming a canopy of red, blue, green, and orange. The sight was such a far cry from the bare white walls of my room that it was hard to believe this was the same city. Dawa and I ordered a simple meal as we waited for Norbu to wrap up his work.

He was a tall, lean man, his skin tan and his jaw sharp. Dawa gazed at him, positively glowing. It was obvious that she was absolutely smitten. The pans sizzled as he added splashes of broth and dashes of spice. Clouds of fragrant steam wafted from the back, and I could see the warm flicker of the stove even from a distance. It was a welcome distraction, better than staring at Dawa and making stilted small talk. In contrast, everyone else in the restaurant was clamoring to speak with Norbu, their voices overlapping.

"Norbu," called a customer. "When are you free? I want to set you up with my niece."

"Thank you, but you don't have to," Norbu replied politely, almost stoic.

"Nonsense! Handsome young man like you, it's a wonder you haven't married yet."

"There's really no need to go to the trouble, sir."

"You sure? Her family's got money, her father has a stable government job—she'd be a perfect wife." The customer glanced at Dawa. "You're a hardworking man, you deserve someone with status."

I flicked my eyes over to Dawa nervously, not sure how she'd react to the dig. But she seemed not to mind, sipping leisurely at her water. Norbu simply offered a polite smile and a murmur. A brush-off, a quiet but firm rejection. Instead, his face lit up whenever he laid his eyes on Dawa, giving her a shy little wave when he caught her eye.

As if sensing my trepidation, Dawa said, "He's helping me move out of the refugee camp once we save up some money." She was blushing to the tips of her ears. "I think . . . I think I want to stay here, in Nepal."

I blinked. That seemed awfully fast. I racked my brain, trying to remember how long we'd been in Kathmandu. My stomach soured at the realization that it had already been three months since we'd arrived. While I was cooped up in my room, Dawa had begun to put down roots.

"I'm happy for you, truly." I knew that I needed to get a job too. The journey to India wouldn't pay for itself. But every day, it was getting harder and harder to drag myself out of my room, let alone leave for work. My wistfulness must've been obvious, because Dawa suddenly looked at me with an intensely hopeful expression.

"You're so lucky to have such a free spirit, Tsultrim," she said fiercely. "You can go anywhere. Nobody to take care of, nothing to tie you down."

Good old Dawa, always looking for the bright side. She made it sound so liberating that I almost believed her. But as I walked back to the refugee center, thinking about the loving couple, I realized just how truly, utterly alone I was in the world.

I didn't want a romantic partner, nor did I want to be a mother. I wanted a home to return to, someone to take care of. I wanted to be known. I wanted to revel in the company of others, without fear that my mere presence put them in danger.

When I returned to my room, the emptiness hit me like a brick wall. Memories of the sights and sounds of Kathmandu seemed to taunt me then: *Look at how empty the room is, how empty you are.*

I was lost, unmoored, and so, so lonely. I yearned for

the color, the noise, the sheer, vibrant life outside. But outside was also where the danger lay. Outside was where there were strangers, bustling crowds whose language I couldn't speak, and happy, hopeful families whose presence reminded me of how alone I was in the world. Now I was more determined than ever to stay in the safe, stifling, suffocating confines of my room.

CHAPTER
THIRTY-TWO

Being a recluse, however, was not a sustainable life-style. The wear and tear on my possessions was starting to show. So, when Chokyi checked in on me again one day, I reluctantly asked for help.

"I need a new blanket," I said, "but I don't think I can go out there alone. I don't speak Nepali." And even if I did, the idea of going outside filled my limbs with lead. If given the choice, I would rather curl up in my room with my tattered blanket. In fact, if Chokyi hadn't checked in on me, I doubt I would've even brought up the issue in the first place. No, I needed someone to accompany me, to make sure I actually went outside.

"No problem, I'll see what I can do," he said with a wide grin.

A few days later, a worker I'd never spoken with approached me. He introduced himself as Lungtok.

"Chokyi told me you needed new blankets," he said, "so I thought I ought to accompany you. It can get quite overwhelming outside. Why don't I buy you a meal while we're out?"

"No, it's okay, I have enough to eat."

"Nonsense! It can't be pleasant to eat the same thing every day."

It felt rude to keep refusing, especially since he occupied an important position at the refugee center. Though I didn't know what exactly his job was, I knew that he managed a team of workers. So finally, I relented.

"Excellent! Let's go eat first. Can't shop on an empty stomach!"

The restaurant he chose was spacious, but there were barely any customers inside. A few servers milled about, and I could hear a cook shouting instructions somewhere in the back. The smell of spices and seasonings drifted from the kitchen—pepper, wild garlic, star anise—giving the restaurant an aroma that warmed me to the core. I was mortified when my stomach grumbled out loud.

Lungtok ushered me toward a table and sat down next to me. The server approached, shooting me odd glances as Lungtok placed our orders in rapid-fire Nepali. They exchanged a few words, and then the server laughed. It was a bright sound, clear and ringing, though there was a note of tension to it. *A mostly sincere customer service laugh*, I thought. Then Lungtok yelled something at the other workers toward the back, which prompted more chuckles. He seemed very comfortable with the staff here.

"I come here often," Lungtok said, as if sensing my train of thought. "The food is outstanding."

Soon, the table was piled high with plates and bowls. I recognized a few dishes. Steamed momo dumplings, thukpa noodle soup, laping cold noodles . . . dishes that Nepal shared with Tibet. Lungtok had gone out of his way to order food that reminded me of home.

I sat through the meal in silence, only picking at the food. My chair was a little rickety, and I rocked back and forth, unable to hold still. The staff were shooting odd looks toward me. I tried not to be too self-conscious of how disheveled I looked, but they were putting me on edge. Maybe they were offended at my lack of appetite. I nibbled at a dumpling, not wanting them to think there was anything wrong with their dishes. The server from before looked particularly uncomfortable, her eyes flicking between me and Lungtok. Meanwhile, Lungtok continued to chatter away, oblivious to my discomfort.

That was when he looped one arm around my shoulders, brushing my breast with one hand and snaking the other up my thigh.

I shoved him away on pure instinct. He turned to me with an incredulous look, as if the possibility of rejection hadn't even occurred to him.

When I glanced at the staff, they didn't seem surprised. Instead, they wore the same expression they'd been shooting me all night. This time, though, I finally understood:

They were looks of pity and helplessness. They turned away when they noticed me looking at them. I wasn't the first girl Lungtok had brought in, and I wouldn't be the last.

"I'd like to go back please." I stared at my plate, keeping my body rigid and my tone firm. The heady aroma of spices now felt more suffocating than warming, like it was clogging up my lungs with every breath I took.

He was silent for a moment, as if processing the situation. When he spoke, it was with an air of genuine bafflement. "I'll have you know that I'm a *very* important person. Who do you think you are? What makes you think *you* could reject *me*?" He gestured toward me in disbelief. As if I should be *thankful* that someone like him had deigned to harass me.

"I want to go back," I repeated, louder this time.

His temper began to rise. "You knew what you were getting into. You can't possibly be this stupid."

"I want to go back."

"I've brought other girls, girls who were thrilled at the attention. What makes you think you're better than them?"

"I want to go back." I wasn't asking anymore. I was positively glaring at the table now, boring holes into the wood grain. I couldn't just run off since I didn't know the way back to the refugee center. But if he dared to make another pass at me, I was going to make him regret it.

He sat there fuming, eyes practically bulging from their sockets. He breathed heavily, and I could almost imagine smoke coming out of his nostrils. I tensed my muscles, bracing myself for whatever violence he was planning. The restaurant was now deathly still, as if the few patrons there were also holding their breath and preparing themselves for Lungtok's reaction. To my surprise, he only snapped, "Fine."

Lungtok grumbled the entire walk back. I kept my eye on him, giving him a wide berth as I trailed behind him. He called me ungrateful, a stupid country girl, a whole assortment of insults that I'd never heard before. But mercifully, he never laid another hand on me. As soon as the refugee center was in sight, I excused myself and all but stormed back to my room.

That night, I stared up at the ceiling, unable to fall asleep even though my whole body was heavy with fatigue. I considered telling the administration about Lungtok's assault. Nothing would change unless I spoke up. It was clear he'd done this to other girls—refugees that he was supposed to help, at that. We were supposed to be on the same side.

When Kewley had asked me for an interview, to speak up against Chinese repression, it had been a no-brainer. But now, faced with the decision of whether or not to report Lungtok, something was blocking the words, making them pile up at my throat.

It was shame, thick and clingy. Despite how much I wanted Lungtok to face the consequences, a touch of shame still lingered at the back of my tongue like a bitter aftertaste. Maybe I really was as stupid as Lungtok had said I was, for believing in the kindness of others. I kept looking at the ceiling, as if the answer was written there.

I can't see the stars from here, I thought dumbly. Of course I couldn't. I was indoors.

For a terrifying moment, I thought I might forget what the night sky looked like, the same way I was beginning to forget how safety felt too.

Did Dawa remember? Did she ever think about how we'd huddle outdoors together in a cluster of blankets—her, me, Wangmo, Pema, Nyima, Thubten, the whole gang? Did she remember the canopy of stars that stretched over us, standing sentinel as we slept? Was that why she was able to move on?

I was supposed to be free here, outside of Tibet. Instead, I felt more trapped than ever in a prison of my own making.

Chokyi held a stack of forms. "We're going to send some people to Switzerland. The government there has offered to take in some refugees soon, and I figured I'd let you know."

"Okay."

He looked at me uncertainly. "Well?"

"Oh, I'm sorry. I didn't realize you were offering." I took a moment to fight through the fog in my head. "Switzerland?"

"Yeah, it's a small country in Europe. It's cold, it's got mountains."

I smiled faintly. That sounded nice. Winter had arrived in Kathmandu, cool and mild. There was no snow on the ground, no frozen-over rivers to slide down. Even Pelbar Dzong in springtime was colder than this. Switzerland sounded like the ideal destination, and yet a part of me hesitated. "Is there nowhere else I could go?"

He put his glasses on and riffled through the papers. "You could go to India. There will be a few buses here in the next few weeks." India. The word felt like a shock to my system that set my heart beating miles per minute. Chokyi continued, still staring intently at his documents. "You might feel safer in Switzerland. It's a neutral country in Europe, so they don't have China breathing down their necks."

"Is it farther than India?"

"Yes, but we'd send you over on an airplane."

"But His Holiness the Dalai Lama is in India, right?"

"Yes, it's where the whole Tibetan government is, actually."

"I want to go there then." I added hastily, "Please."

Just three months ago, Chokyi had been loudly accusing me of lying in this very office. Now he looked up, carefully neutral as he studied me. Finally, he nodded, an action so delicate and out of place on his bold features. He cared, I realized. Despite his brash demeanor and blunt tone, he cared for the refugees here. He'd checked in on us at mealtimes, one by one, not because he was getting paid a salary, but because this was his way of making change in the world. "If that's your choice. I'll get you a seat on that bus."

It was. This was a no-brainer. I was terrified of leaving

Tibet farther behind, of forgetting my roots. But I knew, without a seed of doubt, that I had to meet the Dalai Lama in person.

The next few weeks were a flurry of bureaucracy. Refugees lined up to have their pictures taken for their identification, hunched over stacks of paper. The whole camp was abuzz with anxiety and cautious excitement, yet there was a somber undertone.

Some families were splitting up, sending one person to settle down in India before the rest followed. Others were tired of the constant migration, of drifting for the rest of their lives. It was a moment of mourning, of farewells. Of cutting ties and hoping against hope for a reunion.

My own farewell to Dawa was quiet, pedestrian.

"Do you think you'll ever go to Switzerland?" I asked.

"No. It's too different over there. We won't know anyone, and we won't speak the language. Here, at least, there's a Tibetan settlement. We can be happy," she said quietly. It struck me how she was referring to both herself and Norbu. "Maybe we'll go to Switzerland one day. And . . ." She stopped short, considering her next words. Then she shook her head, a wistful smile on her face. "And maybe one day, I can show him Tibet. But for now, I want to stay here."

I wished we could have spoken more. I could scream myself hoarse at armed guards without a shred of fear, but feelings? Feelings were hard, and I was running out of words that could encompass everything Dawa meant to me. The sleepovers, the excursions, the scent of a damp cave, and the feel of old stone under my fingers. The bleating of sheep, the thud of dull axes on tree stumps, the dark smear of dirt and make-believe blood on our cheeks. Even our treacherous journey was a part of our story, and I hoped that it wouldn't end here.

"Maybe one day."

In December 1990, I packed what few belongings I had left. A backpack, a change of clothes, a metal food bowl covered in dents, a ratty blanket that had more holes than actual fabric.

Five buses were parked in front of the refugee center. They were large commuter buses, lined up one after the other like a dingy metal snake. A crowd had gathered around them, and a team of staff tried to maintain some semblance of order as they went through their rosters.

"Tsultrim, hold on a sec." Chokyi pushed through the crowd and pulled a package out of his bag. "There's a monk in Varanasi, an old friend who teaches at the college. Hand this book to him, will you? Tell him I sent you."

The package was hefty, wrapped in old linen. I traced the straight edges with a careful hand. I could feel creases along the spine even through the fabric, the corners rounded with age and use.

Chokyi wasn't just asking me for a favor. He was doing

a favor for me. He was introducing me to someone at the college, so I wouldn't be completely alone in a foreign place.

All too soon, the worker with the roster called my name. With one last thanks to Chokyi, I hurried onto the bus and headed straight for the back.

"No, no, your seat's up here." The worker stuck her head through the door and gestured to the closest seat. I glanced back at the passengers behind me. The bus was filling up from the back; more passengers brushed past me farther down the aisle. With a shrug, I shuffled toward the window seat and saw Chokyi outside. He gave me a wide grin and a wave, and then nodded to the worker in thanks.

Chokyi had gotten me a seat near the front so I wouldn't get carsick. I'd never gotten carsick before, but he'd cared enough to be thoughtful.

My eyes burned with tears. There were so many people who'd helped me, so many people whom I'd never see again. Chokyi, Chodron, the lama and his wife. My family. I scrubbed at my face with a rough hand. No, maybe I would see my family again. This was just a detour, that was all.

The bus door hissed closed, and the engine roared to life. I heaved a shuddering breath and buried my face in my hands.

CHAPTER
THIRTY-THREE

The Tibetan refugee camp at Varanasi was overwhelming. Thoughts of Phuntsok clouded my mind then. Although I'd received help from plenty of kind people, I was especially terrified this time around. Maybe it was because nothing had prepared me for this leg of my journey.

I'd expected another complex like the one in Kathmandu—a cluster of buildings and bare rooms. Instead, what greeted me was an unofficial camp, just a sea of old white tents spread across an open field. The staff at Kathmandu had told us we'd be welcomed by workers in India, but there were none as far as I could tell. We'd been dropped off with no instructions and no guidance.

Maybe I'd missed an orientation. Maybe I'd somehow gotten on the wrong bus. Maybe I was simply too spoiled, too used to the luxury of a roof over my head for the last three months. Maybe, maybe, maybe. That whisper of self-doubt had been growing steadily over time, but now, it finally came out in full force.

The journey from Mount Kailash to Kathmandu was objectively more difficult. But I had a concrete goal back then, something simple and straightforward to keep me occupied. Head down, one foot in front of the other until I reached safety. I had a new goal now, to see the Dalai Lama, but I didn't have the faintest idea where to start.

Taking a deep breath, I forced myself to think of things I needed to take care of right this moment. That was all I had to think about, not the nebulous idea of receiving an education or meeting the leader of my country. Just the basics: food and shelter. I could do that.

Tentatively, I began snaking my way through camp to find a host, gingerly peeking through tent flaps. Finally, I came across a monk and a nun, who took me in without question. However, food turned out to be much harder to come by.

"You'll have to buy something at the markets," the nun explained with an apologetic look.

But I didn't dare leave camp. I didn't know the language, I didn't know the city, I didn't know anyone. My paranoia grew each day, worsened by the dizziness from malnutrition. I only ever left the tent for the water pump. It was an old, creaky contraption operated by hand, but it was reliable. The problem was that it also served as a social hub.

People snuck looks at me before turning back to their companions, speaking in hushed tones. They giggled and joked around, making the most of a dire situation, finding the humor in their predicament. I should've been moved by the sight, but instead all I felt was an all-consuming dread. Soon, that dread morphed into irritation.

The old Tsultrim would never have gotten so annoyed at a few stares and whispers. The old Tsultrim might've felt self-conscious, but she wouldn't have directed her irritation toward others over something so trivial. Before I knew it, the hollow in my chest had filled up with an ugly tangle of misery.

The paranoia only grew as I approached the water pump. They were laughing at me, surely. They were making fun of my isolation, my clothes, my ignorance. The only way to know for sure was to reach out and ask, but the mere thought made me sick to my stomach. I was thinking the worst of strangers, but distrust kept me safe. Misery loves company, but I only feared it.

One of the monks finally approached me. I braced myself.

"We recognized you from the documentary."

Here it was: the mockery, the distaste, the accusations of seeking attention.

"That was very brave of you."

Oh. I hadn't been expecting that. This was my chance to ask for help.

He smiled. "A lot of people must be taking good care of you for everything you've done."

My words died on my tongue. I'd come so far ignoring

how others might perceive me, but at that moment, I was worried that he'd scoff at me for asking for help, that he'd think me a spoiled child. The fear of judgment began to cloud my thoughts, warping his warm smile into something sinister in my mind's eye.

Wordlessly, I bobbed my head in a half bow, and then returned to the tent alone.

Every now and then, someone came to the refugee camp looking for a relative, and a tearful reunion would follow. A name, whispered in disbelief or yelled in joy; footsteps, halting and unsure or storming across the dirt. Then a frantic embrace.

Many Tibetans shared the same names, and after a few weeks, I'd learned not to get my hopes up at the name Tsultrim. Instead, I averted my eyes away from such private moments.

"Punjun?"

Still, a part of me couldn't help but strain my ears for the sound of my name.

"Punjun, is that you?"

I couldn't fully suppress the hope that maybe next time, I would be the right Tsultrim.

"Punjun!"

I snapped my head toward the voice. It belonged to a young monk a few years older than me. He drew near, as if approaching a wounded animal. I squinted, picturing the young man as an even younger boy, with round cheeks and a full head of hair.

"Sangye?" I whispered. He nodded. It really was him. The young boy from Pelbar Dzong, who used to make fun of me for my runny nose, who lent me his clothing when I hatched my plan to throw yak dung at an officer. We stood there, staring at each other in awe and hesitation, as if the other would disappear if we so much as blinked. Then, as if a switch had been flipped, I broke down in tears.

Everything came pouring out of my chest. The crushing loneliness in Nepal, the harrowing journey from Mount Kailash, the two months in Lhasa where I'd been betrayed and supported in equal measure. Great-Aunt Jampa's death and missing the chance to say goodbye. Leaving my home to keep it safe. Prison. The police at the protests. The unshakable feeling that something had gone deeply wrong in my country. All the terror, the anguish, the bone-deep fear of forgetting and being forgotten. Every unspeakable moment that led to this one.

I sobbed for what seemed like hours, as if my body had finally decided to release every emotion I'd bottled up. Distantly, I registered Sangye holding me like a child, his own body shaking with sobs. I couldn't have cared less what onlookers thought of us.

"How did you find me?" I said, once we'd finally calmed down. I'd picked up my belongings, and we were on our way to the market.

"Whenever new refugees arrive, I always ask for news of anyone coming from our area."

I looked up in surprise. "I remember you being kind of mean to me when we were kids."

He smoothed a hand over his shaved head. "Well, I've changed a lot, as you can see."

"I didn't know you moved to Varanasi." Perhaps the journey would've been easier if I'd known I had a friend on the other side. I shook the thought away. Now was not the time for maybes and what-ifs. I was here, and that was all that mattered.

"There's a Tibetan temple in Sarnath, a place near Varanasi. I've been living there since I became a monk. Come see it for yourself. But first, some food."

Mopeds and bikes swerved around cows, and we ground to a halt as we waited for a herd to cross the street. Sangye explained that cows were sacred in Hinduism, and added, "You won't find beef around here, but there's plenty of other meat and produce."

As if making his point, he steered us to a fruit vendor on the side of the street. He bought a bunch of bananas, chatting with the vendor in Hindi. Then he ushered me toward a tea seller, ordering a drink and all but shoving the cup into my hand.

A blend of aromatic spices filled the air. Cinnamon, clove, something warm and earthy. I eyed Sangye warily. He seemed oddly excited about a cup of tea. I took a tentative sip, and my eyes widened.

"It's sweet," I said. "Indian tea is sweet?"

He nodded. "Weird, isn't it? They call it chai. I've come to enjoy the taste, but I still drink butter tea with salt most of the time. We have to use ghee instead of yak butter, though, so it doesn't taste the same."

We hailed a rickshaw for the final leg of the journey. There was still something hollow in my chest, something that couldn't be filled in by a single pleasant day. But as the trees began to thicken and the hubbub quieted down, I realized that I could be happy. Maybe not today, but someday.

The rickshaw stopped in front of a pair of large red doors. The cream-colored walls were lined with multicolor flags and crowned with a golden dharma wheel and two golden deer. At the front of it all stood two snow lion sculptures with hunter-green manes, stone eyes round and alert as they kept watch. We stepped through the small pedestrian gate that had been built into the front doors, and my jaw dropped at the courtyard within.

Massive date trees reached toward the sky, their branches like hands raised in praise. Low hedges lined the flagstone walkways, leading us past a row of prayer wheels. I reached out to one, the bronze-colored metal cool and solid beneath my palm. Various mantras had been carved around it, and my fingers brushed the dips and curves as I lightly spun the wheel. I could hardly remember the last time I'd even laid eyes on a prayer wheel, let alone spun one with my own hands.

Sangye led me to the living quarters in the basement of another boxy, cream-colored building. Rooms lined the corridor, though a few people lived in the corridor itself, sectioned off with large cloths to preserve some privacy.

"This is where I live," Sangye said, stopping at a door. "It's not much, but you're always welcome here."

Sure enough, the room had only the bare necessities. A cot was pushed against one wall. In the far corner was a portable stove with a canister of gas.

"Come live here, Tsultrim," he said. "You can even have this room. I know I speak for everyone when I say we welcome you with open arms."

The offer was tempting. For starters, I would have my own space, a little haven where I could relearn what safety felt like. And the stove! I could cook my own food, something simple from home. And someone I could speak to. Speak *with*. And yet . . .

"I can't just take your room."

He waved a hand. "Don't worry about it, I can find some space in the monks' lodgings. Make yourself at home."

Maybe it was silly for me to trust him after having my trust betrayed in the past. But I was tired of looking over my shoulder. I wanted to believe in the goodness of others again.

My eyes prickled with fresh tears. Home. For now, this was my new home.

Before I could settle in properly, however, there was just one errand I needed to take care of. With the directions on repeat in my head, I headed out to the nearby college to deliver Chokyi's package.

Like the monastery, the college was rich with greenery. Students milled about, weaving between buildings with a dexterity born of familiarity. They rushed to class and talked among themselves, only sparing me the occasional glance. It seemed that they were no strangers to awestruck visitors. Unlike the students, though, I had no idea where I was going. I only had a name to go by.

I imagined what it would be like to study here, to become so familiar with the school that I could navigate its hallways as confidently as they did. It had been so long since the last time I'd listened to a lecture or read a book. I wasn't even sure I remembered how to read now that I'd gone over a year without practice. I tested the weight of the book in my hands, turning it this way and that. Introducing myself to Chokyi's friend could be my chance to start pursuing my education.

"Excuse me," I finally said to a passing student, "where may I find Samdhong Rinpoche?" The college specialized in Tibetan studies, so language wasn't an issue.

He looked at me strangely. Once again, I had the unsettling feeling that I was missing something important. All I knew was that the monk I was looking for was a high lama and a friend of Chokyi. The student pointed me toward a building, and I hurried away with a muttered thank-you.

I wandered around the building, pausing to ask for directions. Finally, an older man appeared at the top of a long flight of stairs. He was wearing a monk's robes, lips in a straight line. Judging by the way passersby were greeting him, that had to be Samdhong Rinpoche.

I bowed and held out the book with both hands. "For you."

He held himself with such stillness as he regarded me carefully. He reminded me of a calm lake, where not even the faintest ripple disturbed its surface. It was as if our surroundings had quieted down, like not even a whisper of wind dared to blow past. He accepted the book. "Thank you."

"You're welcome."

The lama looked at me. I looked at him. Was I supposed to say something else? Was I missing some sort of etiquette or protocol? I clasped my hands together, and then unclasped them. I let them hang at my sides, but then fidgeted with the hem of my shirt. He cleared his throat. "Well, then. Thank you for bringing this to me."

Finally, I settled on a quick bow, and promptly turned on my heel, making a beeline for the monastery.

It wasn't until later at dinner that I understood how badly I'd messed up.

I recounted my day to Sangye, expecting him to tease me for my timidness. Instead, he gaped at me over his bowl of rice.

"That's not a name, Tsultrim," he said incredulously. "That's a religious title. He's the principal of the Central University for Tibetan Studies."

My cheeks heated up. Embarrassment burned in my stomach. In my haste, I'd even forgotten to introduce myself to him. I'd completely squandered Chokyi's attempt to help me network.

It was clear that I had to work on my shyness. If I wanted to grow, I needed to be more proactive. And now that I was no longer looking over my shoulder for Chinese authorities, this was the time to learn.

CHAPTER
THIRTY-FOUR

We were having some more sweet Indian tea when Sangye broke the news to me.

"His Holiness the Dalai Lama will be giving a series of lectures here."

I choked, bursting into a coughing fit that had me wheezing. "The Dalai Lama?"

"Yes. He lives in Dharamsala with the Tibetan government-in-exile, but he travels around to give speeches."

I wasn't sure what he meant by government-in-exile, but that was the least of my concerns now. "And His Holiness is coming here, to the monastery?"

"He'll be at a venue nearby."

"When?" I all but exclaimed. My excitement was overpowering my usual shyness, and I couldn't find it in myself to care. His Holiness? Here? In the flesh? I had to be dreaming. For a second, I feared that this was just an elaborate fantasy, and that I'd wake up in a scrappy tent.

"Later this week, in the evening. And yes, I'll take you

there," he added, a little amused at my outburst. But I could see the same excitement shining in his eyes too.

In an attempt to calm down, I packed a modest lunch and set out to explore Sarnath, one of the most sacred places for Buddhists. The Buddha had taught his first sermon there and had even named it an important pilgrimage site himself.

I arrived early enough that there were few people with me. A light fog had descended, giving the archeological remains an almost ethereal air. Broken red bricks stuck from the ground, marking where the Buddha had once meditated. I walked down a brick path lined with neatly trimmed hedges, all square angles and clean lines. In the distance, the Dhamek Stupa stood tall and proud.

I stared in awe as I drew closer to the stupa. It was a two-tiered cylindrical structure, wider at the bottom. Scaffolding crept up its brown walls, where little niches had been carved out of stone. Intricate patterns had been engraved into the facade, swirling motifs next to geometric patterns climbing up the building. Though I didn't know what exactly was kept inside, I knew that it contained important relics, as did other stupas. But the Dhamek Stupa in particular marked the exact place of the Buddha's sermon.

I began to circle around the structure clockwise, my heart full of prayer. The sun broke through the fog, and more people filtered in. Some were fellow worshippers who circumambulated with me; others were tourists or locals who simply marveled at the stupa's history.

I thought I couldn't have been happier. That was, until the day of the Dalai Lama's visit.

Sangye and I arrived early to snag better seats, but a sea of worshippers had already gathered in front of the platform, so we ended up in the back. A low murmur rippled through the congregation, a mix of excited chatter and reverent whispers. Even Sangye, who was usually easygoing and laid-back, was practically vibrating with anticipation.

Then a figure walked up to the platform and settled onto a low chair.

It was the Dalai Lama, in the flesh. He wore gold and red robes, the folds of the fabric rippling as he gestured animatedly. His voice boomed from speakers that had been set up around the audience, slow and calm.

I began to weep. As embarrassing as it was to admit, I could barely pay attention to his lecture. I faintly registered something about hope, something about doing good deeds and praying for peace. Some sort of analysis of sacred texts. But the surge of emotion in me was too overpowering, too all-consuming.

His Holiness was essentially a deity made flesh. For so long, I'd thought this man to be dead, the lineage of the Dalai Lama lost to time. I'd only known him from smuggled photographs and hushed whispers. But here he was, far away from me but within view. I was watching his mannerisms in person through tear-blurred eyes, hearing his thoughts and philosophies with my own ears.

Seeing the leader of my religion changed something in me. Even Tibetans who were not particularly religious acknowledged his important role in Tibetan culture. He was a beacon of hope, proof that not all had been lost, that hope would not die as long as we kept surviving, one day at a time.

From that day on, I settled into a tentative routine. The structure provided some relief, something for me to tether myself to. Slowly but surely, I began to come out of my shell.

I woke early in the morning when all was still quiet and spent the day wandering Sarnath or the monastery. Then in the evening, I would attend His Holiness' lectures, his words ringing in my ears even though I was too overwhelmed to fully absorb them. I felt like a person again. Even after the Dalai Lama left, I continued to sit in on lectures from other teachers, drinking in every bit of knowledge.

Sangye even gifted me a prayer book, and I began reading again. It had been so long since I'd last held one, and the script danced on the page, tangling together into an indecipherable mess. I murmured under my breath as I traced the words, each swoop and stroke, each flick and curve. I was rediscovering words and stories, relearning what it meant to be alive after having death looking over my shoulder for so long.

Over the next year, I hungrily took every opportunity to learn more about the city. I still couldn't understand what the locals said very well, but the sounds settled around me like a second skin. Though I rarely initiated conversation, I was no longer the scared young woman who shrank in on herself. When Sangye took me to a gathering of temple donors, I listened intently as I snacked on strips of dried mango. The air filled with the scent of tea and the sound of Hindi and Tibetan. Guests milled about, trading all sorts of small talk. This vendor was having a sale, that restaurant's owner planned to retire. A school was accepting new students, another faced budget cuts. Then Sangye led me toward the lady of the house.

"This is my friend Tsultrim," he said.

"I've heard all about you," the woman said, a warm smile on her lips. She was old enough to be my mother. She was perfectly manicured, the folds of her skirt crisp and clean. She'd painted her face in a light touch of makeup. The dark lines around her eyes made her kind gaze just a little sharper.

The woman and Sangye shared a knowing look, and she laid a gentle hand on my shoulder. "I'd like to discuss something with you in private, Tsultrim." She must've sensed my apprehension, because she immediately added, "It's nothing bad. I'd just like to get to know you more."

She ran through the typical conversation starters: my hometown, my family, and the like. She nodded along as she listened with rapt attention. I could almost see her taking mental notes as she focused those piercing eyes on me. It was almost like being in an office for an intake interview.

Unlike those interviews, though, she never hinted at my reason for leaving Tibet.

"Actually, Tsultrim, I have a gift for you." With a flourish, she shook out a bundle of cloth and held it up with a smile.

It was a yellow dress made of fine silk accented with golden embroidery. The fabric rippled like a golden waterfall as she shifted her hands, showing off all the details. The material looked so smooth and creamy that I didn't dare touch it. There was no way I could accept this. It was too generous, especially from a woman I had just met. I was still searching for the right words when she continued.

"There's another matter I'd like to discuss." She turned to face me fully. "Sangye told me you're nineteen. Is that right?" I nodded. The past few years felt like such a blur, so I couldn't be sure, but that sounded close enough. "And you met my son earlier, yes? He's just a little older than you."

Did I meet him? I racked my brain, trying to figure whom she was referring to. Maybe he was the shopkeeper in the blue shirt, or the politician with a beard. No, it was probably the young clerk in glasses—he had the same hooded eyes as this woman.

"What do you think of him?"

What did I think of him? Nothing, really. But of course, I couldn't just say that to her face. "He seems . . . nice. Accomplished." That answer seemed safe enough.

She radiated pride for her son. "That he is. He earned himself a well-paid job. Nothing too fancy, but a stable, respectable position. What he hasn't found, however, is a suitable bride."

She looked at me pointedly, a glint in her eye. My stomach began to sink. Just when I thought it couldn't sink any lower, she finally came out and said it.

"We'd like you to marry our son."

Every fiber of my being screamed *no*. My reaction was so visceral that I almost shocked myself. Marriage wasn't for me, period. I knew without a shred of doubt that I would only feel trapped, and everyone involved would be miserable. This was exactly why I'd run away from Pelbar Dzong when I was a young girl. Yet here I was, faced with the exact same expectations. She went on, not noticing my discomfort.

"As I mentioned, he has a respectable job, but we would need you to run a small business as well. But I promise it's easy. We own a hand-drawn cart that you would bring to the market each day. Everything you need is in it: the merchandise, the display cloth, everything. Just lay it out and make some sales. We can go over the details later."

"In Varanasi?" I squeaked, shoulders tensing up to my ears as I thought more about the idea. It was true that I was feeling more comfortable here, but I didn't speak Hindi. Even now, it took a little effort to parse through the bits of Hindi that the woman sprinkled into her speech. That was right. Maybe I was drastically misunderstanding her. Maybe she wasn't asking me to marry her son after all. Maybe the

Tibetan word for "marriage" just sounded like the Hindi word for "street" or "cart" or "market," something completely unrelated.

She must've mistaken my tension as enthusiasm, because she was beaming as she plowed on. "You would make a fine wife, Tsultrim, and an even finer mother. I would love for you to be part of our family. Please take some time to consider our proposal."

"I . . . Thank you." I felt my lips move, but I couldn't hear my own voice over the roar in my ears. I stood rigidly and excused myself from the room. Then I made a beeline for the front door, hoping nobody would stop me so I could have a moment to myself.

Accepting it—the dress, the marriage proposal, the money—felt like admitting I would stay here for the rest of my life. Varanasi was lovely. The year I'd spent here was the closest thing to stability that I'd had in a long time. But the sudden proposal was like a shock to the system. I craved stability. I was so tired of wandering and running and leaving. But was this what I truly wanted? My footsteps sped up as I racked my brain, trying to figure out what exactly it was that I wanted to do with my life.

On the way back to the monastery, I spotted a few buses parked nearby. Before I knew it, I was already wandering toward one of the workers.

"Excuse me, where are these buses going?"

"Dharamsala," the driver said.

My heart skipped a beat. Dharamsala. That was right. I'd been planning on going to Dharamsala to meet the Dalai Lama, precisely because I didn't know what to do. I'd grown complacent during the last year, so relieved to have found somewhere safe that I'd forgotten what set me off on this journey in the first place. I was escaping Chinese authorities, protecting my family by staying away. But it went further back than that, it was more than just running away. It was running toward something, toward a future I chose for myself.

That yearning for something *more* came back in full force, hitting me square in the chest. And now, as I stared at the driver in a daze, the universe was showing me a giant, glowing sign.

"They're leaving today?" I asked.

"Yeah, in a few hours."

I turned on my heel, all but running back to the monastery and into my borrowed room. I grabbed my bag and began shoving everything into it: my food bowl, my blanket, the handful of cash I'd managed to save up over the last year. I darted between people in the hallway, muttering apologies as I barreled through. Before I could make it out of the building though, Sangye had already returned. His eyes drifted to the bag in my hand.

"Where are you going?"

"Dharamsala."

"You're going *where*?" he yelped. He had a look of

betrayal on his face. "Tsultrim, do you even know where that is?"

"It's where the Dalai Lama and the government are."

"But do you actually know where it is?"

Silence stretched between us. No. Of course I didn't. I never got the chance to learn that. He took that as an admission of my own ignorance.

"You don't know what you're doing." His voice was devastatingly quiet. "The woman's son—he's from a good family. He's a public servant, so you'll be set for life. No more suffering, no more hardships."

"I don't want to stay here forever."

"If it's travel you want, you'll have plenty of opportunities to do so."

"No, that's not it."

"Then what is it?" He was raising his voice again. "Do you want to go home? Is that it? Dharamsala is even farther away from Kham. You know that, right?"

"I do." I was desperate to return to Pelbar Dzong someday, but at the same time, I ached to see more of the world. I was being pulled in two opposite directions, but I knew for certain that staying here would get me nowhere. His throat worked, as if he was trying to find the right words.

"Don't you want an easy life?"

Of course I did; it was human nature to want stability and peace. But a house and a husband, children and inlaws—that was not an easy life, not for me.

"I want to meet the Dalai Lama," I said, willing myself to stay calm. Sangye only seemed more confused.

"He was just here this year. He does tours all the time, you'll see him again."

"No, I mean . . ." Goodness. Was I being entitled again? Was I being greedy? "I want to meet him, not just look at him from far away."

"You can meet him here! He visits! You're bound to get an audience with him eventually."

"But it's not just the Dalai Lama," I cried. "It's . . . I want . . ." I floundered for a moment, desperate to describe this roiling feeling in my chest. "More."

"More," he echoed. "What is 'more'?"

"I don't know," I admitted. "I can't explain."

"Exactly," Sangye said softly. "You don't know what you're talking about."

He looked like he was soothing a wild animal. But I wasn't just some beast operating on base instinct. I was a person with her own hopes and fears. I had my own goals—nebulous ones, but goals all the same.

Maybe it was unfair of me to think that way. Being a wife and a mother was respectable, crucial. Varanasi wasn't anything less or inferior. But I wanted *more* than that. I wanted to help more people by . . . doing what? All I knew was that I had to meet the Dalai Lama. Surely, he would give me some guidance.

I half expected Sangye to grow annoyed, but instead, the look on his face grew tender, heartbroken. Tears were beginning to well up in his eyes. "You're being impulsive, Tsultrim. I just want what's best for you. Stay here. Stay safe."

Everything he said made perfect sense. But when did I ever make sense?

"*Please.*" His voice cracked, and pushing past him was one of the hardest things I'd ever done.

My mind made up, I clutched my bag to my chest and ran.

Through the corridor and up the stairs. Past the red-bricked temples, past the vendors selling street food and jewelry. Past the large square, where a flock of startled pigeons took flight as I charged by like a storm. Then through the alleyways with their canopies of prayer flags.

I charged past everything that I'd grown used to, that I was now determined to leave behind in some vague pursuit of something more.

"Name?" a worker demanded as I neared the buses. He was an Indian man who spoke Tibetan with a slight accent.

"Tsultrim Dolma."

He scanned his clipboard. "You're not on the list. Where's your ticket?"

"Don't have one," I said, and shoved a handful of money into his hand, not caring how much I gave him. Whatever the cost, it would be worth it. "Here, just take this." I pushed past the worker and marched onto the bus. Since all the seats were already occupied by travelers, I simply plopped myself down onto the aisle. A couple of passengers stared at me in disbelief. Most of them ignored me.

With adrenaline still coursing through my veins, I met the worker's gaze head-on. I wasn't disturbing anyone. I wasn't taking up any seats. I'd paid the fare, if not more. None of the passengers really cared that I had laid claim to the floor of the bus. This bus was *not* leaving without me.

With a roll of his eyes and a mutter to the driver, he stepped off the bus, and the bus doors closed with an irritated hiss.

I more or less starved through the three-day drive. My throat was parched, and I couldn't get any rest while sitting in the aisle. We stopped in Delhi, and I vaguely remember stepping off the bus for a break at some point. I was exhausted beyond belief, and my memory went in and out like a flickering lightbulb.

But I didn't care. I was on my way to Dharamsala, one step closer to seeing the Dalai Lama again. One step closer to *more*.

CHAPTER
THIRTY-FIVE

Like the previous refugee camps, the refugee center in Dharamsala was crowded. Unlike Kathmandu and its separate rooms though, we were placed in a single large hall. A few cots had been placed here and there, but there wasn't nearly enough space for the influx of refugees. The vast majority of us lay on blankets on the floor. The first thing I did was ask for directions to the education department.

A large red arch greeted me at the foot of a hill. It was painted with gold accents, and the sign on top said something about the Tibetan government. Blocky, cream-colored buildings soon came into view, sprawling all over the hillside. There were plenty of trees too, though not the neatly trimmed foliage of the Varanasi monastery.

Gingerly, I stepped through a wooden door and approached the desk, where I was greeted by a staff member. Taking a deep breath, I spoke the words I'd been dreaming of for so long. "I'm here to sign up for school."

"It's too late to enroll," the man said.

"Oh."

He waved the next person forward, a silent dismissal. A part of me knew I should've asked more questions, but I didn't know where to start. Besides, maybe this was how things were done here.

"Okay. Thank you."

My mind flashed back to those three months in Kathmandu, where I'd languished in my room day after day. I needed a reason to get out of bed, to leave my housing. So I set off for the employment office, full of determination. If I couldn't go to school, then I'd get a job. After waiting in line for what seemed like ages, I finally got to speak with the employment office worker. She scratched her nose as she looked through a list.

"There's a desk job available, just some basic office work for the department. You know, filing documents, handling paperwork. That kind of stuff."

I frowned. "I can't read or write very well."

"Then go learn how."

"And where would I do that?"

"At school."

"How do I get started?"

"Go down to the education department."

My frown deepened. "I just did. They said it was too late to enroll."

"Then it's too late to enroll."

"Aren't there other classes I could take?"

She sighed and rubbed her temples. "I don't know. Go ask the education department."

So I went back to the previous office and was met with the same clerk as before.

"Again, it's too late. We don't have any open classes," he said as soon as he saw me.

"But the woman at the employment office said I need to learn to read and write before I can get a job." It was well past noon now. The heat of Dharamsala was fraying my nerves. "What do I do now?"

"Go ask for a job that doesn't require reading or writing."

"There aren't any jobs!" the woman snapped when I went back to her. "You need the requisite skills. Go ask the education department!"

The next few weeks were the same. I'd wake up, have a simple meal provided by the refugee center, and promptly head for the administrative complex. At first, I only visited the education and employment offices. Then I began to ask around different departments as well.

I was bounced between different offices, redirected to different workers. But nobody gave me any indication of what I should be doing. Nobody gave me a solid answer to help me leave the refugee center and start settling down in Dharamsala. I was stuck here, no matter how actively I tried to become independent.

Just as I was about to go absolutely stir-crazy, a staff member came looking for me at the refugee center.

"Tsultrim Dolma?"

I jumped up from my blanket. "That's me."

"A journalist is here to interview some refugees for a documentary. We thought you'd be a good fit, given all you've been through."

My heart thumped against my chest. Now that I'd had more time to process my trauma, I was in a better place than ever to share my journey in full, to get my story off my chest and move on.

We set up in a room in one of the administrative buildings, and the interview went by like any other. *What was your childhood like? How horrible was it? What did they do to you in prison? Tell us all about the bad things that happened to you.*

I knew that the journalists were doing important work. I knew that they wanted stories about Chinese repression to raise awareness. But I couldn't help but feel like I was just a source of sound bites and publicity. It was like I was being paraded around, my pain put on full display. It seemed that nobody wanted anything to do with me outside of my trauma.

The cycle continued. A government worker would come fetch me for an interview with a foreign journalist. Then they would send me back to the refugee camp. I waited for hours at the office for employment assistance, only to be turned away because I didn't have the qualifications needed. To make matters worse, the refugee center was running out of resources, and after a few months, they stopped feeding us altogether. Now I also had to find a way to pay for my meals.

And as if unemployment weren't enough, my health took a turn for the worse. Dharamsala was in many ways the total opposite of Pelbar Dzong. For starters, it was hot. *So hot.* The humidity made the heat all the more unbearable, and I was constantly sticky from sweat. There were all manner of pests that I'd never seen before, and the mosquitoes were the worst.

They buzzed at my ear, swooping in close and immediately darting away when I swatted at them. Seconds later, they would come swooping back in, the buzzing louder than ever. The bites they left were red and angry, swelling up to the size of my fist. I didn't have a mosquito net or any sort of repellant. The only way to prevent myself from getting bitten was to hide under long sleeves or a blanket, but that was obviously out of the question in this heat. Then my skin began to break out with cysts, and I finally gave in and went to the hospital.

"I'm having trouble with my skin," I explained to a nurse. "There are so many inflamed bumps on my face that it's unbearable. I think I'm allergic to mosquitoes, because every time I get bitten, it swells up really badly. See?" I held up an arm to show her the insect bites.

The nurse looked me over for a moment. "Change your moisturizer."

"Excuse me?"

"Your face moisturizer. Or maybe your makeup. It's clogging up your pores, so you'll need something lighter."

"I don't use any cosmetics." I couldn't afford to even if I wanted to.

"Like I said, you need to switch up your products."

Then she promptly walked over to a man with an injured leg. I understood that he had a more serious issue, but he was already surrounded by a crowd of staff.

I left the hospital in confusion. Was that it? Was my condition not serious enough to warrant a hospital visit? Did I sorely misunderstand the health care procedures here?

Once again, I was left feeling absolutely, unutterably stupid.

I was a country girl from the middle of nowhere, Kham. I was nobody.

A worker came looking for me at the refugee center. Another day, another interview, another employment rejection. By now I didn't really need anyone to guide me through the offices. I'd come here so often, it was second nature to weave between desks and squeeze past people. I braced myself and opened the door.

"Hello, Tsultrim. Do you remember me?" Vanya Kewley stood from her chair to greet me. "How have you been?"

I stood there in shock. I'd expected another interview with the same questions and answers, another few hours where I spoke into the void. Instead, here was the first woman who had listened to my story, who was now following up with me, making sure that I was okay.

There was no camera crew with her this time, only a single interpreter who skillfully translated as I rambled on and on. It was such a relief to see a familiar face that it didn't matter that we'd only met briefly twice. She listened closely as I recounted the past few years—everything from the trek through the Himalayas to the awful boiled cucumbers—like I was telling the world's most riveting story.

"And how's life in Dharamsala?"

I bit my lip, trying not to let the bitterness show. "I'm still at the refugee center."

She looked genuinely dismayed, a furrow deep in her brow. "It's been over half a year, hasn't it?"

"Yes. I don't have anywhere else to stay because I can't find a job no matter how hard I try."

"Then I'll speak with the Dalai Lama's sister," she said. "Her office might be able to set something up for you. In the meantime, have this. It should tide you over for a while." Kewley rifled through her pockets and pulled out a handful of bills. "I have some clothing you can have too."

My jaw dropped as she continued to search her belongings. How many times had I been interviewed by now? And how many times had anyone followed up to make sure I was okay? It wasn't that I was expecting payment or special treatment. I'd just felt . . . used. Discarded. Like something to show off to an audience, and then tucked away out of sight until next time.

But now a virtual stranger was offering me money and promising to help me get a job. She was going to speak with His Holiness' sister on my behalf. She'd remembered. She'd *listened*.

With Kewley's generosity, I was finally able to leave the refugee center seven or eight months after arrival. I moved in to a tiny room in a rickety building. The bed was small and hard, and the "kitchen" was a single portable stove. The wall was yellow with water stains, and I could hear my neighbors bickering next door. If I needed to relieve myself, I had to leave the building entirely to use the outhouse. But it was a place to call my own, and for that, I was grateful.

Soon after, I started my new job at the Tibetan Children's Village, and I finally began to gather the pieces of myself back together.

CHAPTER
THIRTY-SIX

"The little one in the back needs a diaper change."

I nodded at my supervisor and hurried over to the baby in question. The baby was fussy, kicking her chubby little legs at me as I tried to remove the dirty diaper. My feet hurt and my back ached from the long hours. But the work was worth it when the baby settled down and let out a gurgled laugh.

The Tibetan Children's Village, also known as the TCV, was a charity founded by Tsering Dolma Takla, the Dalai Lama's older sister. I'd been assigned to the nursery, where I looked after a room full of orphaned babies as part of a small team. Every now and then, a couple would drop by to adopt a child, but for the most part, the orphanage was packed to the brim.

We rotated schedules, and tonight I was on the twelve-hour night shift. I'd always loved children, especially infants. I'd loved the way my siblings babbled when they were babies, the way they grasped my finger in their chubby little fists. But not like this, not a room full of orphans denied a stable life. My heart broke for the ones who were too young to remember but old enough to feel loss. They knew instinctively that the hands that held them were not the ones they'd known before.

"Good work, Tsultrim." My supervisor interrupted my wallowing. Rinchen was a Tibetan woman in her fifties, born and raised in India. Her joints were knobby with arthritis, her voice rough with constant use. Yet she insisted on personally attending to her charges instead of delegating tasks to her team. *Treat them like your own children,* she'd said on my first day, *they deserve to be loved like any other child.*

Now she looked at me with such tenderness in her heavy-lidded eyes. "Once the shift is over, why don't you come visit me for some tea and company?"

Rinchen lived just three or four buildings down the street from me. Our area was rather run-down and a long walk from work. My hair stood on end whenever I walked home alone after a day shift. It seemed like the darkness itself was eager to sink its claws in me. But now we walked at a leisurely pace, savoring the early morning silence until we ambled up the stairs to her apartment.

It was in the same condition as mine, but much cozier. The space felt welcoming and lived-in, full of little signs of the resident. A meticulously maintained shrine, a bed with a vibrantly patterned blanket, and a full stock of snacks, which she set out for me as she prepared the tea.

We carefully skirted around sensitive topics. Rinchen asked about my family, but not why I'd left home. She shared stories about her children when they were little, and I never asked why she didn't have any stories about them as adults. The conversation was surface level, and once upon a time I might've dismissed it as shallow or banal. Yet the care behind each word was real. It was safe. I was safe.

"You're always welcome here," she said in a gentle voice as she saw me out the door, and for the first time in a long while, I truly felt it.

However, walking home late at night alone was wearing me down to the bone. The hair-raising feeling of being watched caused a physical strain on me. Every shadow was a potential assailant, a predator lurking behind a corner. Though I no longer looked over my shoulder during the day, the scars from the rough nights in Lhasa had been burned in my brain. Thankfully, I was soon approved for an apartment in a building closer to work. I'd barely settled into the new space when some workers came knocking.

"We need you to move," they said unceremoniously. "The old woman's apartment is leaking. She'll have to take over your room instead."

"Rinchen's? Can't you fix it?"

"Well, we need to move her into a safe place first. It's already getting moldy in there."

That made sense. "So where are you moving me to?"

The workers looked at me like I'd missed the obvious.

"Into the old lady's place. Weren't you listening? We can't have her in there."

"And that means putting me into that mold-infested death trap instead?" The words burst out of me, and I was almost shocked at my own audacity.

One worker glared hard at me. "So what now? You want us to keep the old woman there?"

"I didn't say that—"

"It's just for a few days, girl. Do it for the old lady."

"No." I could feel my temper rising. "I'm not doing anything of the sort. And you're not guilting me into it either." I'd had enough of making myself small, of people making decisions on my behalf and taking advantage of my eagerness to help others. "I want you to get us both a safe place to live. *Both of us.* And I'm not moving a single inch until you do. Feel free to drag me out of here. Feel free to try, in any case, because I won't make it easy on you. Good luck." I plopped myself down onto my sheets. I didn't care if I was being difficult anymore. If I gave in now, it would only embolden them to do the same to others down the line.

And a few days later, a vacant apartment for Rinchen magically appeared, free of water damage. Word traveled fast, and soon rumors of an unruly troublemaker were flying around the orphanage.

"I appreciate it, Tsultrim," she said, patting my arm. "You stand up for yourself, and I think that's very good."

My face turned red, suddenly aware that I'd been growing bolder each day.

With my housing secure once more, it wasn't long before I began entertaining guests in my apartment too. Most of them were coworkers or some acquaintances from the refugee center. I was walking someone back to the refugee center when I spotted a familiar face I hadn't seen in two years.

It was Lobsang, who'd turned back right before crossing the Tibetan-Nepali border. He was now here in Dharamsala, thousands of miles away from the border. He looked exhausted and much thinner than I remembered. There was an ashen undertone to his skin and deep circles around his eyes. But despite all that, he wore a faint smile. He too had taken the leap and made it in one piece.

"How are the others? The ones who turned back with you?" I asked. I'd ushered him back to my home to chat and was now boiling water for tea.

"I don't know," he said simply. He was looking at the table, not quite meeting my eyes. "I didn't see anyone familiar during my second attempt. I know I'm being hypocritical, but they shouldn't have just given up like that." He let out a harsh chuckle. "I'm being judgmental, but I can't help but think so."

"Maybe a little bit," I said, setting down the tea. "But I'm sure they had their reasons. You know what the trek was like."

"I do." He fiddled with his cup, a wry smile on his face, as if reliving each memory with a dark sense of humor. "That second try was just as terrifying as the first."

"But you made it."

"That I did."

We sat there in relative silence. Car horns blared outside the window and children squealed in delight. A couple was in a heated screaming match, and a car raced by, blasting Bollywood music at full volume. I'd been here for so long that the sounds were almost soothing in their own way.

"Say, Tsultrim," he started. "You heard about the refugee lotto?"

I nodded. Who hadn't heard about it? The entire Tibetan community had been abuzz with news about a new refugee resettlement program in America. "I didn't apply though. I was too busy with everything going on."

"Some winners dropped out, so they're doing another lotto to fill up some spots. You've settled down now, yeah? Why not give it a go? You could go overseas, tell them what's happening back home."

But that was it. I'd been in Dharamsala for over a year now, the longest I'd spent in one location since fleeing from Pelbar Dzong. I'd moved here to meet the Dalai Lama, and that still hadn't happened yet. Should I really dig up the tentative roots that I'd finally begun to lay down here? And did I really want to get my hopes up, only to be disappointed when I wasn't chosen?

As if reading my thoughts, Lobsang fixed me with an intense look. "Come on, what's the worst that can happen? You get rejected? Just put your name down and see what happens."

He was right. I'd been turned down so many times, what was one more rejection?

"What about you? Will you apply?"

He let out a heavy sigh. "America, huh? I'm not sure I'm as brave as you are. But . . ." He shrugged, a smile on his lips. "Can't hurt to try."

A few weeks later, I'd just put a baby down for a nap when Rinchen came looking for me.

"A phone call," she said, and subbed in for me as I headed toward the office.

"Tsultrim Dolma?" said a brusque voice as soon as I picked up the receiver.

"This is she."

"Congratulations. I'm calling to inform you that you've been chosen for the refugee resettlement project."

CHAPTER
THIRTY-SEVEN

As it turned out, winning the lotto was only the first step, and I soon found out why so many people had dropped out.

The fees were exorbitant. There were processing fees, physical exam fees, photograph fees, document fees, transportation fees. I wouldn't have been surprised if they'd charged us for each drop of ink we used to sign the papers. We spent hours waiting in lines that went out the door, and I had no choice but to drop work shifts to complete each step, making my pockets even emptier. When I mentioned it in passing, my friends and coworkers pitched in generously, sparing as much money as they could to help cover the fees. Finally, I was filing the last of my paperwork.

Along with local workers, some American staff were also present in Dharamsala throughout the process. Interpreters were always at the ready, guiding us through the jargon and the language barrier. But this time, the blond woman at the desk directed a few words to me, and then frowned when I didn't respond. She turned back to the interpreter and fired off a string of rapid-fire English.

"What's she saying?" I asked. Was my paperwork wrong? Or maybe they found something wrong with me during my physical exam.

"She says you can't go because you don't speak English," the interpreter said, clearly unhappy at the woman's reaction.

So this was it then. I would be barred from America because I couldn't speak English. Apparently, it didn't matter that I had no opportunity to learn to read or write Tibetan, let alone a foreign language. It didn't matter that I was a refugee, a fugitive who couldn't go home anymore. I was not qualified to be a refugee in America.

The interpreter began arguing with the staff then, and even though I couldn't understand a word, it was clear that the discussion was heating up. I shifted nervously on my feet. It was nerve-racking enough that I couldn't understand a single word of what they were saying about me. The people in line craned their necks at the commotion. Just as I was about to ask the interpreter to let it go, the woman clicked her tongue and threw her hands up in defeat. She looked back down at my documents, grumbling under her breath.

"You're good now," the interpreter said. Though he still had an annoyed furrow in his brow, there was an air of vindication about him. "They're letting you go after all."

"What did you say to them?"

"I told them you're young and full of potential, that you

could learn." He said that so casually that it made my heart skip a beat.

That was right. I was young, only twenty years old. I'd spent so much time scrambling to survive that I'd almost forgotten that I still had the rest of my life ahead of me. But as the reality of my impending departure sank in, so did the anxiety.

I really was leaving. What had started as an attempt to keep my family safe had snowballed into me leaving the continent entirely. Suddenly, I wasn't so sure if going to America was the right thing to do. I already had a stable life here. Then there was my work at the orphanage. I wanted to help my fellow Tibetans, and my job was a way of doing just that. Was it selfish of me to abandon them now? Why did I feel this nagging sense of unfulfillment? Was I ungrateful? Was I too greedy? An American family had graciously sponsored me, so I wouldn't be completely lost in America. But I didn't know anyone there, and I didn't speak the language. Maybe the blond woman was right. Maybe I really didn't belong in America.

I confessed as much to a high lama when I sought out his counsel.

"I don't think you should go," he said. "They spend all their time working in America, just to stay afloat. That's no way to live a life. And you're doing good, honest work here, contributing to society."

But his response wasn't enough to settle the churning

nerves in my stomach. I asked for a second opinion.

"You should absolutely go to America," the second lama said. "You'll have more opportunities there to advocate for Tibet. We need more people to go out and tell the world the truth about the Chinese occupation. I hear it's a good place to raise a family."

His words only made me more conflicted. The options before me were paralyzing. Maybe this was an inevitable downside to having the freedom of choice. But little Punjun would be thrilled to be in this position, so I did what Punjun would do and listed the things I knew. And the one thing I knew was that I wanted more.

I wanted to fight for Tibet and its people. I wanted the world to listen. I wanted to *make* the world listen, to shake everyone by the shoulders until they extended a hand, because this wasn't a fight that we could win by ourselves. I wanted to go home to Pelbar Dzong too, and the only way to do so was to free Tibet first. And this wasn't just a Tibetan problem. China had other neighbors rich in a variety of resources. The Chinese government would not be satisfied with just occupying Tibet.

I wanted to explore what the world had to offer. Despite my homesickness, I wanted to meet new people, hear new languages, taste new foods. I wanted to learn. I wanted to know. I wanted to see where my village stream converged with other rivers, until it formed a single endless blue.

I had my answer.

❖

Before departing for the airport, the refugees gathered in a large room. A white screen had been set up in front of some plastic stools. I sat at the back, near the projector. It was whirring furiously, emanating heat like it had been in use nonstop all day.

"Before you leave us, we want you to watch this documentary," a worker said. "We want you to remember everything that's been happening at home."

He pressed play, and some upbeat, brassy music filled the room. A narrator spoke with a clipped tone over shaky footage of marching Chinese soldiers. A blue van drove through a shallow river and pedestrians milled about in Lhasa. I tried my hardest to concentrate as the images flashed across the screen, but the voiceover was in a foreign language. Even the Tibetan-speaking interviewees had been dubbed over in what sounded like English. I closed my eyes to focus on catching the snippets of Tibetan that came through.

"I was taken, handcuffed, to the police station. I was thrown on the floor," said a high, wispy voice in Tibetan. She was crying, gasping out every word as she recounted every horror that she'd endured. I blinked at the projection. She had not been dubbed over in English. I recognized that voice.

"We were prodded countless times by seven or eight people," a second girl said, voice distorted from the speakers. She was hiccupping. "We were stripped naked and told that as you oppose the communist system, you will be executed."

Suddenly, heads turned, and I found myself looking back at dozens of curious eyes as the documentary continued to play.

"That's her," someone whispered.

I turned my gaze back to the giant face projected onto the screen.

It was me, three or four years ago, heavy bags beneath swollen eyes, wheezing and trying to get through my testimony. A pressure grew in my chest. It was disorienting to see myself projected on a screen like that. Film was reserved for big stories, important stories. But I wasn't a brave soldier fighting evil. I wasn't a monk on his way to India or his mischievous monkey king companion. I was just a Khampa girl. And my story mattered. The pressure turned into a comforting weight.

I never doubted for a moment that speaking out was important. But to have that conviction reflected back at me, to feel acknowledgment, to receive confirmation that I'd been heard, that I wasn't just screaming into the uncaring void... To hear my own words for the first time.

"That's me," I muttered in disbelief. My eyes prickled with tears as I watched past-me recount the horrors she'd experienced in prison. She pushed through the interview. And after the camera stopped, she would push through another ordeal and another. For a moment, I imagined reaching out to cup her face. I'd swipe her tears away with a thumb, give her shoulder a comforting squeeze. I'd listen to everything she had to say, for as long as it took. And then I would look her in the eye and say, "I am so, so proud of you, Tsultrim."

I saved myself.

I had plenty of help along the way—my family, my friends, the most unbelievably kind strangers. I was driven by my faith in the Dalai Lama, the conviction that he would point me in the right direction, if only I could meet him.

But at the end of the day, I was the one who stared at a patch of grass outside a barred window. I was the one who walked across mountains on frostbitten feet. I was the one who dragged myself to where I was now, bloody and broken in body and mind, but somehow still alive.

A few days later, I finally met the Dalai Lama. Not during a lecture from afar but during a private audience with a group of fellow refugees.

He had the same youthful air about him as I'd seen in photographs, as if he were a much younger man. He still gesticulated broadly, even though he was solemn as he spoke.

"You are now all ambassadors for Tibet," he said. "It'll be hard at first. You'll be without friends or family in a foreign land. But remember the people who stayed behind. We are all praying for you."

I mulled over his words as we lined up to speak with him

directly. We were now all ambassadors for Tibet, he'd said. It sounded like such a fanciful notion, that an uneducated country girl like me could represent an entire country like an esteemed diplomat. But then again, if a country was made up of countless people, then it made sense that a country's story was made up of countless stories, including mine. All I had to do then was share my own story and listen to others as they shared theirs. And if someone couldn't speak up, I'd do my best to help them find their voice. Our perspectives and opinions were all different, and even directly contradicted one another at times, but Tibet wasn't just one thing.

Tibet wasn't just a wasteland of pain and oppression; it wasn't just a mystical land of spiritual secrets. Tibet was Great-Aunt Jampa, who had devoted her life to Buddhism. It was Lhamo, who'd renounced his monastic vows. It was Nyima with her curt replies and eye rolls; Dawa with her little giggles and encouragement. But it was also Phuntsok, who gladly sheltered dissidents yet took advantage of young women. It was the Tibetan guards who sided with the oppressor for reasons I would never fully understand.

Tibet was beautiful and ugly and breathtaking and nauseating and kind and cruel. Tibet was home, and I would share every facet, every detail with the world.

I was scared. Every day, it seemed that I was leaving Tibet even farther behind. Every step I took pulled me in a different direction. But those clamoring thoughts quieted when I finally stood in front of the Dalai Lama.

I'd been dreaming of this moment for years, thinking about what I'd say, what I'd ask. Every time I'd hit a crossroad, I thought to ask the Dalai Lama for guidance. But now, instead of offering advice, he asked in a gentle voice, "Where do you want to go? Do you want to go to school?"

He asked me because only I could decide where to go next.

I opened my mouth to answer him, but all that came out was garbled sobs. So I nodded. I wanted to go to school. I wanted to see the world. I wanted to decide for myself what my future looked like. I wanted to fight so that all Tibetans could do the same. He cupped my face with a wrinkled hand. And he looked at me, *really* looked at me, even though I was a weeping, incoherent mess.

"Do not forget us," he said, and offered me a small golden Buddha statue. I lifted it with shaking hands, barely seeing past the tears in my eyes. "No matter where you go, do not forget us."

I kept crying, unable to form words. So instead, I replied in my heart, over and over like a mantra, like a prayer.

I won't forget. I won't.

CHAPTER
THIRTY-EIGHT

When I was a child, airplanes would fly over our village. Father had told us that people traveled long distances in them, but the planes never seemed to be in a rush. They seemed to move so slowly, crawling across the sky like ants.

Now, as we waited at the airport, the planes zipped past us with loud roars that made my ears ring. Security guards had checked us and our luggage for contraband, though I barely carried anything at all. I had a change of clothes, a folder of important documents, and the gold Buddha statue stowed safely in my single bag. Announcements crackled overhead in a dozen languages.

Then, we were led down a long tunnel. The air smelled stale and sterile, recycled through vents over and over. An attendant greeted us at the doorway at the end of the hall and directed us to another seating area. I settled into a straight-backed seat and watched as workers walked up and down the length of the aisle in their neat uniforms. They inspected the cabinets that had been built into the walls, making sure the latches were secure. Another announcement blared over the speakers, and the attendants disappeared down the aisle.

The ground trembled under my feet, but I paid it no mind. Was I supposed to be doing something right now? It felt like all I'd done all day was sit around and wait. A weight started pressing on my chest and my ears began to roar. A spike of nerves shot through my spine. Did I somehow miss an important part of the process? Was I in the wrong place? Did I not bring the right documents?

I turned to my neighbor. "Um, excuse me?" No response. The girl seated next to me had her face practically glued to the window.

"We're flying." It was the man across the aisle. He was gripping the armrests, his knuckles turned to white peaks. His forehead shone with sweat.

"What?"

The man visibly steeled himself, gulping dramatically before repeating himself. "We're flying. In the sky. Off the ground." He clamped his mouth shut with an audible *clack* of teeth.

With a start, I craned my neck to look through the oval window. The horizon was tilted at an odd angle, and soon there was nothing but blue sky. Clouds drifted past, close enough to touch. I could see my neighbor's reflection in the thick glass, a mix of complicated emotions dancing across her face.

We were flying.

I couldn't see much with the girl blocking my view, but I imagined the airport shrinking into little blocks, like the toys children play with. The colors starting to blend the farther up we went, higher even than the mountains I'd climbed. The ground fading into a dull green and brown. I wondered if it would have been worse to watch as my home dropped away from my feet.

But home was still there, alive. Surviving in small spaces carved out of sheer stubbornness and tenacity, caverns where it endured like stone statues, waiting patiently to see sunlight again.

I relaxed back into the chair, now aware of the weird pressure that pressed me into my seat. My heart ached.

I was relieved to put distance between myself and the Chinese government. I was relieved to know that they couldn't touch me with an ocean between us, that I was no longer directly endangering my family. But there was more to my life than defying China, more to my story than endless pain wrought by occupiers who showed no mercy. I'd been shaped by my time in prison and in refugee camps; I'd also been shaped by soft morning prayers, mildly embarrassing festival mishaps, and a heart so full that it threatened to burst open. If only I could pack those moments into my bag and take them with me. Instead, I clutched my memories close to my chest as the airplane brought me to a foreign land.

The Earth is a sphere so vast that we perceive its curves as a single, stable line. I knew as much when I first stepped outside Pelbar Dzong, the setting sun making my eyes water as I headed west for Lhasa. I kept my eyes trained on that horizon, sneaking past guards on the Tibetan-Nepali border, then farther west to India. I boarded a plane whose pilots used that same line as a guide as they flew us to the U.S.

I'd eventually settle on the East Coast, in a place called Amherst, Massachusetts.

Now, if I head west—on foot or by plane or cramped on the floor of a shuddering bus—my journey would take me across North America. I'd reach the West Coast to marvel at the Pacific Ocean and wonder if my village stream fed that endless stretch of blue. On the other side of that ocean is Asia, in all its breathtaking diversity. My trip might take me to Japan for a connecting flight, or perhaps even a detour to the Philippines farther south. And then I'll continue westward, past Taiwan, over Hong Kong, through East Turkestan, like a kora around the globe.

And maybe one day, on my never-ending journey west, I'll finally reach Tibet once more.

AUTHORS' NOTE

Since invading Tibet in 1950, the People's Republic of China (PRC) has amassed a long list of human rights abuses. Though many people and organizations have spoken out, these issues sadly still persist in modern-day Tibet.

It's important to note that what the PRC government refers to as the Tibetan Autonomous Region (TAR) is actually much smaller than historical Tibet. The government divvied up Tibet's original three provinces and incorporated them into Chinese provinces. For example, Tsultrim's home, Kham, was broken up and partially incorporated into Sichuan, Yunnan, and Qinghai. The Free Tibet Movement calls for the liberation of all of historical Tibet, not just the TAR.

Tsultrim was unable to acquire a passport due to both cost and red tape. Although the PRC insists that Tibet is part of China, Tibetans are not entitled to passports, making it difficult for them to travel internationally and domestically. One Tibetan writer, Tsering Woeser, waited seven years for her passport application to be reviewed. The application was ultimately denied.

PRC exploitation of natural resources has caused extensive damage to Tibet's ecosystem. Kham is in east Tibet, a region that is facing mass deforestation. Extensive mining has caused wastewater to flow into local rivers, polluting important water sources. Hydropower dams also cut off access to rivers. Many international corporations rely on these exploitative practices to gain profit, including major electric car companies and billionaire investors.

The school in Pelbar Dzong was shut down before Tsultrim had a chance to attend. Many Tibetan children still don't have access to Tibetan education. According to experts from the United Nations, almost one million Tibetan children have been taken from their families and forced into residential schools. There, they receive schooling in Mandarin Chinese and curriculum that focuses on Han Chinese culture. As of 2022, 78 percent of Tibetan children between the ages of six and eighteen are in residential schools. By doing so, the PRC aims to erase Tibetan language and culture.

Tibetans are religious to varying degrees, but Tibetan Buddhist customs are widely observed. The PRC often targets monks and nuns in particular. Some monastics have resorted to self-immolation as a form of protest against persecution. In 1995, the PRC government even abducted the reincarnated Panchen Lama when he was six years old. The Panchen Lama is another important figure in Tibetan Buddhism. The government then selected their own Panchen Lama, disregarding the long history of Tibetan reincarnation. The whereabouts of the true Panchen Lama remain unknown.

To this day, the PRC government still imprisons Tibetans who speak out, or who simply want to embrace their traditions, often without trial. Tsultrim was lucky enough to be released, but many prisoners die in captivity. Gutsa Detention Center, where Tsultrim was unlawfully detained, is still operating. According to the International Campaign for Tibet, a British company has built a luxury hotel right next to the detention center. They named the hotel Lhasa Paradise.

Tsultrim mentions that China has many other neighbors, and that the Free Tibet Movement is part of an international struggle. The PRC has employed similar tactics in Southern Mongolia ("Inner Mongolia") and East Turkestan ("Xinjiang"). It has violently suppressed protests in Hong Kong and threatens to invade Taiwan. The PRC government even harms its own citizens, by imprisoning activists and silencing dissent.

If you'd like to learn more about Tibet, we encourage you to check out organizations like Free Tibet, Students for a Free Tibet, International Campaign for Tibet, and High Asia Research Center, among many others around the world that prioritize Tibetan voices.

We hope that *Defying China* serves as a reminder that these are not mere statistics or headlines. Behind each number and each word is a person with hopes and dreams, who experiences joy as well as sorrow. Their stories deserve to be heard too.

ACKNOWLEDGMENTS

Tsultrim and Rebecca would like to thank editors Rosie Ahmed and Michelle Lee for their tireless guidance; our agent, Claire Draper, for their endless faith in us; and the rest of the incredible team at Dial Books for supporting us on this journey. Special thanks to Channel 4 and Screenocean for providing documentary footage of "Tibet: A Case to Answer" from their *Dispatches* series.

Tsultrim would also like to thank:

My father, Bhuchung Tsang, and my mother, Tsetar Dolkar, for everything they've given me. May your names never be forgotten. Thank you to friends, family, and strangers in Tibet, Nepal, and India who offered kindness when I needed it. Thanks also to Rebecca for helping me share my story, and to the U.S. for welcoming me as a refugee in 1992. Diversity, equity, and inclusion make this country truly beautiful. Last but not least, my deepest, heartfelt gratitude to the Dalai Lama, for his model of faith and keeping Tibet alive.

Rebecca would also like to thank:

Tsultrim, for entrusting me with her story; my writing buddies Ariel Rada, KJ Scott, and Roslyn Talusan, for their late-night encouragement; and Andie, Cris, and Hannah, for being my people. Last, I'd like to thank Rue and Yukimi, without whom I would not be here right now.